Berkeley Castle Tales

Berkeley Castle Tales

Edited by

Stuart J. Prior
Mark Horton
Konstantinos Trimmis

Archaeopress Archaeology

ARCHAEOPRESS PUBLISHING LTD
Summertown Pavilion
18-24 Middle Way
Summertown
Oxford OX2 7LG
www.archaeopress.com

ISBN 978-1-80327-568-0
ISBN 978-1-80327-569-7 (e-Pdf)

Cover: An Anglo-Saxon gold ring that was first recorded in Berkeley Castle's collections in 1860. (photo BCP - Department of Anthropology and Archaeology);
The inner gatehouse of Berkeley Castle (photo by Aerial Cam 2008).
Back cover: Berkeley castle front approach by Leonard Knyff, c.1676 (Berkeley Castle Archives)

This book is available direct from Archaeopress or from our website www.archaeopress.com

Contents

Foreword by Charles Berkeley

It gives me great pleasure in contributing an introduction to this wonderful book on the Berkeley Castle Project undertaken by University of Bristol's archaeology students. My father, when approached, was very keen that this important study was to be done; he discussed with Dr Stuart Prior and Professor Mark Horton what they were proposing and how the dig might work, over 15 years ago. To know that 900 years of family history at Berkeley has been augmented through the University dig is tremendous.

Before William FitzOsbern and his timber framed motte-and-bailey castle, there existed a Minster, possibly housing monks and nuns. After this came down, stone from this was used in construction for the foundation of the shell keep of the castle. Berkeley has a rich layer of history that is connected to many great events in this country, and to know that early Roman, Anglo-Saxon, Norman and Tudor artefacts have been found along with more recent Civil War defences is for us proof of a rich social history in the town and surrounding countryside. My family is proud to be associated with this historic site and owe a huge thank you to everyone who has been involved in the project over the last 15 years.

The enthusiasm shown at all times by Professor Horton and Dr Prior, and the senior team at the University with their passion and knowledge of the site, has been there for us all to see. It has been a privilege for the family to have followed the work and seen the results of this extraordinary uncovering of our archaeology.

Berkeley has always had a story to tell the world, and now we have another layer or two that will excite and be of great interest to many in the future.

Charles Berkeley

Foreword by Roland Brown

I am delighted to see the results of 15 years of hard work put into print to record the findings of the University's Berkeley Project. The team at Berkeley Castle have always looked forward to the arrival of the University of Bristol undergraduates for a few weeks each year, and it has been very rewarding to see the project develop over that period. The staff and students were met by all types of weather during their project but remained cheerful and productive throughout. Following the completion of the programme, we will miss the buzz around the Castle arising when something significant was found. The picture of the site kept evolving as layer after layer of history was carefully uncovered and each year provided something of interest or excitement. I hope that the many, many students who first cut their teeth in practical archaeology at the site will remember Berkeley fondly.

I am particularly grateful to Dr Stuart Prior and his team for engaging so proactively with Berkeley Castle during their time on site. Stuart, Mark, Siân, Emily and many others were always ready to share their knowledge of the site with the Friends of Berkeley Castle, our visitors, staff and many other groups who had an interest. We were also particularly pleased when the dig's social media team became based at the Castle so that they could provide updates to visitors as the project developed. These measures were very important in making the dig relevant to today's visitors, and I hope that the findings of this study will continue to be of interest and benefit to visitors to Berkeley Castle for many years to come.

Roland Brown BSc (Hons) MRICS FAAV
Estate Director

Foreword by Professor Graeme Were

Before arriving in Bristol in January 2018, there were several things I had discovered about the Department of Anthropology and Archaeology in my preparation for my return to UK academia. The first was that Bristol archaeologists are highly regarded amongst their peers; their fieldwork skills are considered second to none and the graduates produced are eagerly snapped up for archaeology jobs around the world. The second thing I found out was that the department had adopted a four-field approach to anthropology. This approach – widespread in American anthropology departments – blends social, linguistic, and biological anthropology with archaeology. Naturally, material culture figured prominently within this matrix and I saw my own research interests strongly reflected by staff in the department. These two reasons, not to mention Bristol's links to museum and heritage sites in the region, provided further incentives to be excited about my new move.

Yet, beside these two significant factors, there was in addition one other feature of the department that really stood out – the Berkeley dig – the annual fieldwork excavation that tied together the department's key strengths in anthropology and archaeology that takes place over three weeks towards the end of the academic term each year.

Berkeley – as it is familiarly known in the department – encapsulates all the positive aspects of four-field anthropology. Not only does it produce some remarkable finds each year, from gardener's glasses dating back to the mid-twentieth century to artefacts from the Roman period and the English Civil War – it also involves engagement with the local Gloucestershire community. In the village of Berkeley, students had set up a pop-up exhibition of finds in local shops and residents' windows. This went on to win a prestigious national award in 2015–2016. It is precisely this diverse skillset that students on the course experience that makes Berkeley what it is and what brought me to Bristol. In the first year I visited, students had interpreted finds and displayed them in one of the most significant rooms in the castle. I found the display case of archaeological finds surrounded by visitors, while a painting by the great English artist George Stubbs (best known for his studies of horses), seemed almost unnoticed. This moment made me reflect on the advice of an English archaeologist friend of mine who said to me when I was about to depart Queensland: 'One thing you really must do when in Bristol is to visit this Medieval castle up the M5 in Gloucestershire.' It was only when visiting the dig and the exhibition in May 2018 that I put two and two together.

This report is the fruition of over a decade of fieldwork and brings to a close a chapter in the life of the Department of Anthropology and Archaeology. The rich findings underline the continued importance of archaeology and anthropology in shedding light on our past. Yet what makes this so special is how the project has reached out beyond academia, impacting in positive ways on students, communities, visitors, and schoolchildren, all of whom participated in this project and contributed in some way to what we now know Berkeley to be. As of all great projects, when they finally come to a close, I am certain we will take inspiration from Berkeley's collaborative model to develop future projects which deepen our understanding of the past.

Graeme Were,
Professor and Chair of Anthropology,
Head of Anthropology and Archaeology
August 2020

Chapter 1

Tales from an Excavation: University of Bristol and the Berkeley Castle Project 2005–2019

Stuart J. Prior

Introduction

In 2003, in light of proposed development and heritage conservation work in and around the town and castle of Berkeley, Gloucestershire, Elizabeth Halls, the then Castle Director, approached staff at the Department of Archaeology and Anthropology, University of Bristol, with the offer of a long-term research project. Elizabeth was keen to see serious academic research carried out on the castle and its environs. The research proposal was readily accepted by the university and the Berkeley Castle Project (BCP) was established (Fig. 1).

The project began with an initial visit by the late Prof. Mick Aston, Prof. Mark Horton and Dr Stuart Prior back in 2003, and the first season of fieldwork at the castle was conducted in 2005. This subsequently turned into a 14-year archaeological research project for students from the university, surrounding schools and colleges, and local volunteers of all ages until the final season of excavation by the university in the summer of 2019.

With Berkeley Castle (Fig. 2) as a locus for the fieldwork, the project was initially established as a joint venture between the Berkeley Castle Charitable Trust and the Department of Anthropology and Archaeology, University of Bristol. Then, in 2007, following further documentary and cartographic research, the BCP extended its fieldwork into the Edward Jenner Museum Garden, working with the Edward Jenner Museum Board of Trustees and, in 2009, with further fieldwork undertaken in Saint Mary's churchyard, working with the St Mary's Berkeley PCC. The projects were fully supported by the late Mr John Berkeley and, more recently, by Mr Charles Berkeley, the owner and occupier of the castle.

From the outset the project's objective was to build up a detailed picture of the history and archaeology of the castle and associated settlement of Berkeley and the focus for the project was described as 'Minster, Manor and Town'. The project aimed to achieve its objective by combining the results of detailed archaeological fieldwork with information contained in the castle's impressive collection of 20,000 historical documents; 6000 of which relate specifically to the medieval period. It was anticipated that the project, on such an important, prestigious and largely undisturbed site, would add to our knowledge and understanding of the early medieval period and subsequent changes in landscape and society with the coming of the Normans, and the erection of a castle on the former Saxon site.

In 2005, excavations in the Walled Garden to the north of the castle (at ST 6850 9930) – Trench 1 – recorded evidence for a ditch containing late 9th to early 11th century pottery and a Saxon millstone. This highlighted that Berkeley was an important 'central place' in the late Saxon period, the ditch seemingly being a boundary ditch for the suspected minster and the pottery and millstone found, with their late 9th–early 11th century dates, correspond perfectly with the known historic dates for the minster itself. The first authenticated evidence for a minster at Berkeley comes from an Anglo-Saxon charter of 824, which is a record of the settlement of a dispute between Bishop Heahberht and the familia

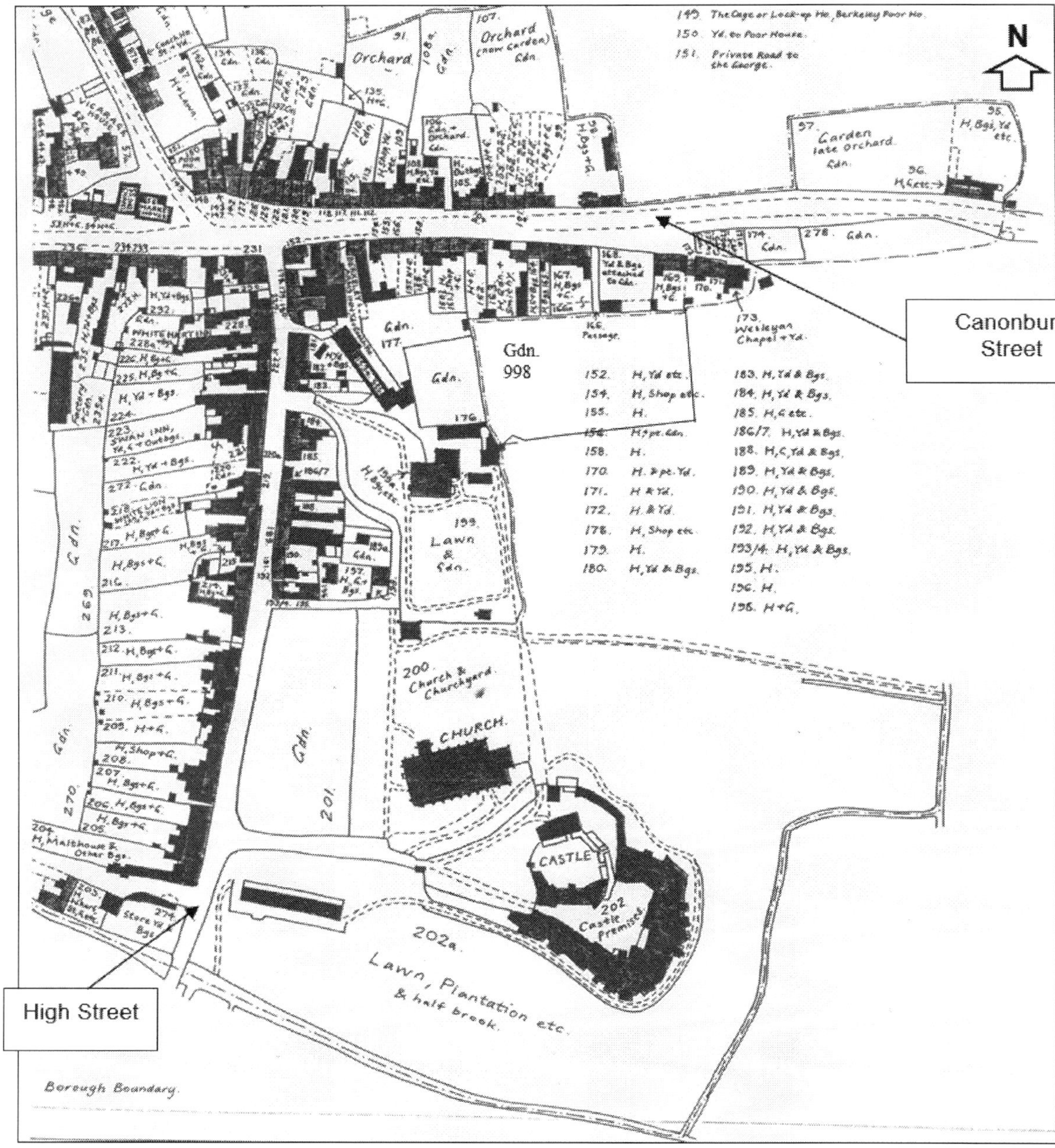

Figure 1. Section of Berkeley town and castle from 1840 Tithe Map

at Berkeley concerning land at Westbury on Trym (S1433 – misc. texts), while the minster appears to have been destroyed sometime between 1019 and 1051, at the hands of Earl Godwin.

Historical background

A detailed and comprehensive account of the history of the castle and town of Berkeley were included in BCP Report No 1 (Prior 2005) and a detailed map regression analysis of relevant historic maps was also undertaken and the results of the exercise were discussed at length in BCP Report No.1 (Prior 2005a). Below is a summary of the results and discussions from both studies. Names followed by Roman numerals in square brackets, used throughout this report, refer to members of the Berkeley family: e.g. Thomas [IV] (1352–1417) was the 10th Baron of Berkeley, but the fourth Thomas in the family line.

The town

Historically, a settlement at Berkeley can be traced back to the Domesday survey of 1086, though its origins appear to lie in the Saxon period, as early sources refer to a settlement named *Beorkenlau* or *Beorclea.* The name *Beorclea* may derive from *Berk*, 'a birch', and *Lea*, 'a pasture'; whilst *Beorkenlau*, when translated, means 'the birch clearing' (Tandy 2003, 1). An alternative interpretation of the town's name is *Beorcleah* or *Beorclingas*, where *leah* is a word used to describe 'a woodland clearing' and *ingas* means 'to belong to someone'. Importantly however, the word *ingas* can also refer to 'religious communities or monastic sites'. According to Tandy (2003, 237) documentary sources record the presence of an abbey at Berkeley from the 8th century onwards and *Beorclingas* may be a reference to it. There are also numerous references to a nunnery, and even a minster, at Berkeley during this period.

The first recorded abbot at Berkeley is reputed to be *Tilhere*, who is seemingly mentioned in a deed of 759, which was witnessed by King Offa (Tandy 2003, 237). There are several authenticated references to abbots or abbesses at Berkeley in the 9th and early 10th centuries, in Anglo-Saxon charters. The abbey built up the estate which became known as Berkeley Hundred, which was the largest estate in the county prior to the Norman Conquest. It has been suggested that in 833, lands in or around Berkeley may have been owned by some of King Alfred's family, as part of the dominion of Ethelred and Eathelflaed (Tandy 2003, 216). Smyth states that the Hundred was established by 890 (Smyth 1639). By 1086, the abbey and its estate had been dissolved (Leech 1981, 4).

Berkeley appears to have been a Royal Demesne during the reign of Edward the Confessor (1042–1066) (Tandy 2003, 218) and a town was in existence by this time. The evidence for this comprises a small collection of coins minted at Berkeley during this period (Leech 1981, 4). Domesday Book (1086) records that Berkeley had 'a market in which 17 men live and pay dues', indicating that a market was in existence in the reign of Edward the Confessor, and had probably existed long before. This makes Berkeley the only market-town in Gloucestershire at this time, besides Tewkesbury. Domesday also mentions the castle at Berkeley: 'In SHARPNESS 5 hides which belong to Berkeley, which Earl William placed outside to build a small castle. Roger claims them' (Morris 1982, 163b).

Smyth, in his *Lives of the Berkeley's*, written 1639, states that '*in many old deeds*' the town was called '*nova villa*', and an undated deed in the Public Records Office (Ancient Deeds V) refers to a tenement in 'the new town of Berkeley'. This suggests that the town, or a large part of it, rather than developing around the Saxon market in a somewhat *ad hoc* fashion, was actually a Norman 'New Town' that would have been laid out sometime between the 11th and 13th centuries. The regularity of property boundaries on the west side of High Street seem to support this notion and it is likely that the majority of the town plan can be attributed to the Normans (Leech 1981, 5).

In 1159, Henry II granted permission to Robert FitzHarding (*d.* 1170) and his heirs the right to hold a market at Berkeley. Smyth suggests that Berkeley became a borough by 1171, during the reign of Henry II (Tandy 2003, 5); while Fisher suggests that the date was slightly later, 1236–1262, during the reign of Henry III (Fisher 1865, 7–8). The town was granted a Royal Charter by Edward I (1272–1307). From the 13th century onwards, the town of Berkeley sought to established itself as an important market and trading centre, although its prosperity was often overshadowed by the wool and cloth producing towns of the Cotswolds nearby.

The town layout has changed little since the medieval period with the four main streets, Canonbury Street, High Street, Salter Street and Marybrook Street, first referenced in 1492, 1575, 1575 and 1516 respectively (Leech 1981, 4). The main trading street during the medieval period was probably High

Figure 2. A depiction of the inner ward of Berkeley Castle by F. W. Hulme (1845)

Street. Many buildings within this street are earlier than the buildings along Canonbury Street and adjoining Salter Street.

Moyle's 1544 Survey of Berkeley (Fig. 3) and the Tithe Map of 1840 show a series of regular medieval burgage plots to either side of High Street, from the Canonbury Street junction to The Pill. In contrast, the plots in Salter Street are larger and more irregular which suggests, in combination with the dates of the buildings in the area, that the commercial centre shifted from High Street to Salter Street and Canonbury Street during the 17th–18th centuries: when the town became a prosperous trading centre. Many buildings in Salter Street and Canonbury Street date to this period and there are a number of buildings along Canonbury Street which, although now dwellings, were once shop frontages. The same can be said of medieval buildings in High Street.

Smyth suggests that in 1422 the town may have comprised as many as 240 houses (Smyth 1639, III, 84), but this number was greatly reduced by 1483, as a result of rival claims to the castle, which saw it attacked, taken and retaken on numerous occasions, half destroying the town in the process. In 1639, Berkeley consisted of a castle, a church and just 80 houses. In 1804, it consisted of 99 houses and 658 inhabitants (Fig. 4).

The town lost its borough status in 1886 when the corporation lost its charter and was annulled. The town and district, from that point on, came under the jurisdiction of the county magistrates, with the status of a parish. In the 19th century the town declined in importance as it was not situated on any through roads or rail routes.

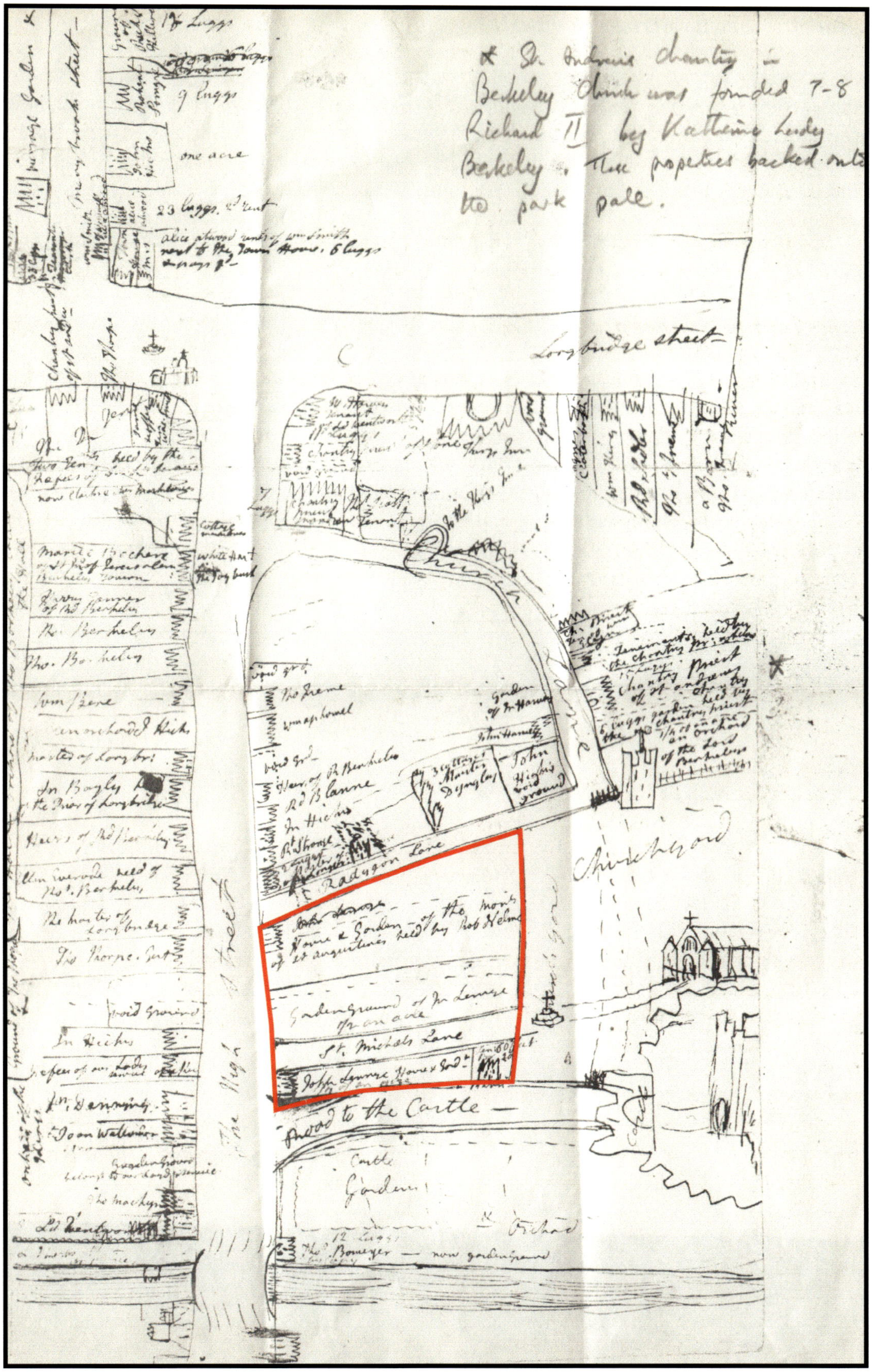

Figure 3. Detail from Moyle's 1544 map of Berkeley (section in red was target of BCP work on High Street)

Longbridge Street and Holy Trinity Hospital

On the 1544 Moyle Survey of Berkeley, Canonbury Street is named Longbridge Street. At the east end of Canonbury Street, where the road crosses the rivulet that flows to the east of the town, was an area called Longbridge. It was named after a long wooden bridge which, by the 17th century, had been replaced with a causeway pitched with stone. At Longbridge, there was a medieval hospital of Holy Trinity, founded by Maurice de Berkeley [I] *c.* 1170–1189. The complex comprised chapel, priory and hospital, along with a series of fishponds. It was dissolved at the time of the Dissolution of the Monasteries, under the *Chantries Act* of 1547. Smyth (1639) records that all the buildings were demolished before the end of the 16th century (Leech 1981, 5; GSMR 5116).

Little Park and Castle Worthy

All the properties that front onto the eastern side of Church Lane, along with those that front onto the southern side of Longbridge Street, back onto a feature listed as 'Park Pale' on the 1544 Moyle Survey of Berkeley. In 1544 an area bounded to the north by Canonbury Street, to the east by the Longbridge rivulet, to the south by the perimeter boundary of the castle, and to the west by the eastern boundaries of the Churchyard, Chantry and Vicarage, was a deer park known as 'Little Park' or 'Kings Park'. The word 'Pale' describes the paling or fencing that was used to enclose the park. Adjacent to Little Park was another park called Castle Park.

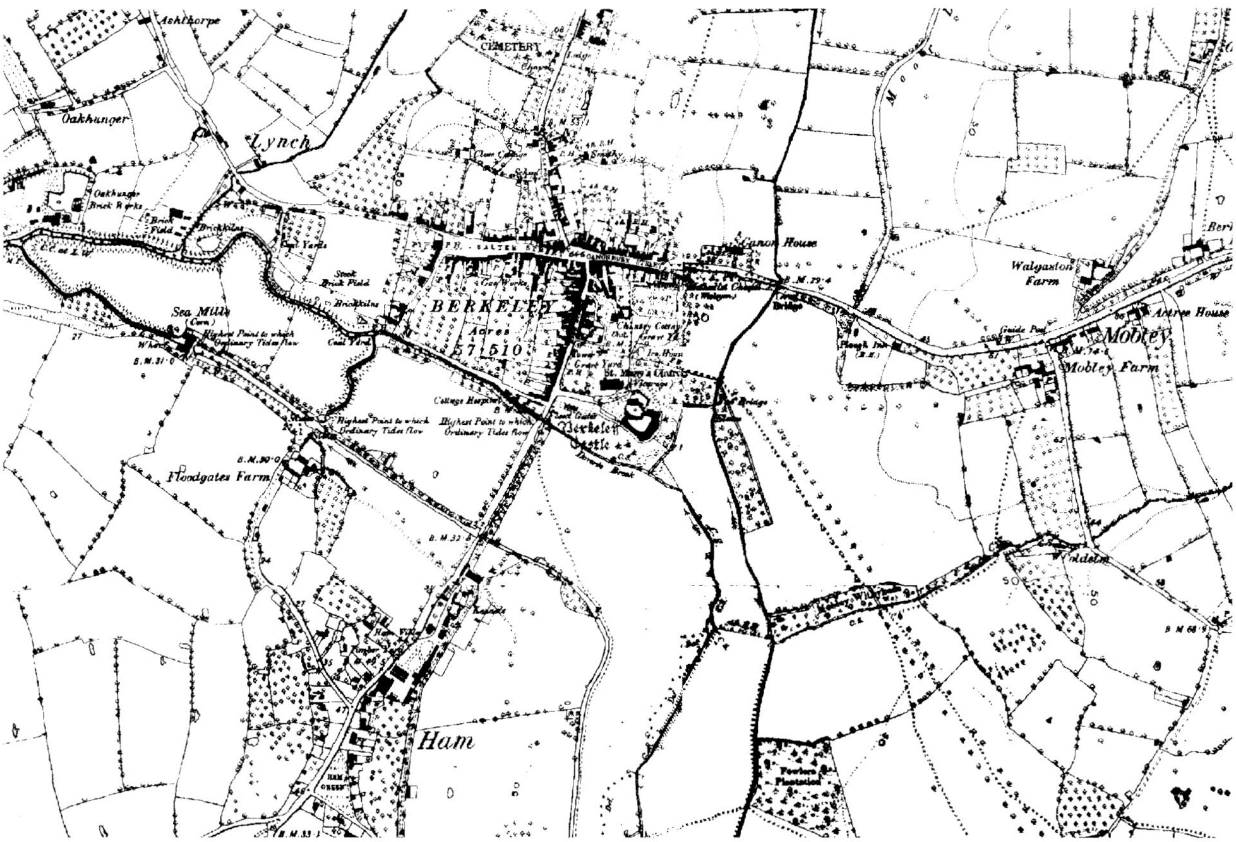

Figure 4. OS first edition map of Berkeley

The first record of 'Little Park' and 'Castle Park' dates from 1522, when the tenants of Berkeley wrote to Henry VIII to complain that his deer had escaped from the two parks and had eaten/damaged their crops. Henry's reply was that 'Castle Park' was to be enlarged and another large deer park created. The new park, which went away from the town towards the village of Newport, was named 'Worthy Park' or 'Castle Worthy Park' (Tandy 2003, 60–1, 229).

The Walled Garden

In 1544, and from at least 1533, the area which comprised a walled garden (Fig. 4) to the north of the castle was part of a deer park named 'Little Park'. The Walled Garden first appeared on the 1840 Tithe Map and plot 998 was a 'garden'. The owner of the garden was Lord Segrave (Lord of the Manor) and the occupier at the time was the Berkeley Free School. The construction of the walled garden is the first visible enclosure of the former 'Little Park' deer park. On the OS 1st edition map (1880–1885 above) the layout of the walled garden is indicated.. On later maps, depicted in the garden, in the north-west corner, is a large greenhouse and two more stand against the north wall. There is also a series of formal paths, which run around the perimeter and cross the garden centrally in two directions, dividing the internal area into quadrants. The paths are lined with trees. Outside the eastern wall of the garden are several other greenhouses, oriented roughly east–west.

Church Lane and Jenner's Garden

Moyle's 1544 map of Berkeley (Fig. 3) shows Church Lane as a neat arc curving north-west to south-east which continues through the churchyard to the castle gatehouse but, on all later maps, the course of the lane has completely altered. A plan in the Gloucester Records Office (GRO, Q/SRh 1828A/2), dated 1828, shows a proposed alteration to Church Lane to the course of the present day route. The alteration was carried out and a new lane was constructed to give Captain Jenner a larger frontage to his house (plot 199 on the 1840 Tithe Map). The Chantry was newly built as a residence in *c.* 1707 and Edward Jennner (famous for inventing the procedure of vaccination) moved into the house *c.* 1785. The Edward Jenner Museum building served as the Vicarage from 1854 to 1983, at which point a new vicarage was built in the former garden.

Nelme's Paddock

At present, the area enclosed by Radigon Lane to the north, St Mary's churchyard to the east, the road to the castle to the south (called 'King's Highway'), and High Street to the west, is an empty paddock. On Moyle's 1544 survey of Berkeley, however, this paddock is shown bisected by a lane called St Michael's Lane that ran from High Street to the west door of the church; and opposite the church door, in the entrance to the lane, is depicted a large stone cross.

The paddock, as portrayed on the 1544 map, is further subdivided into four plots: two to the north and two to the south of St Michael's Lane. The entries in the plots, from north to south, read: *Home and Garden, of the monks of St Augustine's, held by Robert Nelme; Garden, Ground of Robert Nelme, ½ an acre; John Lennye, House and Garden, ¼ of an acre; Barn, length 60 feet × width 20 feet.* Thus, in 1544, there were houses in the north-west and south-west corners of the paddock, fronting onto High Street, and in the south-east corner there stood a large barn, fronting onto the 'King's Highway' to the castle. As Robert Nelme was in possession of the majority of land that today comprises the paddock, the area quickly gained the nick-name 'Nelme's Paddock': this name has been used throughout the report to distinguish this piece of ground.

On the 1840 Tithe Map, there is no sign of the buildings, St Michael's Lane or the large stone cross depicted in 1544; and these features are not visible today. Smyth (1639, III, 84) states that St Michael's Lane had gone before his lifetime which, if true, means that it disappeared sometime between 1544 and 1567, and it is perhaps possible that the houses were destroyed in September 1645, in the English Civil War, during a three day siege on the castle. On the 1840 Tithe Map, 'Nelme's Paddock' is labelled Plot 201 and is listed in the Apportionments as a 'garden'. This was a walled garden that produced fruit and vegetables for the castle household. On the OS 1st edition map (1880–1885) the walled garden has been filled in to create the paddock.

Quarf Mead and Home Ground

South-west of Berkeley Castle, on the opposite side of the road to the stables and kennels of Berkeley hunt, there is a large meadow, which measures *c.* 200 m north-east to south-west × *c.* 200 m north-west to south-east. It is bounded to the north by the Little Avon River, to the east by the road to Ham, to the south by the northern boundaries of various properties that front onto Hamfield Lane, and to the west by the eastern boundary of Floodgates Farm. Unsurprisingly, since the meadow borders the Little Avon River and is only 8–10 m AOD, it has been known to flood during high tides at Sharpness. The meadow contains numerous earthworks, some rectangular, which may represent house platforms. Tandy (2003, 175–90) suggests that the bridge at the north-east corner of the field is the original site of the 'Lockfast Bridge', first recorded in 1165–1220, and hence the castle's two water mills, mentioned in Domesday, were located at nearby Brown's Mill, 500 m to the south-east, and Sea Mills, 280 m to the north-west. The earliest map that shows the meadow is the 1840 Tithe Map which depicts it divided into two plots: adjacent to the Little Avon River is the smaller 'Quarf Mead' plot, the southern boundary of which follows the 10.00 m contour line, and south of this is the larger 'Home Ground' plot. On the OS 1st edition map, 'the highest point to which ordinary tides flow' is marked in the meadow's north-west corner and it is possible that 'Quarf Mead' translates as 'Wharf Meadow', and may have numbered among Berkeley's many wharfs. The numerous earthworks in the meadow are not depicted on any historic or modern maps. These findings led to several years of research that attempted to identify positively the external boundaries of the Anglo-Saxon minster as well as further investigation of the interior of the Anglo-Saxon minster itself, and additionally, excavation and survey work in and around the castle.

Previous archaeological work in Berkeley

Between 1917 and 1937, the 8th Earl of Berkeley carried out a series of archaeological excavations in the Outer Ward and within the shell-keep at Berkeley Castle (GSMR 5112). Reports on these excavations are published in *Transactions of the Bristol and Gloucestershire Archaeological Society* 1927, vol. 49, 183–93 and 1938, vol. 60, 308–39, and the results have been reinterpreted in BCP Report No. 1, 35 (Prior 2005a). The most important conclusions reached were: (1) that a moat surrounded a major portion of the shell-keep – the moat ran around the base of the shell-keep on the south-west, north-west and north-east sides; (2) that the moat was not concentric with the shell-keep and was therefore earlier in date – which suggests that it was a moat surrounding one of the earlier mottes [1067 or 1121] (Fig. 5).

An archaeological watching brief was also undertaken between February 2002 and March 2003, by M Cook, in St Mary's churchyard (GSMR 5117). In addition to recording 10th–14th century Saxon and medieval pottery, a section of stone paving, when lifted, was found to comprise gravestones turned face downwards. Five had legible inscriptions and dated between 1791 and 1853.

Finally, an archaeological evaluation was undertaken by George Nash for Border Archaeology during February 2003 (GSMR 22165 and 22166). Eight trenches were excavated in the Walled Garden close to the medieval street frontages of Canonbury Street. Three of these revealed sections of medieval building foundations which fronted onto Canonbury Street. Associated with these structures was a significant finds assemblage including medieval glazed pottery. Other trenching located within the walled garden revealed evidence of an earlier formal garden layout including the foundations of a 19th century greenhouse, together with the remains of an under-floor heating system (Nash 2003, 16–17).

Bristol excavations at the Berkeley Castle estate

From 2005 to 2007 research and excavation concentrated mainly on identifying the boundaries of the Anglo-Saxon minster at Berkeley digging firstly in the Walled Garden [ST 685 991] to the north of the castle and then focusing upon the buildings themselves inside the minster (Fig. 6).

In 2006, a large trench (Trench 3) was opened inside the remains of the castle's Walled Garden complex, commonly known as the Butterfly Garden [ST 685 991], located near the medieval street frontages of Canonbury Street. Trench 3 was cut adjacent to Trench 1 to explore a longer section of Anglo-Saxon ditch that was discovered in the 2005 excavations. A further 8.00 m of truncated mid-9th to early 11th century ditch was uncovered. The ditch profile was wider than that recorded in 2005, and the ditch is now estimated to have been *c.* 2.00 m wide at the top when first cut. Thus we knew we had located one

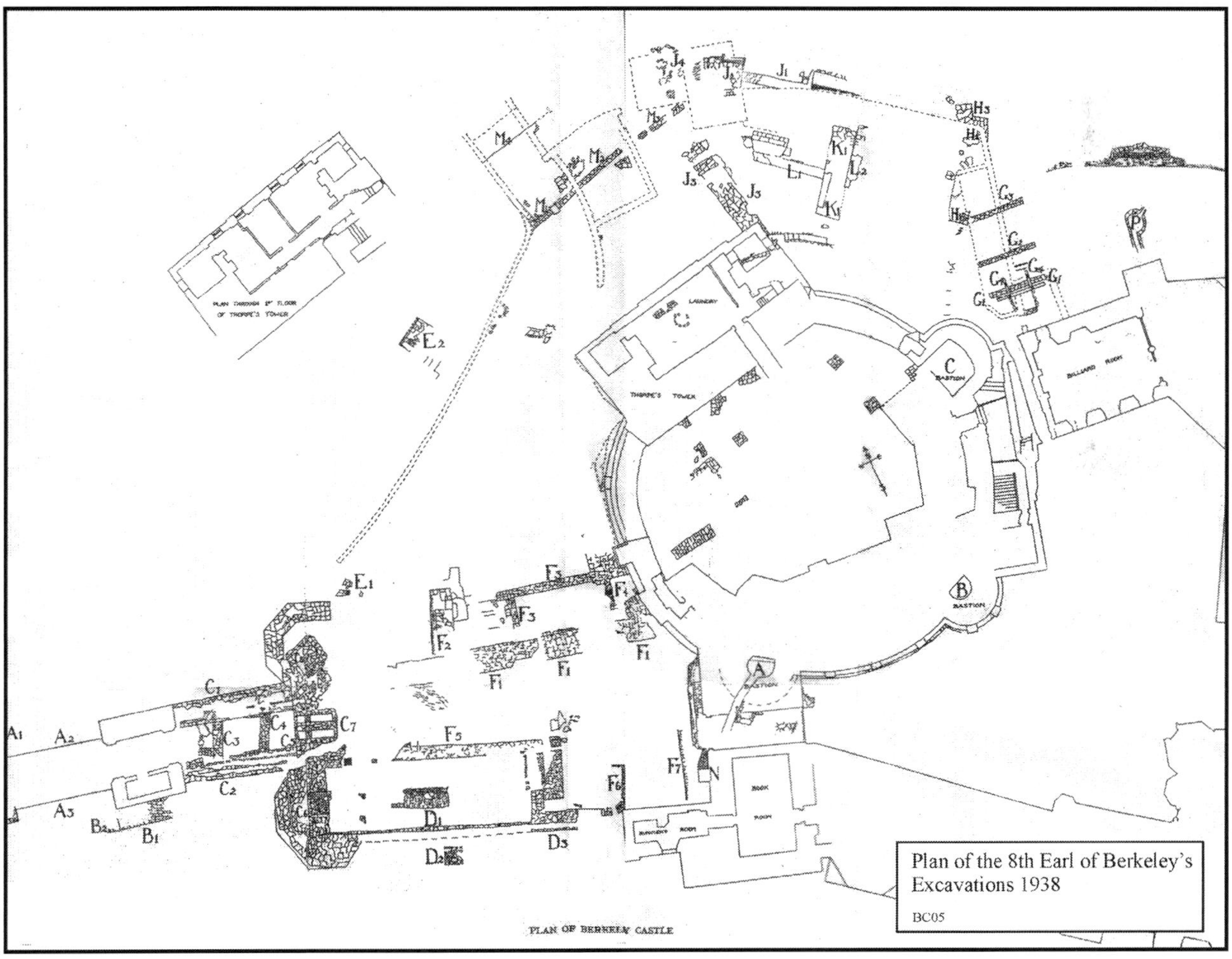

Figure 5. Plan of the 8th Earl Berkeley excavations in 1938

side of the minster's enclosure ditch, and for the next few years the goal was to ascertain the external boundaries of the minster. The real boundaries were not realized, however, until the final year of excavations in 2019.

In 2006, the ditch fill in the Walled Garden was found to contained two sherds of mid-9th to early 11th century pottery; a further two sherds were also recorded in adjacent contexts, and an Anglo-Saxon coin was recovered. The coin was a silver halfpenny of King Edgar (the Peaceable) 959–975; the Great Great Grandson of Alfred the Great.

The size, location and alignment of the ditch recorded in Trench 3, along with the finds contained in the ditch fill and adjacent contexts, support the suggestion made in the 2005 excavation report that there was a Saxon Minster at Berkeley which appears to have gone into decline towards the end of the 10th century.

In addition to the excavations in 2006, two large, detailed earthwork surveys were undertaken. In Quarf Mead and Home Ground [ST 680 987] a survey recorded a complex palimpsest of earthworks associated with the Little Avon River and possibly connected to river transport, waterpower or flood defence, as well as the vestigial remains of old field boundaries and areas of ridge and furrow ploughing. The earthwork survey in Little Park and Castle Worthy (Longbridge) [ST 687 992] respectively recorded a sizeable L-shaped platform and a couple of large rectangular sunken features bordering a well-defined rectangular platform: the latter appears to be the remnants of two fishponds and a building which may possibly be associated with the medieval hospital complex of Holy Trinity (*c.* 1170–1547), whilst the former may be a protective or defensive structure linked to the northern approach to the castle.

From 2007 to 2009, research and excavation concentrated mainly on the interior of the minster with work undertaken in Nelme's Paddock [ST 684 990] and the Edward Jenner Museum Garden [ST 685 990]. Excavations in 2007 investigated what is presumed to be the nun's church (BCP Report Number 7; 'Archaeological Fieldwork in the Jenner Museum Garden', 2007 – Trench 9) for the double-house minster; St Mary's church (extant) conversely forming the monk's church (with an Anglo-Saxon string course still visible in the present church). In the Edward Jenner Museum garden excavations (Trench 5, 7, 10 and 11) also investigated other Anglo-Saxon buildings that were probably small dwelling houses for the nuns.

Two burials were uncovered in 2007, during excavation of Trench 5 (BC07 – Trench No 5; BCP Report Number 7; 'Archaeological Fieldwork Jenner Museum Garden' 2007 – Trench No 5) alongside the south wall of the Jenner Museum garden, which revealed clear evidence of late Saxon or Saxo-Norman use of the site. It is tempting to attribute these burials to the Anglo-Saxon nunnery recorded historically as having been founded *c.* 883 and demolished *c.* 1043. The nunnery appears to have formed an integral component of the minster, whose chapel, sources suggest, was located adjacent to the site where the two burials were unearthed.

Also undertaken in 2007, in Nelme's Paddock [ST 684 990], was an open-area excavation that recorded the remains of the now-vanished St Michael's Lane and two Tudor houses, which are shown on Moyle's 1544 map of Berkeley and, additionally, the remains of the castle's Medieval Barn. Remnants of the east wall of the barn have been identified – and recorded – in the present churchyard wall to the west of St Mary's Church. A geophysical survey was undertaken on a number of visible earthwork features in Quarf Mead and Home Ground [ST 680 987]. A detailed earthwork survey undertaken during the Project's 2006 fieldwork, suggested that these features may be the remains of house platforms, wharf side structures or one, possibly two, medieval watermills that are known to have existed in the area. Furthermore, in the Castle Moat [ST 686 990], a detailed earthwork survey was undertaken of two areas: (a) the ditch/

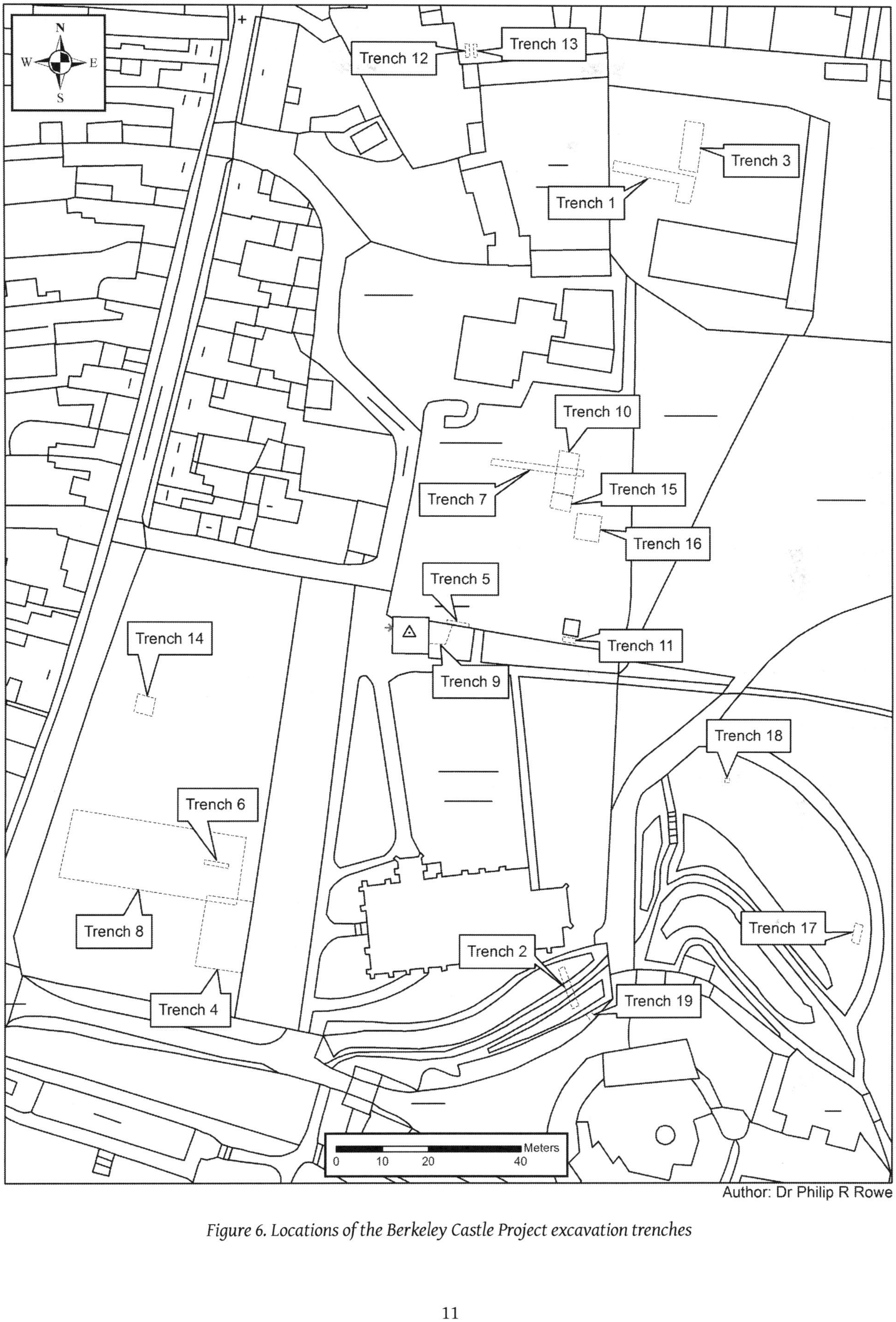

Figure 6. Locations of the Berkeley Castle Project excavation trenches

moat that lies between the castle's Outer Ward and St Mary's church; (b) the area to the north and east of the castle keep, which is bounded by a terraced garden to the south, a brook to the east, Little Park to the north, and a pathway from the main visitor car park to the castle in the west. The survey built upon the excavation work undertaken during the Project's 2005 fieldwork, which demonstrated that the ditch between the castle's Outer Ward and St Mary's church was a defensive feature from the English Civil War (*c.* 1645) rather than a medieval castle moat. In 2008, excavations continued in Nelme's Paddock [ST 684 990] looking for the western ditch of the minster but it was not until 2015 that the true external west ditch of the minster was finally recorded in Nelme's Paddock; and excavated from 2015 to 2019. In 2009, however, an excavation in the *Berkeley Arms* Hotel (Trench 12) recorded the Anglo-Saxon boundary ditch running along the rear of the gardens that front onto Canonbury Street. Thus, we knew we had the east and north sides of the minster enclosure at that point, and from 2009 to 2019 excavations were targeted to try to find the minster's western and southern extremities and to investigate some of the structures and buildings of the interior. It is not hard to ascertain the southern extent of the minster, however, as the ditch must run up the private drive to the castle, otherwise you fall off the end of the hill that Berkeley sits atop.

In 2009, excavations continued in Nelme's Paddock, where Trench 4 (15 m north–south × 10 m east–west) and Trench 6 (5 m east–west × 1 m north–south), which were opened in 2007, were combined to form one large trench (Trench 8); and this trench was further extended west towards High Street. Also in 2009, excavations continued in St Mary's Churchyard [ST 684 993] in an area adjacent to the east side of the free standing Church tower. If Berkeley was indeed a double house minster it would have had two churches, one for the monks and one for the nuns, and the excavations here set out to prove this. At St Mary's there is a separate bell tower at the north end of the churchyard which was rebuilt in 1753 after it was damaged during the Civil War (GSMR 9344). This bell tower was constructed on the site of an earlier church with tower (Bigland 1791; Fosbroke 1821, 49; Fisher 1865, 10; Leech 1981, 5; Tandy, 2003, 108, 236–40). Early references specify that the previous church was a nunnery chapel (Bigland 1791; Fosbroke 1821, 49) and that the minster either decayed or was incorporated into the newly established parochial system sometime between 1019 and 1051. The objective of the work undertaken in St Mary's Churchyard was to locate the foundations of the nunnery chapel. The excavations uncovered walls and floor layers that were clearly part of the fabric of a medieval church/tower, which was subsequently robbed to provide building stone during the reconstruction of the replacement tower in 1753. Excavations also revealing that the later church tower did not sit atop of the footprint of the earlier one, and that it was clearly moved several metres to the west, which of course means that the nunnery chapel, or earlier church that adjoined the medieval tower, was several metres to the east, just outside the edge of the excavated trench cut (and so remains a mystery for another time).

Between 2008 to 2010 excavations were conducted in Nelme's Paddock (Trench 8), St Mary's Churchyard (Trench 9) and in the Jenner Museum Garden (Trench 10). These trenches were also focused upon identifying the interior of the minster and in addition to create a broader understanding of the landscape evolution around Berkeley. In 2012 and 2013, excavations were mainly concentrated in the Jenner Garden, with the extensions of Trench 10 and Trench 15, again to try to understand the interior of the Anglo-Saxon Minster and the potential buildings within. In 2013 two trenches were opened in the area of Castle Gateway (Trench 17 – north-east of the castle and Trench 18) to assess changes to the castle's entrance. The results highlighted that the original entrance to the castle had shifted away from being northfacing with castle visitors now approaching from the south-west resulting from a newly constructed private driveway. The last trench opened at Berkeley was that dug by the University of Bristol team in 2015 (Trench 19) in the Castle's Outer Ward (next to footbridge) as, with the conclusion of the excavations in Trench 19, we were finally beginning to understand the early origins of the castle and the great donjon that was constructed when the castle was built in stone by Robert FitzHarding in 1153–1154.

Community and heritage in Berkeley

From the very early days of the Berkeley Castle Project the Bristol team, which was already experienced in the aspects of public and community archaeology, put this at the forefront of its approach to the engagement with the local communities. Community engagement is a major concern for education and heritage sectors alike. The diversity of engagement strategies employed by these bodies is context dependent and, as such, there is no single best practice guidance that can be applied to all projects. The demand for community engagement comes from multiple directions: the community themselves; the educational institution, such as a university; and may also extend to include heritage partners, like museums. Engagement activities can serve to bring academic research into the wider world in a tangible manner. In Berkeley the university students were positioned as drivers in engagement showing an important contribution to fieldwork-based learning.

At Berkeley, the project has launched an onsite social media team which communicated in real time the excavation achievements to the public, and a blog, still available (in 2021) through the departmental website. These activities were completely student led providing them with valuable skills. The community aspect of the Berkeley Castle Project though was really showcased with the 'Town Museum Project', one of the many 'mini- projects' co-run by students. Students were taking their knowledge of archaeological research and hands-on fieldwork experience at Berkeley Castle, combined with their classroom learning, and transforming it into a tangible engagement output.

The Town Museum Project aimed to identify an effective way to bring archaeology to the community of Berkeley, to provide opportunities for students to enhance their engagement skills and to showcase the archaeological research undertaken by the Department of Anthropology and Archaeology. The objectives centred on plans to design a temporary exhibition of artefacts for public display around the town of Berkeley. This would lead to an invitation to the community to participate in hosting a temporary display of excavated artefacts and place students at the heart of all activities. We also sought to evaluate all aspects of the project, including student, stakeholder and participant reflections and feedback and to work with our heritage stakeholder (owner of the artefacts), Berkeley Castle, and consider what activities could support their efforts and concerns. The design, implementation and feedback were developed into a project model with the goal to share outcomes and impacts as widely as possible.

The Town Museum Project ran from 2013 to 2015. Berkeley Castle, our key heritage stakeholder, facilitated and supported the project from its inception, giving permission for artefacts to go on public display and printing information materials as requested by the Engagement Team. In the first instance, a notice was posted through the letterboxes of residents informing them of our excavation season along with an invitation to apply to host a display tray for the Town Museum. In small teams, students went door to door in the centre of the town, introducing the project and asking residents if they were interested in applying. This personal approach worked much more effectively than the printed flyers and resulted in 20 community participants, including private residences and commercial businesses, signing up in just one day. The face-to-face engagement was an important experience for the students and taught them the value of inter-personal relationships with the community.

Once the community demonstrated their interest in the project, students extracted 250 artefacts from the archaeological assemblage for display. To ensure that items would not become mis-catalogued later, each item was hand-labelled. Students then arranged the artefacts into trays on coloured paper, to make a pleasing display, and designed information sheets to display alongside the trays. Both elements required them to use a range of archaeological skills, drawing on their existing academic knowledge and research abilities. Students also took care to design an agreement form for the community to sign, leaving them with a copy of the form for their records. The agreement was very simple and served to remind participants to take reasonable care so that the artefacts would not be damaged during the project.

The Town Museum Project outcomes concentrated on three main aspects: first, placing trust in both students and the community helped to develop better relationships between the different stakeholders; secondly, within a supervised and supportive framework the students were able to take creative charge of managing a project to produce effectively impressive and professional result; finally, inviting community participation in both private and commercial venues lead to better and more effective engagement.

The aims and objectives of the project were met and then exceeded. The research efforts of the Department of Anthropology and Archaeology were showcased to great effect in a public venue. Berkeley Castle were delighted to be able to share their history within the community, to enhance community relations, which is a priority for them. They also welcomed the possibility of increased publicity of their heritage site. The project proved to be an effective way to bring archaeology into community life at Berkeley. The community were pleased to be so actively included within our research efforts and applauded the project vocally. Local businesses also saw the project and associated media coverage as a means to promote their business and support the local economy. The community also improved their knowledge of history, archaeology of their local area, and artefact analysis. Students developed an extensive range of transferable engagement-related skills, from communication to time management, and also greatly enjoyed the experience. They valued the trust placed in them to lead the project and invested much personal time. Likewise, the community valued the trust given to them to become temporary curators of the artefacts.

The Berkeley Tales volume

Research in Berkeley is far from complete and this volume does not aim to be a definitive publication of the archaeological research for the Castle and the town. The scope of the publication is to communicate the outcomes of the 15 years of University of Bristol research in the area and to pave the road for future research in the evolution on town landscapes in Britain. Kostas Trimmis, Gareth Dickinson and Jenifer Muller in Chapter 2 tackle exactly this aspect of the landscape evolution in Berkeley, building on the earlier work by Phil Rowe and Jim Pimpernell. Geophysics and landscape research were core components of the BCP from the very first to the very last season. A series of archaeology technicians, landscape archaeology students and professional providers working for all these years at Berkeley is summarised in chapter two. In Chapter 3, building specialist and archaeology project manager Rachel Morgan and the current author attempt to create a biography of the castle itself, based upon building recording, historic research and archaeological information from the Bristol excavations. Chapter 4 presents a summary of the excavation's main findings with a brief report for every trench at Berkeley reconstructing the narrative of the excavation and the past events. The reporting of Trench 8, where work had not yet been completed by the end of BCP's time on site, is also presented as a preliminary work.

The second part of the volume focuses on the presentation, assessment and analysis of the finds assemblages from BCP. In Chapter 5, Paul Blinkhorn, a long-time project collaborator, presents analysis of the pottery assemblage from the BCP. The pottery reports are presented by trench with the overall discussion in the last chapter. In Chapter 6 all the small finds from the project are presented by Emma Firth, incorporating previous work by Leslie Webster. Chapters 7 and 8 focus on the analysis of animal and human skeletal remains from Berkeley, respectively. Sarah Gosling, another long-time project partner presents a first account of the animal bones from the Walled Garden, Castle Worthy and the

Jenner Garden excavations. The Nelme's Paddock material is also assessed. Christianne Fernée follows, with a detailed analysis of the human bone finds, mainly from Trench 4 in Nelme's Paddock but also from the Jenner Garden excavations, incorporating earlier work by Annsofie Witkin. Kostas Trimmis joins the present author for the last chapter to present the narrative and evolution of Berkeley Castle and town based upon the archaeological finds and features.

Bibliography

Bigland, R. 1791–1792. *Historical, Monumental and Genealogical Collections, Relative to the County of Gloucester.* London.

Earl of Berkeley, 1927. Berkeley Castle. *Transactions of the Bristol and Gloucestershire Archaeological Society* 49, 183-193.

Earl of Berkeley, 1938. Excavations At Berkeley Castle. *Transactions of the Bristol and Gloucestershire Archaeological Society* 60, 308-339.

Fisher, J., 1865. *History of Berkeley, its Church, Castle, etc.* Bristol.

Fosbroke, T.D. 1821 Berkeley Manuscripts. *Abstracts and Extracts of Smyth's Lives of the Berkeleys.* London.

Leech, R. 1981. *Historic Towns in Gloucestershire: Archaeology and planning.* Stroud: Sutton

Morris, J. (ed.) 1982. *Domesday Book - Gloucestershire.* Chichester: Phillimore.

Nash, G.H. 2003. *Walled Gardens at Berkeley Castle, Berkeley, Gloucestershire.* Unpublished Evaluation Report.

Prior, S.J. 2005. *Archaeological Excavation & Earthwork Survey in The Butterfly Garden, Castle Moat & Water Meadow, Berkeley Castle, Gloucestershire, 2005.* Bristol University: unpublished Report (BC05), BCP Report 1.

Prior, S.J 2007. *Archaeological Excavations in the Edward Jenner Museum Garden. BCP Report No 7. 2007: Archaeological Excavation Report for the Edward Jenner Museum, Gloucestershire, 2007* (Unpublished archaeological report).

Smyth, J. (of Nibley). 1639 [1883]. The Berkeley Manuscripts: Lives of the Berkeleys = Maclean, J. (ed.) *Transaction of Bristol and Gloucestershire Archaeological Society* 8.

Tandy, D. 2003. *Berkeley: A town in the marshes.* Privately Published.

Chapter 2

Tales from the Land: An Account of the Landscape and Geophysical Research of the Berkeley Castle Project

Konstantinos P. Trimmis, Gareth Dickinson, and Jennifer Muller

The Berkeley landscape

Berkeley sits at the head of the fertile 'Vale of Berkeley' and the surrounding countryside consists of rich meadow and pastureland. The parish of Berkeley includes the town and a small area around it and the pattern of the adjacent parish boundaries indicates that it was carved out of the surrounding, and much larger, parish of Hamfallow (Leech 1981, 4).

The ridge upon which both town and castle reside is *c.* 800 m wide at its south-western end, tapers to a rounded point in the north-east, and measures *c.*1.65 km (1 mile) in length from north-east to south-west. Waterways flank the base of the Berkeley ridge on all sides. A spring in the north-east of the town separates into fluvial channels east and west of the ridge. While the channel to the west is unnamed the one to the east is known as Newport Brook. These in turn run into Berkeley Pill, known as Doverte Brook, beyond Lockfast Bridge at the south end of High Street, a tributary of the River Severn which runs 4 km west. The Little Avon River, known locally as the Matford (Tandy 2003, 179), joins the Berkeley Pill channel to the west of town. These waterways not only form physical bounds within which the town is contained but constitute a part of Berkeley's social identity as 'It has been said for generations that to be a true inhabitant of the town of Berkeley one has to be born within the four bridges' (Tandy 2003, 11). The bedrock geology to the west of Berkeley ridge is composed of mudstones from the Micklewood Formation and Wenlock Rocks while the course of Berkeley Pill and the Little Avon follow the boundary between the Raglan Mudstone Formation and Mercia Mudstone Group. The superficial geology of the waterways surrounding Berkeley ridge is composed of Flandrian alluvial clays, silts, sands and gravels (Fig. 1).

The castle is located to the south-east of the town of Berkeley, at a height of *c.* 23 m AOD, overlooking water meadows to the east and south, some 15–17 m below. The site for the castle was well chosen, as the location affords good visibility of the surrounding countryside and would have offered good defensive potential. Berkeley castle and town are situated on a low ridge of Red Marl with intermittent bands of sandstone. The Soil Survey of England & Wales (1983) identifies the soil around Berkeley as Fladbury 1 813b, consisting of stoneless clayey soils, some of which are calcareous and affected by groundwater. Underlying is primarily solid Silurian (with Limestones), Ludlow, Wenlock and Llandovery Bed geology. To the west, this is surrounded by undulating solid Devonian (with Limestone's) and Old Red Sandstone, and to the east by alluvial deposits and solid Lias geology.

Landscape research in Berkeley Castle Project (BCP)

Landscape research, with a bi-fold aim to understand the evolution of the anthropogenic landscape and fluvioscape of Berkeley and the training to archaeology students, was core component to the Berkeley Castle project from its inception in 2005 to the final season in 2019. Landscape research in BCP was

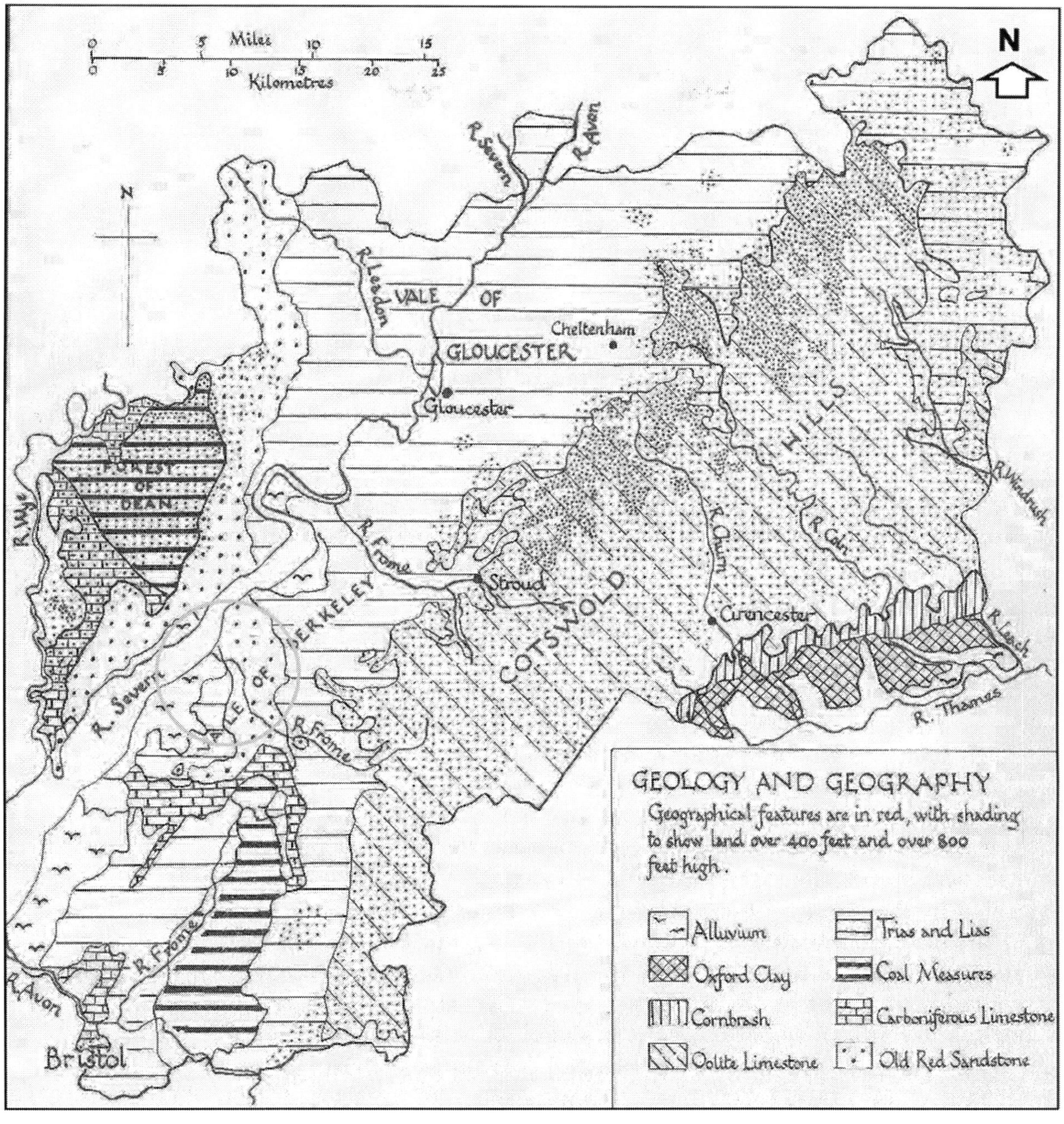

Figure 1. A simplified geological map of Berkeley.

undertaken with a combination of earthwork and geophysical survey in and around Berkeley Castle and the town (Fig. 2). Earthwork survey was conducted by several surveyors between 2005 and 2008, with a second phase by K. Trimmis in 2019, with the objective of recording any earthworks in the BCP area of study and to assess their date, character, and extent.

Geophysical survey played a complementary role during the field school excavations in Berkeley, between 2005 and 2019, again with several surveyors leading the works. Magnetometry and resistivity techniques that detect anomalies underground through different methods were sometimes used together as complementary methods. Surveys were carried out in different areas of Berkeley as student training exercises but also to explore the evolution of the wider landscape around Berkeley Castle.

The temporal span of the landscape research in BCP covered a broad period of approximately 2000 years from the Romano-British period to the end of the 20th century. The spatial extent of the research was, however, quite narrow, concentrating on the single fluvial landscape of Berkeley. However, it is hoped that the multidisciplinary methodology, developed and tested in BCP, can work as a guide for similar studies, that can create a more comprehensive picture of waterway modification and exploitation on a larger analytical level.

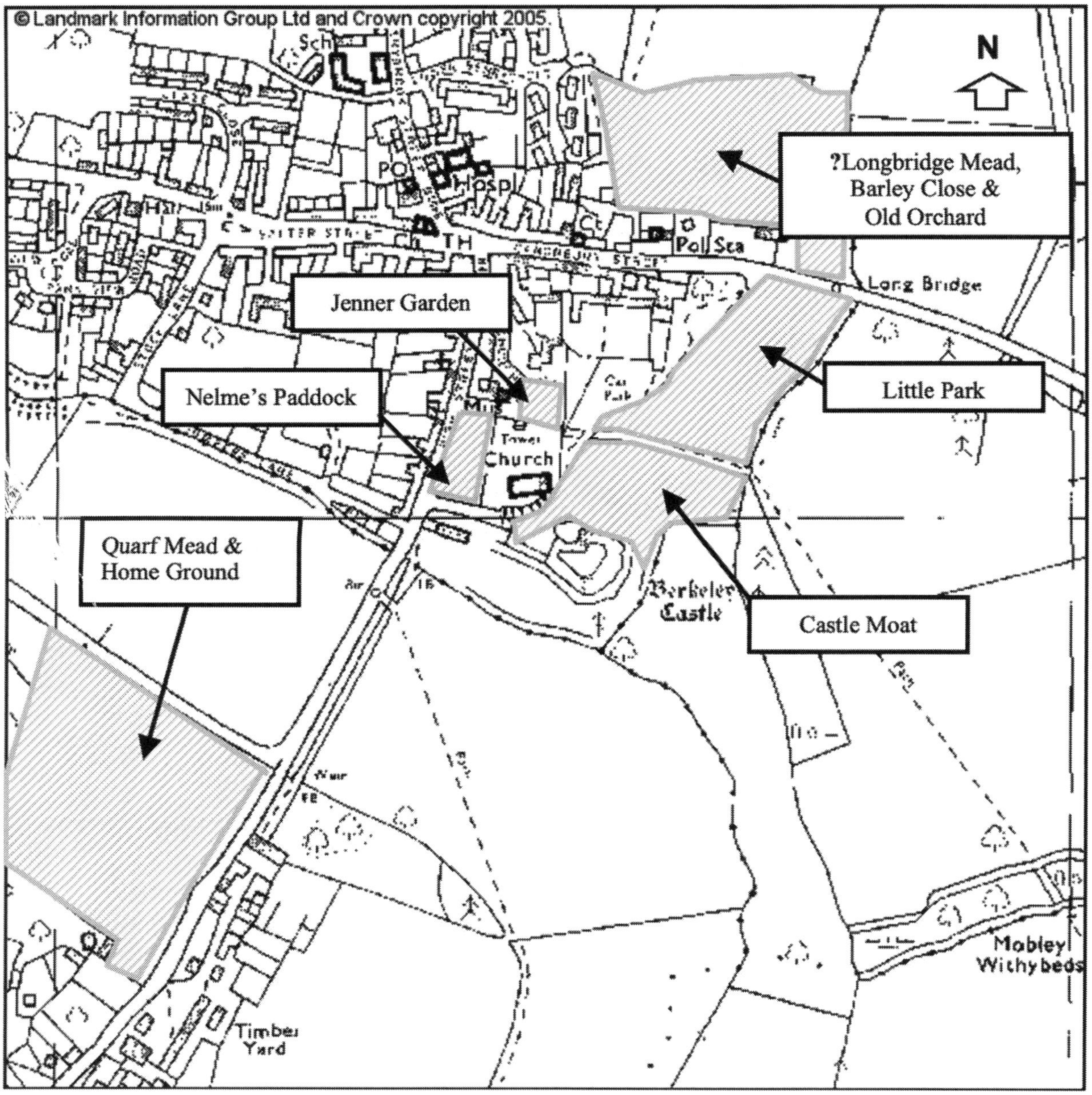

Figure 2. The area covered from Berkeley Castle Project with the landscape study areas annotated.

Methods

Data collection

For the earthwork surveys at Berkeley a combination of tools and methods was employed. Early surveys were undertaken using a Topcon GTS 210 (EDM) with the results plotted in the field. Survey control points were established using the EDM with the survey data logged manually. Control points were used to take off-sets using hand-tapes, which enabled rich details and features to be accurately plotted. Some linear features were plotted using the EDM alone. Later surveys conducted with a combination of a Topcon HIPER SR with classic tacheometry using a dumpy level, for teaching purposes. The principal control points were tied into the national grid (OSGB36) to allow the completed earthwork survey to be related to Ordnance Survey maps and recording systems based upon them. The heights of principal control points AOD were also established. In addition to the earthwork survey drawing, notebooks were kept in which all control point and tape and offset measurements were recorded.

Instruments used for resistivity and magnetometry surveys were the Geoscan RM15-D Resistance Meter, the TR/CIA Resistance Meter and Geoscan FM36 Fluxgate Gradiometer. Both methods rely on the contrast existing between archaeological features and the soil matrix for the anomalies to be visible (Schmidt 2013).

Just as buried archaeological features 'interrupt' the soil, they also interrupt the flow of the electrical current injected into the ground through electrodes during resistivity. The current is carried through the ground by ions, which are what remain of salt crystals from water that has passed through the soil; therefore, resistivity is strongly influenced by the moisture content in the ground. When it is neither oversaturated nor very dry, high resistance responses will usually indicate solid materials, like stone, that make up walls, made-up surfaces, roads and sometimes even coffins. Low resistance anomalies will create less resistance than the soil around them, indicative of ditches/gullies, pits/postholes, drains and graves (Gaffney and Gater 2011; Schmidt 2013). Modern services, like metal pipes and drains, will also show up in this category. However, an abundance of water in the ground will lower the overall electrical resistivity of materials like soil, clay and sand, therefore making it more difficult to 'see' low resistance anomalies. Alternatively, high resistance anomalies are difficult to detect when the soil around them is excessively dry and there is little difference between them. In some cases, such as an infilled pit that would normally have low resistance, water can sink to the bottom, leaving the top dry and resulting in it being undetectable from the soil around it. As a generality, the combination of soil types (loam, clay, sand) and underlying geology will also cause variations in moisture content at any time.

RM15 and TR/CIA resistivity meters involve the paring of electrodes (one current/one potential) being passed over a measured grid, with the results being compared to a background reading obtained from a pair of electrodes placed in a 'fixed' position at least 15 m away. Results are measured in Ohms and calculated resistivity in Ohm–Metres. The effective depth of penetration is approximately 0.75 m.

Magnetometry relies on contrasts in the magnetic field to see features underground. Topsoil and subsoil will usually have different iron contents, and when soil has been moved around, such as to create a pit or ditch, that area will produce a higher or lower magnetic response to the natural soil around it. This enables the detection of infilled sub-surface archaeological features such as ditches, postholes and pits. Strong magnetic anomalies will be generated by iron-based objects or areas modified by intense heat, such as hearths, kilns, and ovens, whose properties have been magnetically altered permanently (thermoremanence) in association with their relative position in the Earth's magnetic field from the time they cooled (Gaffney and Gater 2011).

Issues with magnetometry can arise from the surveyor having undetected metallic objects on their person, which will result in the gradiometer detecting the magnetic item rather than what is underground. Iron-rich items on the surface, not always visible while surveying, or even underground services, can also create strong responses that may hide other, more subtle features. Geology plays a large part in the results as well, with sedimentary and metamorphic rocks generally known to be less responsive than igneous due to their thermoremanent magnetism.

A Fluxgate Gradiometer, one type of magnetometer, comprises two fluxgates, or tubes, which measure the difference between the two detections of an anomaly underground (Oswin 2009). Carried by hand with the bottom sensor approximately 0.1–0.3 m from the ground, two high stability fluxgate sensors are suspended on a single frame 1 m apart and accurately aligned. Reading the difference in the magnetic field at each survey station, results are measured in nanoTeslas (nT). The effective depth of penetration is approximately 1 m, with the fluxgate gradiometer suppressing any diurnal/regional effects.

All surveys were carried out in grids of 20 × 20 m or 30 × 30 m along zig-zag and parallel traverses spaced at 1 m intervals, recording data points spaced at 0.25 m intervals to a maximum instrument sensitivity of 0.1 nT. The survey mode was set to bi-directional. Incomplete survey lines resulting from irregular area boundaries or obstacles were completed using the 'dummy log' key.

Complimentary to earthwork and geophysics survey, aerial imaging was also employed for the landscape research of the BCP. The last few seasons in Berkeley showed an increase in the use of UAVs (drones) and digital 3D dense cloud airborne photogrammetry that was used to create a 3D model of the castle and also for further recording of the excavation trenches and landscape features.

Data processing and presentation

For the earthwork surveys at Berkeley, in the early phase of recording (2005–2008) the finished plans were inked-up, scanned into Adobe Photoshop Elements, cleaned-up and imported as a layer into the ArcGIS Geographical Information System before scaling to a size appropriate for publication. Earthwork surveys of 2019 were all illustrated in the field, and then later digitised with the use of Affinity designer. Again, surveys have been incorporated as layers in a GIS environment, this time using the open source QGIS application.

Following the completion of the detailed geophysical surveys, processing and analysis took place using the Geoplot software package for the gradiometer and resistivity meters. A composite of each detailed survey area was created and processed using Geoplot. Every effort was made to reduce the instrument directional sensitivity in the field rather than reliance on post data-collection processing.

The most typical method of visualising the data is as a greyscale image. In a greyscale plot, each data point is represented as a shade of grey, from black to white at either extreme of the data range. A limited number of standard operations can be carried out to process the data, including clipping and despiking. The results of the survey were then overlaid onto a digital map of the study area. This was then used to produce interpretation figures. The final results have been presented at an appropriate scale tied to the Ordnance Survey National Grid.

Results summary: earthwork survey

The Castle Grounds: surveys run by J. Pimpernell and K.P. Trimmis

The castle sits in a commanding position on the south-eastern corner of a wedge-shaped ridge, which rises out of a relatively flat, low-lying, watery landscape. A ditch (feature A) running between the castle and the parish church is the main feature in the area (Fig. 3). The ditch runs west–east, is some 70 m long, 11 m wide at its widest and a maximum of 3 m deep. A pathway runs along the bottom of the ditch connecting to the gully (feature B) via a tunnel under the roadway connecting the car park and the castle, and to the formal gardens via a tunnel under the road leading up to the castle gatehouse. A short flight of steps leads up to the Outer Ward. The bank on the church side is substantially higher than that on the castle side.

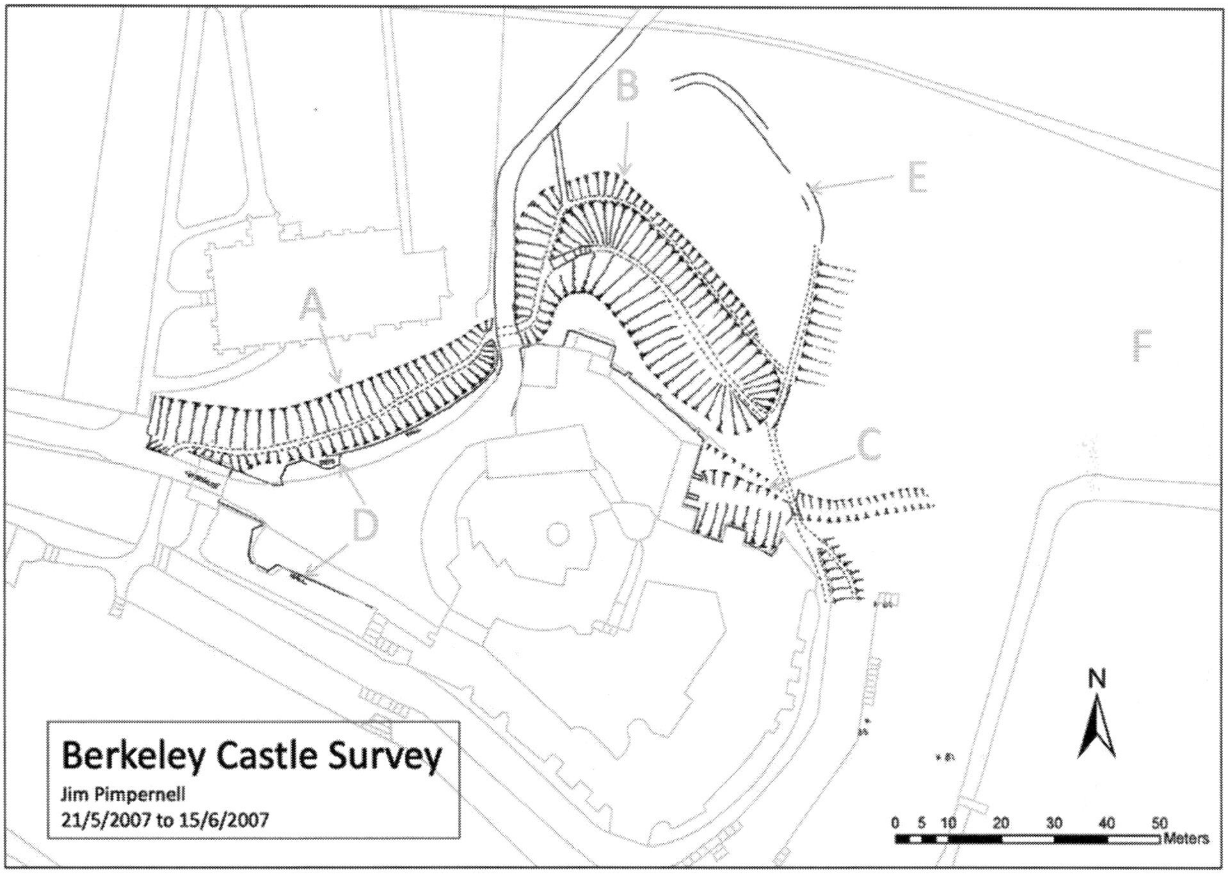

Figure 3. Earthwork survey of the castle grounds

A deep gully (feature B) to the north of the castle is the second feature in the area. The gully runs for 58 m from south-east to north-west before turning sharply south to south-west and joining the ditch (A) described above. It is 21 m wide at its widest point and up to 5.5 m deep. Two pathways run through the gully: one which drops down a gentle slope from the south-east into the centre of the gully and exits via steps into the continuation of ditch A; the other runs close to the top of the north-east side of the gully before turning south to join the first pathway above the steps. A further set of steps leads from this second pathway up to the roadway that connects the car park to the castle.

A shallow ditch-like feature (C) runs west to east adjacent to the north side of Curtain Wall of the Inner Ward of the castle. The ditch is 45 m long, 12 m wide at its widest and 1.5 m deep at its deepest. It is crossed by a bridge carrying a footpath. It becomes significantly both narrower and shallower to the east of the bridge. Lastly, a boundary wall around the edge of the Outer Ward has also been surveyed.

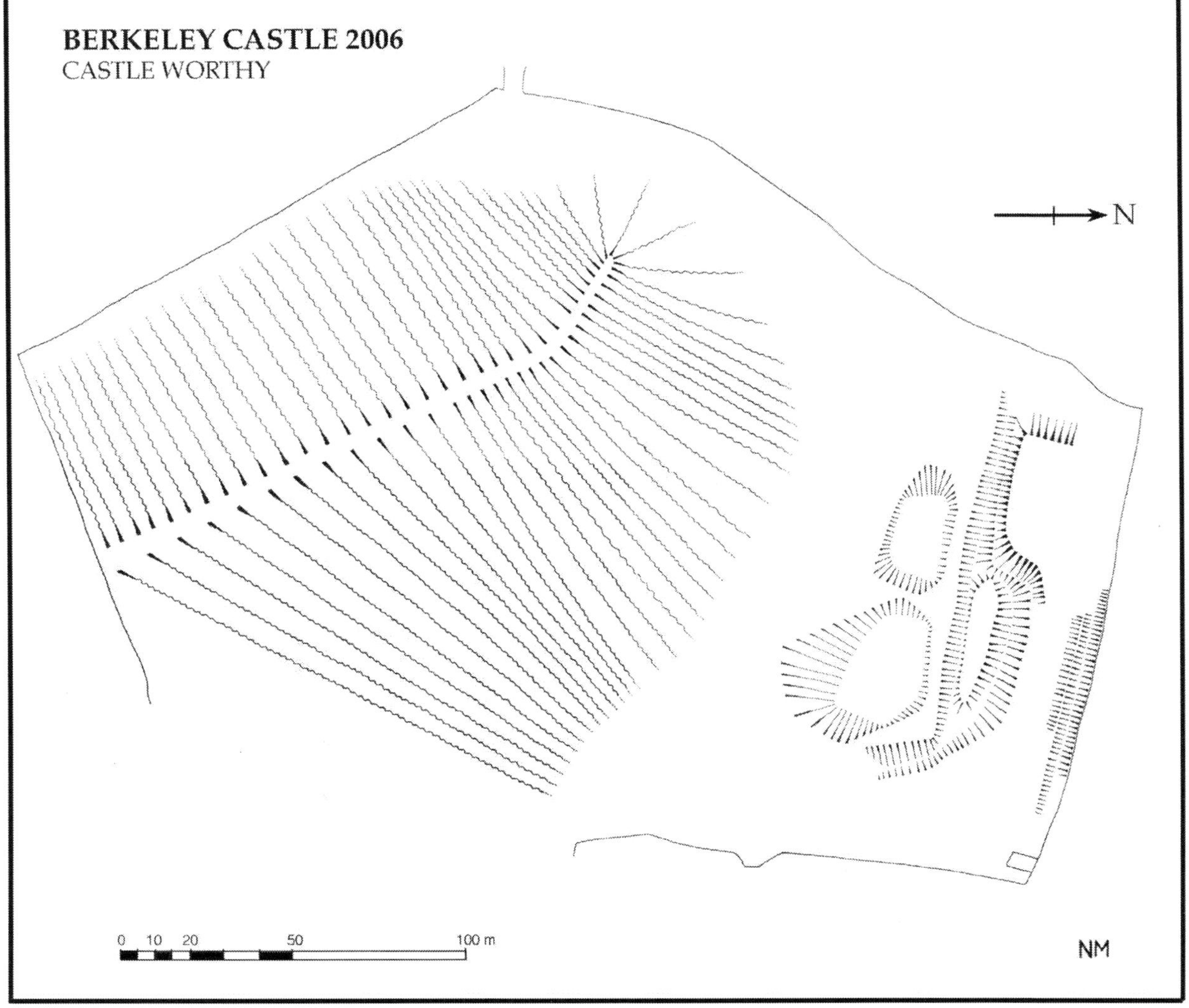

Figure 4. Earthwork survey of the study area at Castle Worthy

Less obvious, but visible after closer inspection, is a 1.75 m wide trackway composed of shaped stone blocks running for 80 m, mostly north–south, and leading towards the north face of the castle. Most of the stones making up the bed of the track have either been removed or are below the surface; however, the edging stones are clearly visible in the areas indicated on the survey. In addition, the area marked F is covered by a mixture of mature trees and shrubs with clearings and footpaths. Much of area is prone to flooding and is not maintained as part of the castle gardens as such. Earthen embankments run along the edge of streams but appear to be the result of regular removal of silt from the stream and are not part of any flood prevention scheme. They were not surveyed. In addition, the area has been used to dump significant amounts of garden waste and building rubble. These features were also not surveyed.

Castle Worthy and Little Park: survey run by N. Morris

Little Park and Castle Worthy lie to the north-east of Berkeley Castle and immediately south of 'Long Bridge': the bridge crossed by Canonbury Street as it heads east out of Berkeley (Fig. 2). The two fields are separated by a rivulet but are linked by a small footbridge to the south. Little Park adjoins Berkeley Castle visitor's car park, which is situated to its west. The field of Castle Worthy approximates to a

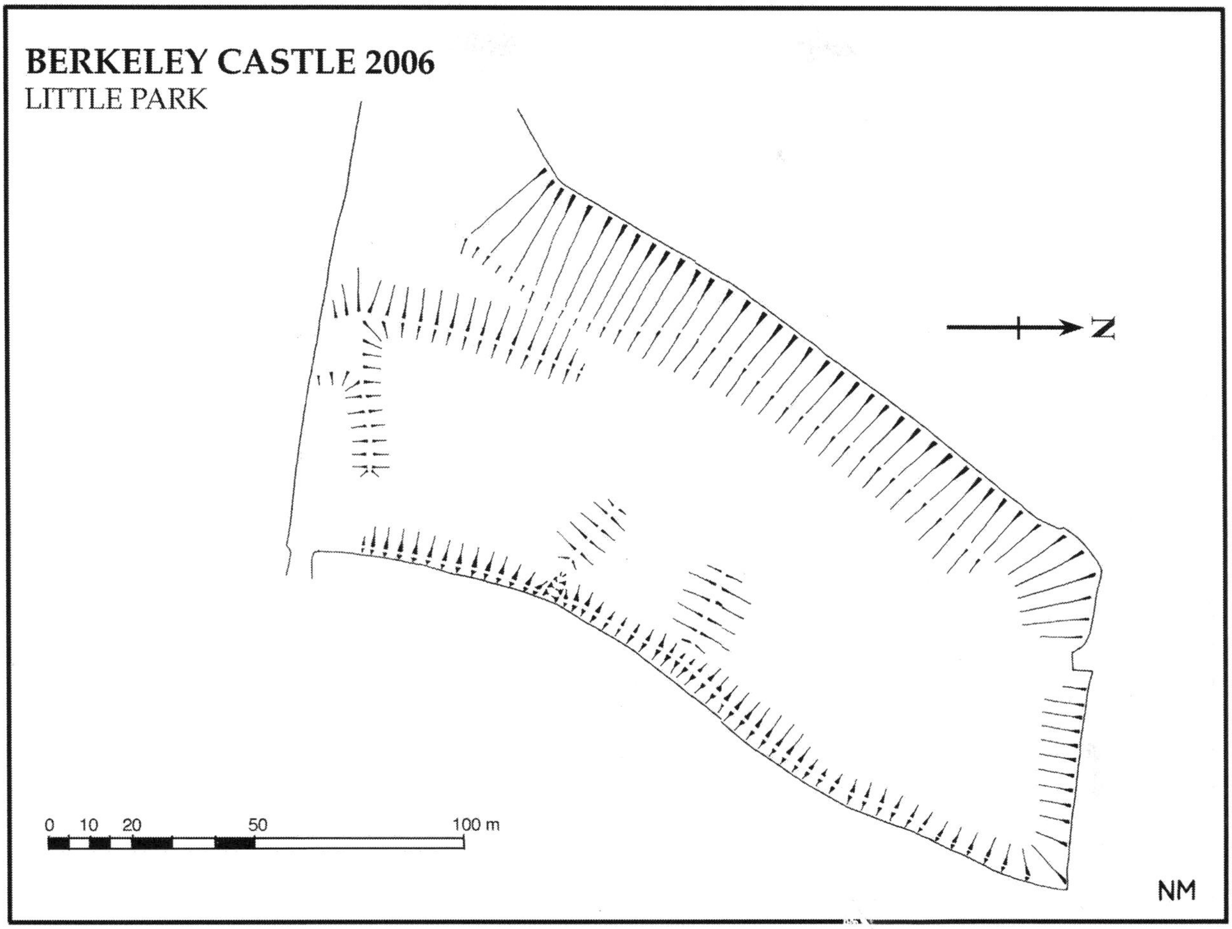

Figure 5. Earthwork survey of the study area at Little Park

almost a rectangular feature, with the apex at the southernmost corner. There is a narrow-wooded strip running along the northern boundary. A short ridge of higher ground runs parallel to the south-western edge and appears to be entirely natural. The eastern arm of the field follows the curve of this ridge, with the incline rising to the east. This area lacked any obvious earthworks, so was omitted from the survey. A small ridge of earth noted running along the western edge of the field, adjacent to the rivulet, was also omitted from the survey as it was clearly a modern deposit connected with the regular scouring of the rivulet to ensure reliable drainage.

Earthworks visible in Castle Worthy (Fig. 4) included: (i) a well-defined rectangular platform in the north-west corner, measuring *c.* 35 × 25 m; (ii) north-east of the rectangular platform, running alongside the road, was a small ditch and bank feature which, although partially obscured by undergrowth, appeared to run from the platform eastward for around 70 m, dissipating as it approached the electric substation in the north-east corner of the field. Both the platform and the ditch and bank earthwork were associated with a significant quantity of scattered stone, either partially buried or on the surface, some of which, upon cursory examination, appeared to be dressed.

Immediately south of the platform but again running eastwards parallel to the road, were a number of more ephemeral features, which consisted of: (iii) a long linear channel, running west–east from the edge of the rectangular platform for approximately 110 m, with a southerly curve at the eastern end;

(iv) a shorter crescent-shaped channel, approximately 40 m long, which abutted the eastern edge of the rectangular platform and adjoined the longer channel at both ends, thereby forming an oval 'island' to the east of the rectangular platform; (v) two roughly rectangular depressions, aligned west–east immediately south of the long linear channel. The two roughly rectangular depressions were the most visible features at the outset of the fieldwork as a period of prolonged rain had filled them with water. During the course of the survey, however, the weather improved and the water abated, leaving the long linear channel as the most pronounced of the features.

Levels taken at the base of the long linear channel failed to demonstrate a clear inclination of axis, although the general slope of the land in Castle Worthy field strongly suggests that the base of the channel must have sloped from east to west. A pond situated on higher ground to the north-east, visible on early OS maps, suggests that the channel could have served as an overflow to carry excess water to the rivulet, however the substantial nature of the channel makes this scenario unlikely. If the channel was designed to funnel water across the field then it is probable that the water was intended to end up in the rectangular depressions to the south which are almost certainly the remains of two small fishponds associated with the medieval hospital.

The field known as Little Park is roughly rectangular, with the long axis running north-north-east to south-south-west. The western edge of the field is marked by a steep slope to a stone wall which separates it from castle visitor's car park and access road. In the south-west corner of the field a public footpath passes underneath a small stone bridge and continues on into St Mary's churchyard. A small area by the northern boundary is wooded, and another grouping of large trees stands towards the south-west corner of the field. The second group of trees was substantial enough to interfere with the plotting of the field boundary during earthwork survey but the area surveyed was adequate enough to allow comparison with the OS maps of the area.

Earthworks visible in Little Park comprised: (i) a low bank along the field's eastern edge which was partially interrupted at one point by a shallow hollow leading down to the rivulet; (ii) a steep incline towards the northern boundary, which brings the level of the field up to that of the adjacent road; (iii) a steep incline towards the western boundary, which brings the level of the field up to that of the adjacent access road and car park; (iv) a shallow L-shaped ridge measuring *c.* 60 north–south × 30 m west–east, situated in the south of the field, that terminated in a rectangular platform 15 m north–south × 20 m west–east, which may continue beyond the southern boundary wall.

The small incline recorded in the north of Little Park is likely associated with either the construction of the modern B4066 road or its predecessors. Similarly, the eastern bank recorded adjacent to the rivulet is either a modern deposit connected with the regular scouring of the rivulet or a form of flood defence; although the shallow hollow which interrupts the bank, that was no doubt cut to give livestock access to the potable water supply, renders the defences practically useless. On the opposite side of the field the steep incline to the west undoubtedly resulted from the construction of the car park and driveway.

Quarf Mead and Home Ground: surveys run by J. Pimpernell and K.P. Trimmis

The surveyed field is of rough pasture, bounded by Little Avon River to the north, the Berkeley to Ham Road to the east, Floodgates Farm orchard to the west and fields and gardens on the outskirts of Ham to the South (Fig. 2). The field comprises 5.4 ha of land. There is a general slope running from the higher southern ground to the river on the northern boundary. The field is not well drained, particularly in the area close to the river. The following features were immediately visible: A) A raised bank running alongside the Little Avon river; B) a scarp, a little further south, running parallel to the river; C) a gully/ depression intersecting with the scarp and running roughly north–south down the centre of the field;

D) a sinuous embanked feature running broadly Southwest - Northeast on the east side of the field; E) three areas of ridge-and-furrow running broadly north–south. Less obvious, but visible after closer inspection, were the following features: F) a slight ridge extending for 100 m in the south-west of the field and running approximately west–east; and G) a rectangular 'platform' area to the west of the southern end of gully C.

The raised bank (A) is a levee of unknown date constructed alongside the southern bank of the current course of the Little Avon to protect the low-lying part of the field from flooding during the extreme high tides that occur in the Severn Estuary. The scarp (B) appears to be the original southern bank of the river. The route of the Little Avon has clearly been straightened to its current course at some point in the past. Tandy (2003, 175–90) suggests that the bridge at the north-east corner of Quarf Mead is the original site of the 'Lockfast Bridge', first recorded in 1165–1220, and hence the castle's two water mills, mentioned in Domesday, were located at nearby Brown's Mill, 500 m to the south-east, and Sea Mills,

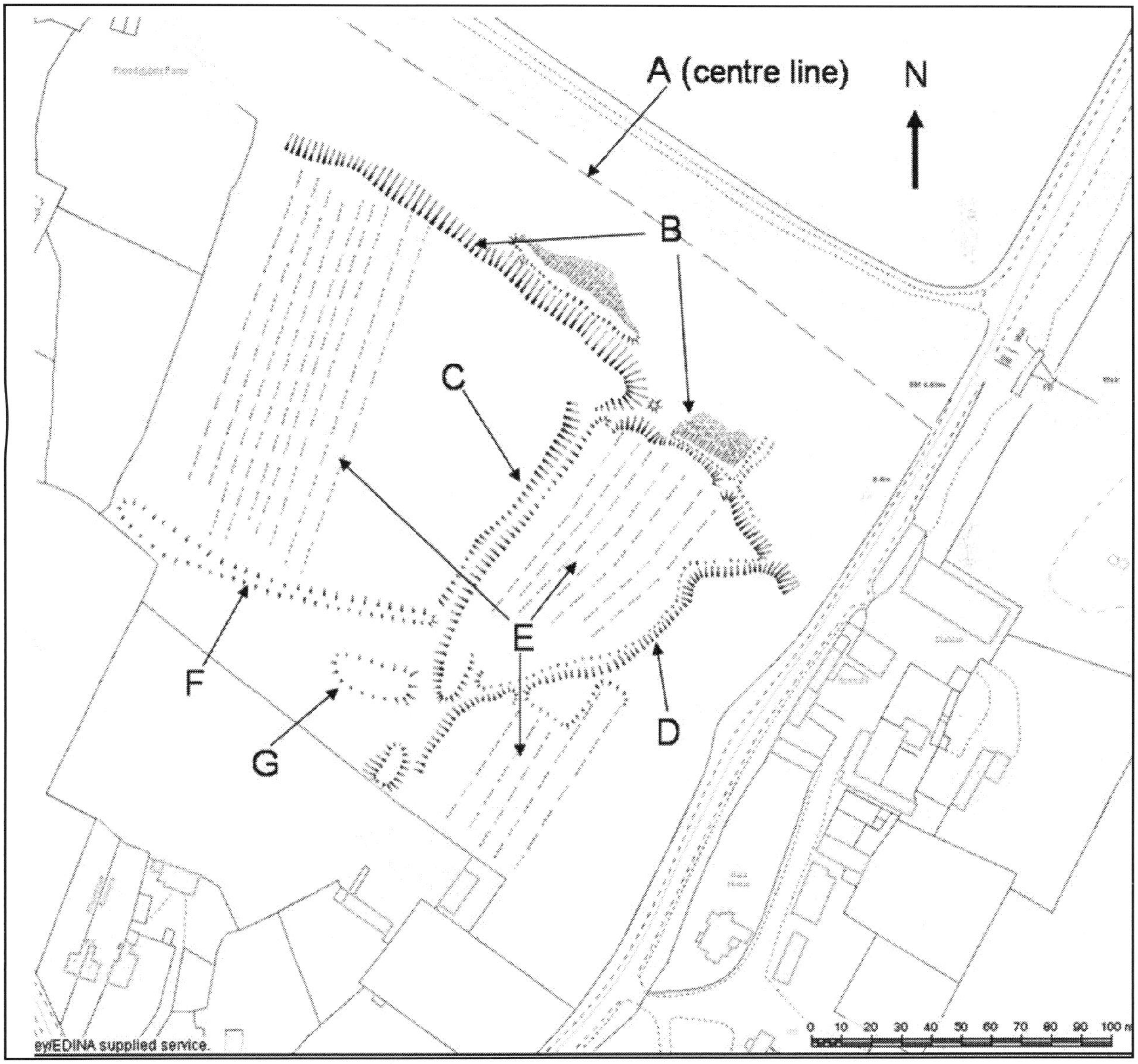

Figure 6. Earthwork survey of the study area at Quarf Mead

280 m to the north-west. If Tandy is correct, it is feasible that the Little Avon River was straightened in the later Anglo-Saxon period when a leat was constructed to provide water to the mill at Sea Mills. Alternatively, with the death of Robert FitzHarding in 1170, Berkeley Castle passed to his son, Maurice I (1120–1190), who is known to have constructed a series of sluices and locks about the castle, which enabled him to flood the flat low-lying surrounding fields. This served a dual purpose, it was useful for defence, but also made possible the creation of ponds and lush gardens and it is viable that the river was straightened *c.* 1170 as part of these works.

Gully C, leading to the scarp is probably a partially filled-in hollow-way running down to the original river bank and was the point where travellers using the Severn could gain access to Ham by bringing their boats up the Little Avon and drawing them onto the lower part of the hollow-way or perhaps alongside a wooden pier. The line of the hollow-way appears to continue into the field to the south of the surveyed field towards the centre of Ham. The land between Ham and Berkeley was, in earlier times, marshy and would have been difficult if not impossible to cross at certain times of the year, particularly during the winter. This barrier was eventually overcome by, amongst other things, the building of the causeway and bridges linking the two. However, prior to this, the original course of the Little Avon would have provided a convenient ferry route for those needing transport between the two settlements. The original course of the river joined Berkeley Pill close to what is now the junction of Jumpers Lane and Stock Lane as shown below. This original waterway only disappeared during the 1970s when the course now followed by the Little Avon was constructed and the mill leat to the mill at Sea Mills infilled.

The embanked feature (D) appears to be an old field boundary of up to 0.6 m high. It pre-dates the areas of ridge-and-furrow which respect its course. Berkeley Estate maps of the early 19th century show the area to the east of the embankment as orchard. The course of the embankment at its northern end is particularly interesting having an almost rectangular aspect which may indicate a now vanished structure.

Three areas of ridge-and-furrow (E) are present with widths ranging from 5 m to 7 m. The area to the west of the gully is slightly more extensive than shown on the survey plot since, at the time of the survey, the field was heavily covered with high-growing flowers which camouflaged the more degraded ridges. The long slight ridge feature (F) is over 100 m in length and is respected by the ridge-and-furrow to the north. It is probably the vestigial remains of a field boundary; perhaps an extension of the boundary on the south side of what was the orchard at Floodgates Farm.

Finally, the 'platform' (G) is broadly rectangular and was subject to a geophysical survey during the course of the earthwork survey. Using a TR/CIA Resistivity Meter, an area of low resistance was found to run in conjunction with the rectangular earthwork that was visible on the ground. Not archaeologically conclusive, it is recommended that further evaluation work is undertaken in this area to fully establish its significance.

Results summary: geophysical survey

Walled Garden: survey run by P. Rowe

A flat, grassy patch of land within the old walled kitchen garden at Berkeley Castle was one of the first areas to be surveyed with the RM15 Resistance Meter. This area was known to contain an original 18th/19th century kitchen garden feature. Located approximately 300 m north of the main castle site and adjacent (19 m north) to the Butterfly House [ST 685991], the survey site encompassed a total area of 40 × 40 m (5.5 × 10 m^2 grids) and was orientated in a north-west–south-east direction.

A high resistance linear feature running north-east to south-west was clearly identified about 25 m north of the current main greenhouse, indicating possible building foundations or a wall. South-east of this feature were two low resistance linears, one running parallel to the high resistance feature and the other perpendicular to it. These low resistance linears form a corner of what appears to be a rectangular, outlined area. Another feature of high resistance sits approximately 10 m north-east of the main greenhouse. Its square shape measuring *c.* 4 m^2 suggests a possible hard surface or possibly building material. An irregular high resistance feature, located 5 m west of the greenhouse, is slightly cryptic in shape. It may imply further possible building material foundations or wall footings, or even a garden feature.

Though the survey could not capture the entire area it looks as if the low resistance linear running north-west to south-east continues to intersect the high resistance feature. As these features are of low resistance, they may represent foundation trenches or even more likely the dug borders of one section of planting often seen in other historic, walled kitchen gardens.

The 1st Edition Ordnance Survey map shows only the outline of the kitchen gardens split into four main sections that were bordered with trees. A long greenhouse lined the northern wall. By 1902 the 1st Revision OS map, shows another greenhouse sat in the north-west corner of the gardens and this grew to a larger structure by the 1930s and remained there at least until the 1970s. It is very likely that the high resistance structure in the northern corner of the survey is the foundations of this structure.

An archaeological excavation also conducted in 2005 (Prior 2005) immediately south of grid 1 revealed evidence of activity on this site since at least the Neolithic period. The excavation also revealed the remains of a palmhouse running north–south on the western end of the site, which is recorded as having been brought to the site in the 1920s–1930s (Prior 2005). This is likely the high resistance linear feature.

Inner Keep Garden: survey run by P. Rowe

The inner keep garden, a flat, grassy area within the main shell keep of Berkeley Castle, was surveyed to investigate the possible site of an early castle well, in addition to a 19th/20th century water feature. A RM15 resistance survey of a total area of 20 × 10 m (2 × 10 m^2 grids) was completed in May 2005 [ST 685989]. A small part of the survey area was obstructed by bushes and a partially-metalled footpath that resulted in the logging of 'dummy' readings.

A high resistance, curved feature was clearly identified at the western end of the survey, approximately 3 m east of the current main wall. This feature is suggestive of buried building material pertaining to the collapsed Shell Keep wall breached during the Civil War. However, its shape is distinct and could indicate the foundation of another wall rather than buried building material. An area of low resistance about 3 m^2, 5 m east of the centre of the gridded area, is suggestive of an oval feature. This may be the 19th/20th century garden water feature. Due north, in the centre of the gridded area, a 0.5 m^2 feature of low resistance indicates the site of the early castle well.

Watermeadow 1: survey run by P. Rowe

Approximately 100 m south-west from the main castle site, a wide grassy area adjacent to the main complex and gardens was surveyed several times, both with resistivity and magnetometry. Features investigated were possible fishponds and watercourse, suggested by an earthwork analysis conducted in 2005 by undergraduate students. In May 2005, a RM15 resistance survey of a total area of 140 × 40 m (13 × 20 m^2 grids) was completed [ST 683988]. An FM36 fluxgate gradiometer survey was conducted over the same area, covering 140 × 60 m (20 × 20 m^2 grids). The site sits on a floodplain, and therefore alluvium deposits from former flooding could potentially obscure all but recent archaeology.

Resistivity

The slight linear depression that runs north–south in a diagonal across the survey site was visible by mid–low resistance results banked by parallel lines of higher resistance. The feature could be seen starting mid-field from a present watercourse, giving credence to the theory of an earlier linear watercourse crossing the site. However, the feature is also suggestive of a possible trackway.

Situated *c.* 50 m to the east of the linear depression and running parallel another linear feature of high resistance with a high resistance linear running perpendicular from it in a westerly direction. Also concurrent with surviving low-lying earthworks, it has been suggested as banking for castle fishponds though, as previously stated, this is purely speculative with limited evidence to support it. This same area was revisited in June 2014, when an RM15 resistance survey of a total area of 120 × 30 m (4 × 30 m^2 grids) was completed, this time to span the terminus of the linear depression noted in 2005 to establish whether it was the location of a water mill. However, the data recovered was too poor due to changeable weather with intense periods of rainfall. The only feature apparent in the results is an area of high resistance in the far south-western corner of the survey, though this can be attributed to an area of gravel metalling, deposited to enable vehicular access on and off the site.

Magnetometry

Most commonly visible throughout the survey site were discrete dipolar anomalies suggestive of ferrous material on or near the surface. There was no sign of magnetic variation on the north-western side of the survey where resistivity had picked up the possible watercourse, which suggests an absence of disturbed soils normally associated with banks/ditches. Situated *c.* 25 m east of the depression was a concentrated area of positive responses that were initially interpreted as the result of burnt ground or metal. However, a positive response without an associated negative response is indicative of an infilled, cut feature. Whether it is archaeological or natural, such as a tree bowl, is impossible to know without excavation.

Further east, *c.* 60 m from the depression towards the northern end of the survey are a set of positive responses set out in a staggered vertical, rectangular pattern. The results are likely the outcome of the data not being collected at a steady rate. If destaggered, this may have shown up as a similar shape to the anomaly just south of it, however rotated. The more southern anomaly appears as a horizontal, rectangular pattern orientated west–east, but with a distinct bipolar response that indicates it is probably a metallic item. It has been suggested that these two features may relate to 20th century horse jumps.

Watermeadow 2: survey run by P. Rowe

Immediately south-west of the Watermeadow 1 survey, another survey was conducted with resistivity and magnetometry in May/June 2005, about 350 m south-west from the main castle site [ST 683987]. The RM15 resistance survey covered a total area 140 × 60 m (16 × 20 m^2 grids) and the FM36 fluxgate gradiometer overlapped this, covering a total area of 140 × 100 m (31 × 20 m^2 grids).

Resistivity

The slight linear depression noted from the earthwork survey, which was present in the northern section of the field, continued through Watermeadow 2. This appeared as a mid–low resistance linear banked by parallel lines of higher resistance. This feature is similar to the potential watercourse noted before in Watermeadow 1. One grid, *c.* 60–80 m along the base line, displayed high levels of resistance, suggesting the possibility of buried building material. However, when compared to the other grids in the survey there is a possibility of it being the consequence of poor data collection.

Additionally, on the west side of the survey area is a faint line of mid-resistance that appears to run possibly in a semicircular pattern vertically for *c.* 40 m, though again as before this could be down to the quality of the raw data collected. Without a resurvey or excavation, archaeological interpretation is unable to be made. No other archaeological features appear present within the results.

Magnetometry

Like the magnetometry survey of Watermeadow 1, the survey site contained a large number of discrete dipolar anomalies, suggestive of ferrous objects on or near the surface. In the places where these responses are stronger, such as at the centre and south-western end of the survey site, the ferrous material was likely on the surface. At the north-west corner were curvilinear striations with a slight positive response. These could be natural in origin, potentially representing paleochannels that have filled with soil over time. Other faint positive responses towards the eastern side of the survey could also related to natural features.

Overall, the results of this site seem to be affected by the underlying geology, or possibly alluvium, throughout. The northern end of the survey shows poorly collected data and it is recommended that the survey is redone in order to establish the presence of any features. The north-eastern end of the survey shows a strongly positive sub-square anomaly, which is likely the result of poor data collection.

Nelmes Paddock: surveys run by RPM Smisson, H. Weber, P. Rowe and K.P. Trimmis

Nelmes Paddock is a south-westerly-sloping grassed area used for the grazing of livestock. It is a long field, running 94 m in a north-north-east direction parallel to High Street (Fig. 2). The field is approximately 230 m west of the main castle site between Berkeley churchyard and High Street [ST 683990]. Resistance and magnetometry surveys covering a total area of 90 × 40 m (32 × 10 m^2 grids) were completed in May/June 2006. The field was surveyed again with both methods over two weeks in 2013 to compare with the 2006 results (Fig. 7).

RM 15 Resistivity

Limited areas of high resistance were identified at the north-north-east, east-south-east and south-south-west parts of the survey area, possibly relating to building material. Transecting the site in an east-south-east direction was a line of high resistance, suggesting the possible course of the historic St Michael's Lane, while an area of low resistance parallel to High Street in a north-north-east direction has been interpreted as soil creep or a pipeline.

Overall, limited archaeological data recovered for the site has made interpretation difficult. Varying factors may have contributed to the lack of positive geophysical data, with both extreme weather conditions making the collection of data difficult, as well as probable soil overburden following the removal of the medieval/Tudor buildings depicted on 16th century cartographic documents, to a level beyond the range of the instrument (>0.75 m).

TR/CIA Resistivity

The TR/CIA resistivity survey revealed similar findings. High resistance in the south-east corner was suggested to mark the location of suspected former barn. High resistance may mark a stone spread or paved area. Low resistance near the retaining wall along the High Street boundary at the north-west may be due to a pipeline or soil creep. The survey showed a linear of high resistance running east-west at the south-east end of the field. This may be the route of St Michael's Lane leading up to the church to the east. Generally the lack of detail suggests either the ground has been made up so any archaeology has been buried in soil beyond the range of the instrument, or it has been removed. No evidence was found for the suspected medieval buildings along the High Street boundary to the west.

Magnetometry

At the north-east end of the survey area were several discrete dipolar responses. These appear to lie on the edge of a spread of magnetic debris. The strength of the response was moderate and could therefore be an indication of building rubble or small ferrous debris. Toward the northern end of the survey was a series of positive responses in a horseshoe pattern, apparent in the 2006 survey. Without any associated negative response these are likely to be infilled, cut features. Whether they are natural depressions in the ground or humanly made, this would need to be determined by further exploration. However, their location correlates with one of the high resistance areas observed in the RM15 Resistance survey. In the 2013 survey this is the one area that greatly differs from that of 2006. The results show several dipolar anomalies in place of the positive ones, with none of the features visible.

One other difference between the two surveys appears at the centre of the site, where three shadowed areas that look like a geological response appeared in the 2013 survey. All along the western boundary, running in a north-north-east direction parallel to the High Street, is magnetic disturbance caused by the cast-iron railing running along the boundary of the field. Another area with strong dipolar responses is at the south-east end of the site where the response has been attributed to ferrous anomalies created by barbed wire attached to the trees.

It was concluded in 2006 that extreme weather conditions and potential overburden of soil on the site affected the results of the survey. By 2013, a trench within the paddock was being excavated, and due to the depth of the archaeology within this trench it was further concluded that any features would be beyond the range of the instrument (>0.75–1 m).

Dr Jenner's Museum and Gardens: surveys run by P. Rowe, H. Webber, RPM Smisson and K.P. Trimmis

Dr Jenner's Museum and gardens are located approximately 220 m south-east of Berkeley town centre and approximately 230 m east of the castle complex, on the south-east end of the spur (*c.* 19–21 m AOD; Fig. 2) [ST 684991]. The garden is an area of cut grass situated due south of the main house/museum. Part of the garden was purposefully flattened under the ownership of Edward Jenner to create a lawn tennis area. This sits directly adjacent to the south side of the building making for an ideal location for students to practice their geophysical recording skills. Two resistance surveys were conducted in June 2006 within a total area of 40 × 30 m. The Geoscan RM15 resistance survey was carried out over 11 × 10 m^2 grids. The TR/CIA resistance survey was carried out in 2 × 20 m^2 grids and 1 × 10 m^2 grid. In 2013, another resistance survey was conducted to compare with the results from 2006 (Fig. 8).

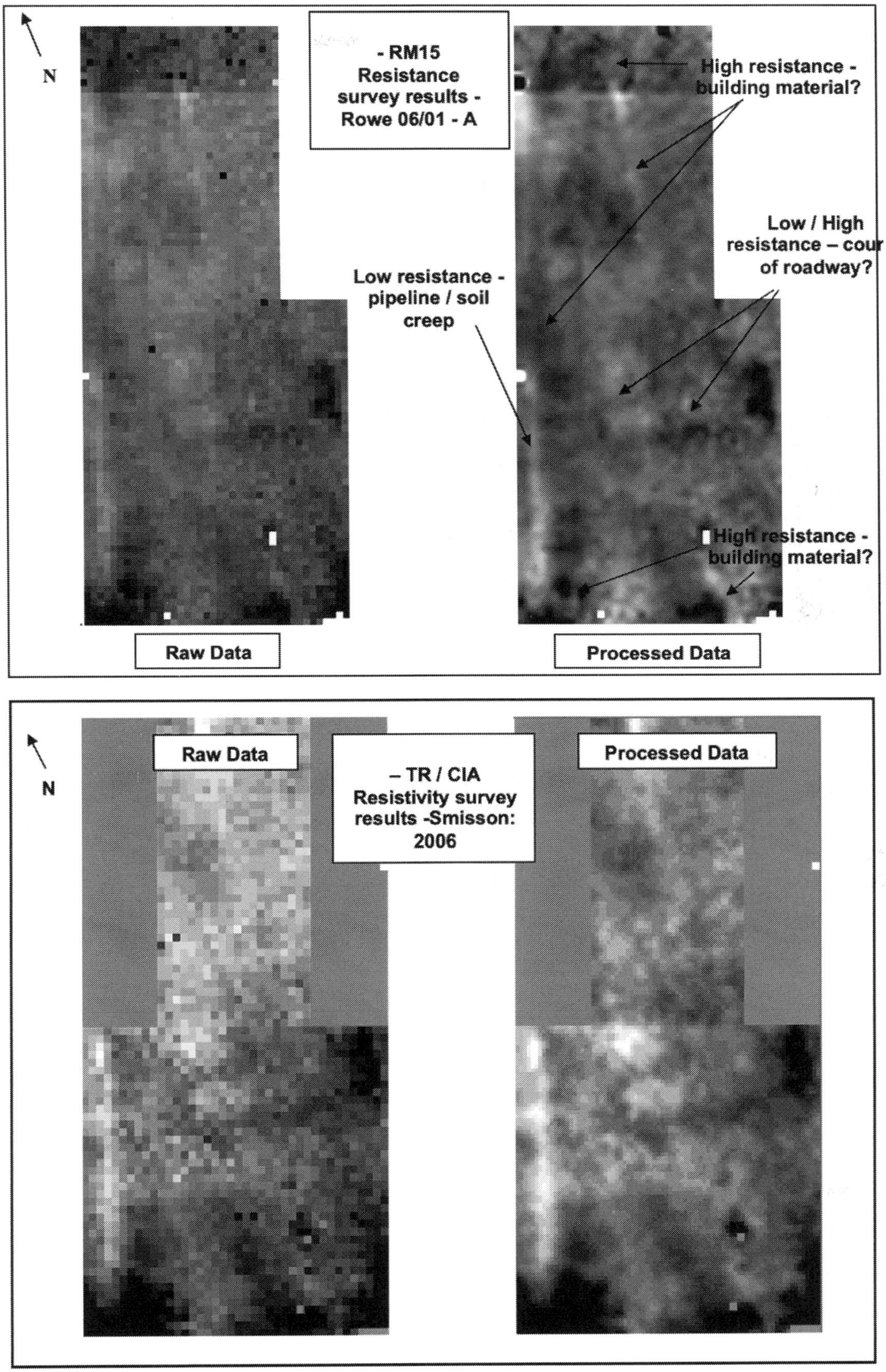

Figure 7. Resistivity survey results at Nelme's Paddock

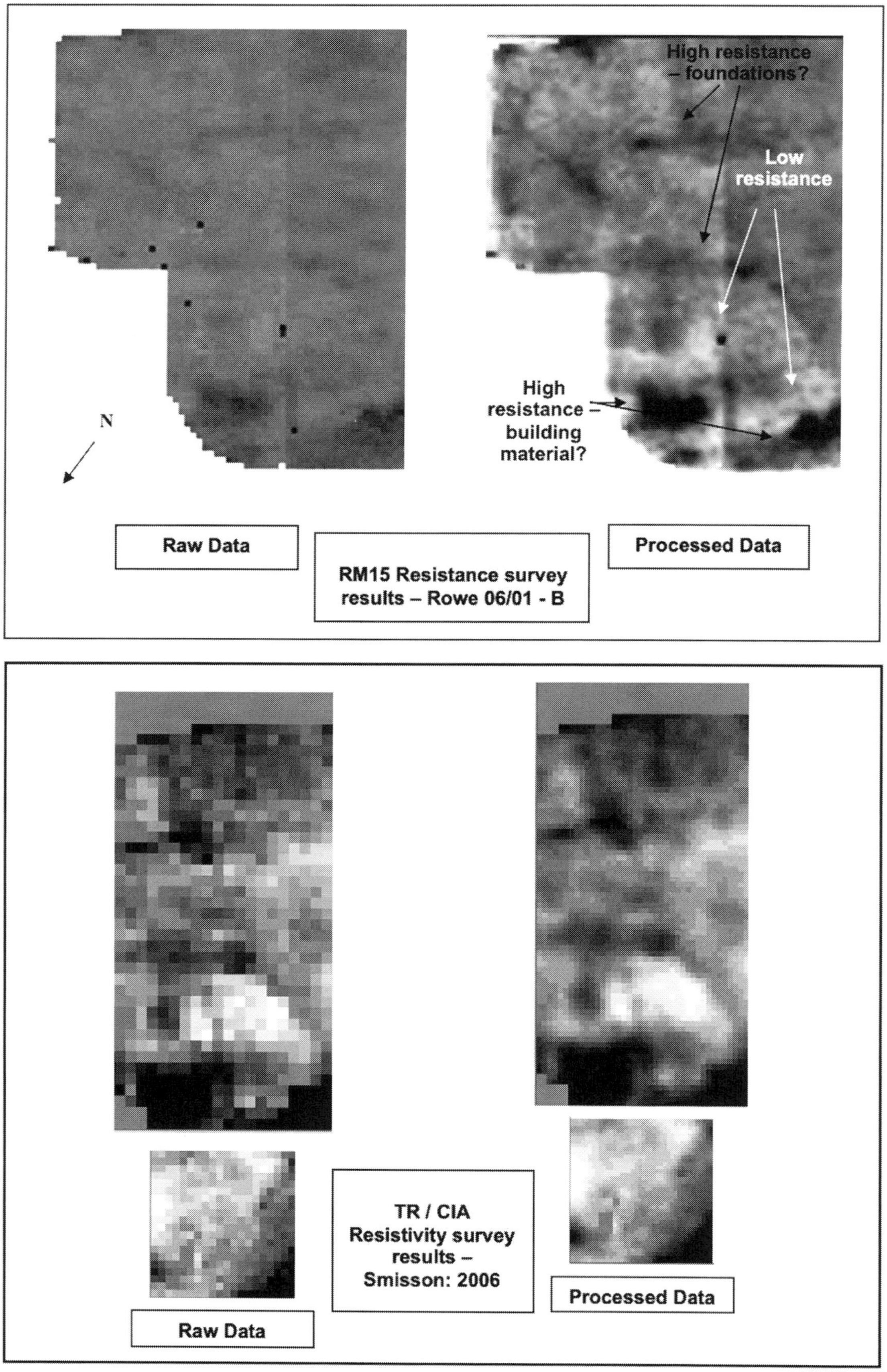

Figure 8. Resistivity survey results at Jenner Garden

RM15 Resistivity

Several high resistance linears could be clearly identified throughout the survey area. These ran in several directions without any clear pattern of connection except in two cases where linears running north-east to south-west intersected with another running north-west to south-east. These features are potentially associated with the 18th/19th century formal garden. However, there is a possibility that they could relate to foundations of the earlier chantry known to have once stood on the site and even, possibly, the Anglo-Saxon nunnery that was once within this site vicinity.

In the 2013 survey all features that were visible within the 2006 survey could still be seen. In addition, a linear of high resistance appeared that runs from west to east. This is most likely a part of the early drainage of the garden. However, a significant response on both surveys lay in the north-west section. This large oval high resistance response is likely to be a spread of some sort of material and has potential to be of some archaeological interest.

TR/CIA Resistivity

The TR/CIA resistivity meter also found evidence of considerable activity under the lawn, and also suggested the possibly of foundations of buildings or the remains of the formal 18th century garden. It is suspected that buildings associated with an Anglo-Saxon nunnery may be close to the southern boundary of the garden, if as suspected the Tower is built on Anglo-Saxon foundations.

Little Park/Castle Worthy (Longbridge): surveys run by P. Rowe and RPM Smisson

Little Park/Castle Worthy is located on level ground approximately 400 m from Berkeley town centre and 300 m north-east of the castle complex (Fig. 2) [ST 687992]. Today it is used for the grazing livestock though it is believed to be the area where the hospital complex of Holy Trinity (*c.* 1170–1547) once stood. An archaeological earthwork survey completed during the Berkeley Castle Research Excavation in 2006 located possible platforms, an interpretation that the geophysical evidence possibly supports. A resistance survey of a total area of 100 × 40 m (10 × 20 m^2 grids) was completed in June 2006 (Fig. 9).

RM15 Resistivity

Areas of high resistance could be seen to run parallel to the road in a north-west to south-east direction, suggesting the possibility of either building material or a pipeline associated with the sewage pumping station nearby. A sub-square area of mid–low resistance, interspersed by patches of higher resistance, was discovered in the south-west area of the survey site. This corresponds with surviving earthwork platforms, and could be indicative of building material/foundations.

TR/CIA Resistivity

On a possible platform in the field, a number of features can be made out in the resistivity data, including what looks like a clear building outline with internal divisions. The area of strong response in the centre of the survey area was characterised on the ground by a quantity of dressed stone blocks within which no modern materials such as brick were visible. Potentially these cover other building foundations.

When surveyed there was very little variation in response from the field outside the area of the platform visible on the ground. The only feature seemed to be a line of individual, high resistance readings in the raw data running diagonally from the north-east corner of the field that were thought to be modern and associated with a rising main from the sewage pumping station. Potentially the survey has located the Augustinian Chapel and Hospital, but excavation would be needed to confirm this.

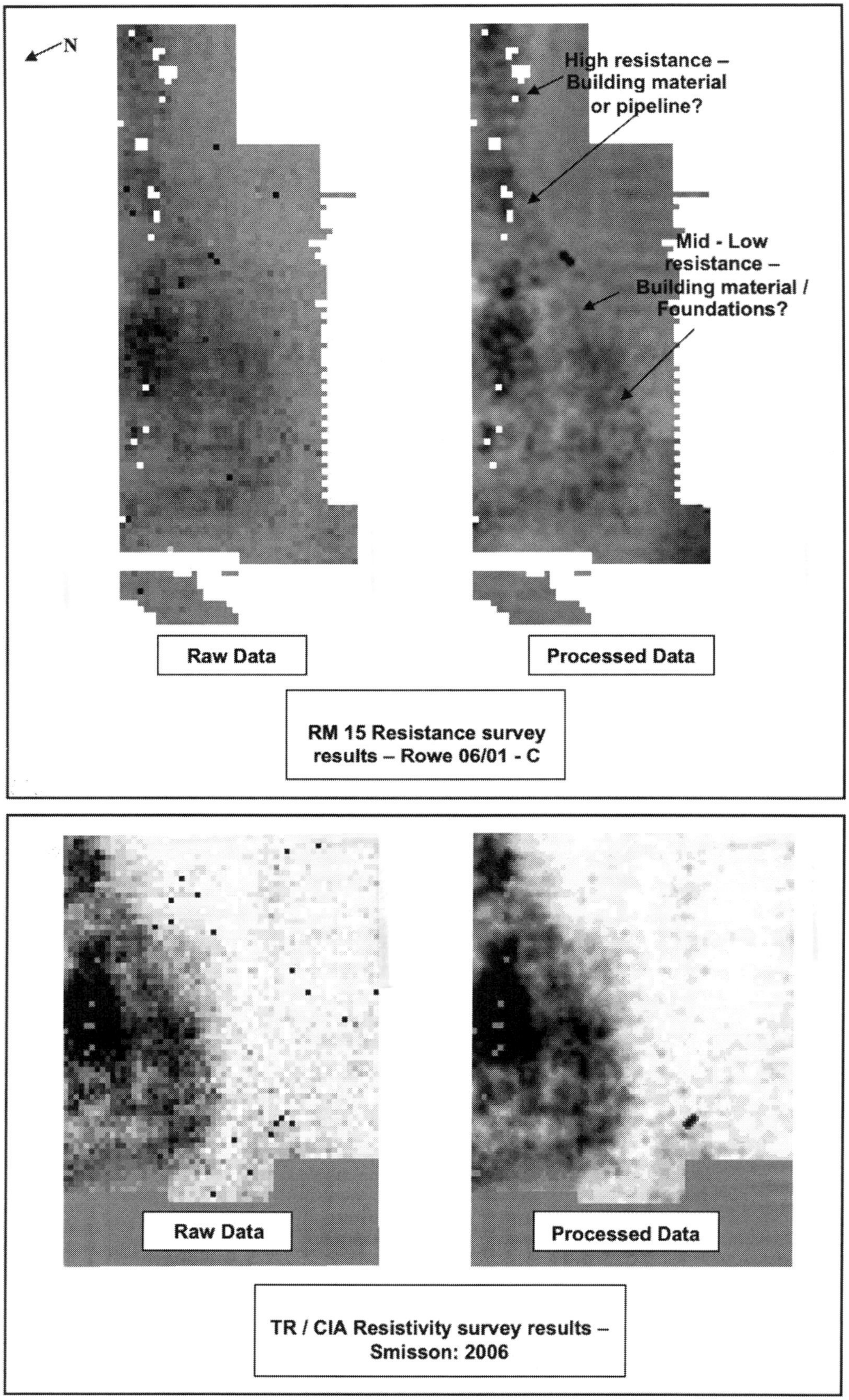

Figure 9. Resistivity survey results at Little Park area

Quarf Mead/Home Guard: Survey run by RPM Smisson

Quarf Mead/Home Guard (referred to as Home Ground in figure 2.2) is a field situated approximately 620 m south-west of the main castle complex/gardens and about 650 m south-south-west of Berkeley village [ST 6850 9118]. It sits at 11 m AOD on a slight south-west incline (Fig. 2). The surveyed area contains various unknown earthworks. A grid area consisting of 6 × 20 m² grids and 1 × 20 m² grid was completed over a 60 × 40 m area and surveyed in June 2006. Within the area covered by the six 20 m square grids, the geophysics results appeared to locate a field boundary that terminates at a hollow-way. Some 10 m south of this a low resistance rectangle appears that coincides with the rectangular earthwork visible on the ground. This may be significant or the parallel responses may be indicating this is all simply ridge-and-furrow on a new orientation not visible on the ground.

The single grid was surveyed over a small area where an entrance seems to appear on the ground together with a possible triangular platform. The resistance survey showed that the ridge-and-furrow, here running north–south, terminates at this platform, although it continues past it on the east side. High resistances here may indicate a building. It is recommended that this site be considered for further investigation work; only a full archaeological excavation of the site would fully establish the presence of buildings or other features in this area.

Discussion

There are numerous problems encountered when trying to reconstruct a prehistoric fluvial landscape involving the interaction between physical processes such as the deposition of alluvial material, changing water levels and human processes of drainage and land reclamation. The following section will attempt to look at these physical and human processes and place them within a chronological framework.

Hydrology, geoarchaeology and morphodynamics

Berkeley Pill and its associated channels are part of a broader hydrological system centred on the Severn Estuary. The dynamic processes of the estuary including the wide tidal range, mean spring range of 12.3 m at Avonmouth (Allen 1985, 849) and the powerful nature of these tides has created a broad range of riverine landscapes. As discussed above, Berkeley is located in the lower part of the inner Severn, an area of wide and irregular coastal strips (Crowther and Dickson 2008, 24). The channels entering the Severn are also part of the tidal zone; their formation inevitably derives from a combination of normal inland hydrological systems and dynamic tidal processes. Prior to fluvial modification in the form of sluices and flood gates the tidal range of Berkeley Pill was said to be as far inland as Newport (Tandy 2003, 179) 4 km inland of the Severn. Other physical processes involved in channel formation along the Severn Estuary include the underlying geology and increasing sea levels (Allen 1985, 849). Prior to human drainage schemes the natural courses of the inland waterways would have consisted of a number of largely stable pills with smaller more dynamic plan channels, in the form of rills and extensional fractures, on the lower marshes (Allen 1985, 860).

Narrower plains and marshes are present approximately 1.5 km from the Severn where the channels likely demonstrate a more stable course. Defences and land reclamation have mitigated some of the risks of coastal flooding on the lower ground approaching the Severn and have largely masked the braided network of tidal channels which would have formed the prehistoric marsh (Allen and Rippon 1997, 328). There is no standard horizontal plan type for Severn Estuary tributaries. Berkeley demonstrates a strongly meandering channel type while others are remarkable straight, or moderately sinuous (Allen 1985, 853). Channel cross-sections show less variation in form tending to have steep symmetrical banks, of 30–50°, a V-shaped base and tend to completely empty somewhere between half and low tide (Allen and Rippon 2007, 335).

The channel silting observed today is primarily a result of disruption of the saltwater and freshwater flow. Freshwater flow is particularly important in this regard as it flushes some of the silt brought in by the tidal waters, otherwise deposited on the channel edges, out into the parent channel (Allen and Rippon 2007, 336). Rotational slipping, still visible on the tidally influenced mouth of Berkeley Pill, would likely have constituted the prime morphodynamic erosional process; moving sediment slowly down the bank in narrow, but thick, bowl-shaped fault surfaces (*ibid.*). The morphodynamic processes discussed above also have implications for understanding site formation processes and artefact distribution. Allen and Rippon (2007, 338–9) highlight six mechanisms for artefact distribution within paleochannels such as Berkeley: deliberate placement; dumping from rotational slipping; fluvial transport from the land; or transportation by tidal currents or storms. Any archaeological excavation or survey within the zone of fluvial influence must consider these processes if the interpretations are to be valid.

The development of the agricultural landscape

The alluvial lands which formed the prehistoric wetlands of the Severn margin were almost certainly reclaimed through sea defences and land drainage systems during the Roman period, however, due to erosion and depositional processes on the Severn and its tributaries, the location of these defences may be different to those seen today (Allen 1992, 88). Figure 10 illustrates the locations of sea/tidal banks on Berkeley Pill although the date of these earthworks is unclear. While the locations of Romano-British and Saxon reclamation of the marsh zone are still to be confirmed, the medieval systems have left traces on the landscape in the form of field boundaries and ridge and furrow.

A study of the field boundaries on alluvial lands reveals a number of triangular fields with points facing west towards the Severn. This pattern is indicative of an advance and retreat form of agriculture (Allen 1992, 95) whereby defensive lines are established further inland than the operational field systems of the period. Allen (*ibid.*, 89) states that two types of ridge-and-furrow can be identified; older ridge-and-furrow corresponding to medieval open-field cultivation and younger ridge-and-furrow which is generally a product of post-medieval enclosure (*ibid.*, 93). Figure 10 shows that marsh south of Berkeley Pill is dominated by the older type (HER38345, NMR1466986) while a basin formed by higher topographic ridges close of the Severn appears to have been traditionally used as open gras land with some later style ridge-and-furrow encroachment as the land was drained. Earthworks recorded as part of the NMP show that the older style ridge-and-furrow close to Berkeley Pill respect the boundaries of the earthwork flood defence bank, suggesting that a single channel course was established for Berkeley Pill by the medieval period, adding further weight to the Romano-British, and possibly Saxon, period reclamation of the marsh. Furthermore, nearly all of the ditches recorded are within the bounds of the older style ridge-and-furrow. The orientation of both the ridge-and-furrow and the ditches correspond to either known watercourses or the direction of the receding Severn.

The upkeep of the drainage system was a constant process (Wells-Furby 2012, 284). Sea-wall defences appear to be concentrated into phases of construction or maintenance, beginning in the mid-1330s and reaching a peak in approximately 1350–1. The nature and location of these works is unknown, however the dating of this phase falls within the lordship of Thomas III (1292–1361), who is known to have carried out numerous modifications to the castle. The results of this analysis indicate that Thomas, in addition to castle improvements, also undertook substantial improvement works to the estate.

Numerous sinuous channels, suggesting natural formation processes, are visible on LIDAR images of the meads south of Berkeley town. The channels generally form sharp angles with the parent channels of Berkeley Pill and the Little Avon, suggesting that the specific channels have been canalised to some degree, or at the very least dredged and maintained over time. A characteristic feature of these rivulets is the presence of ovoid depressions towards the south of the channels.

A *c.* 1800 drainage plan (GRO PC/401) shows for the first time the channel running along the western edge of Castle Mead from the base of High Street to the bridge into Ham. This channel, now containing approximately 1 m of silt in the base, has limestone walls either side and was clearly intended to allow excess water to flow from Berkeley Pill into the Little Avon. A sluice to the east of Lockfast Bridge, which

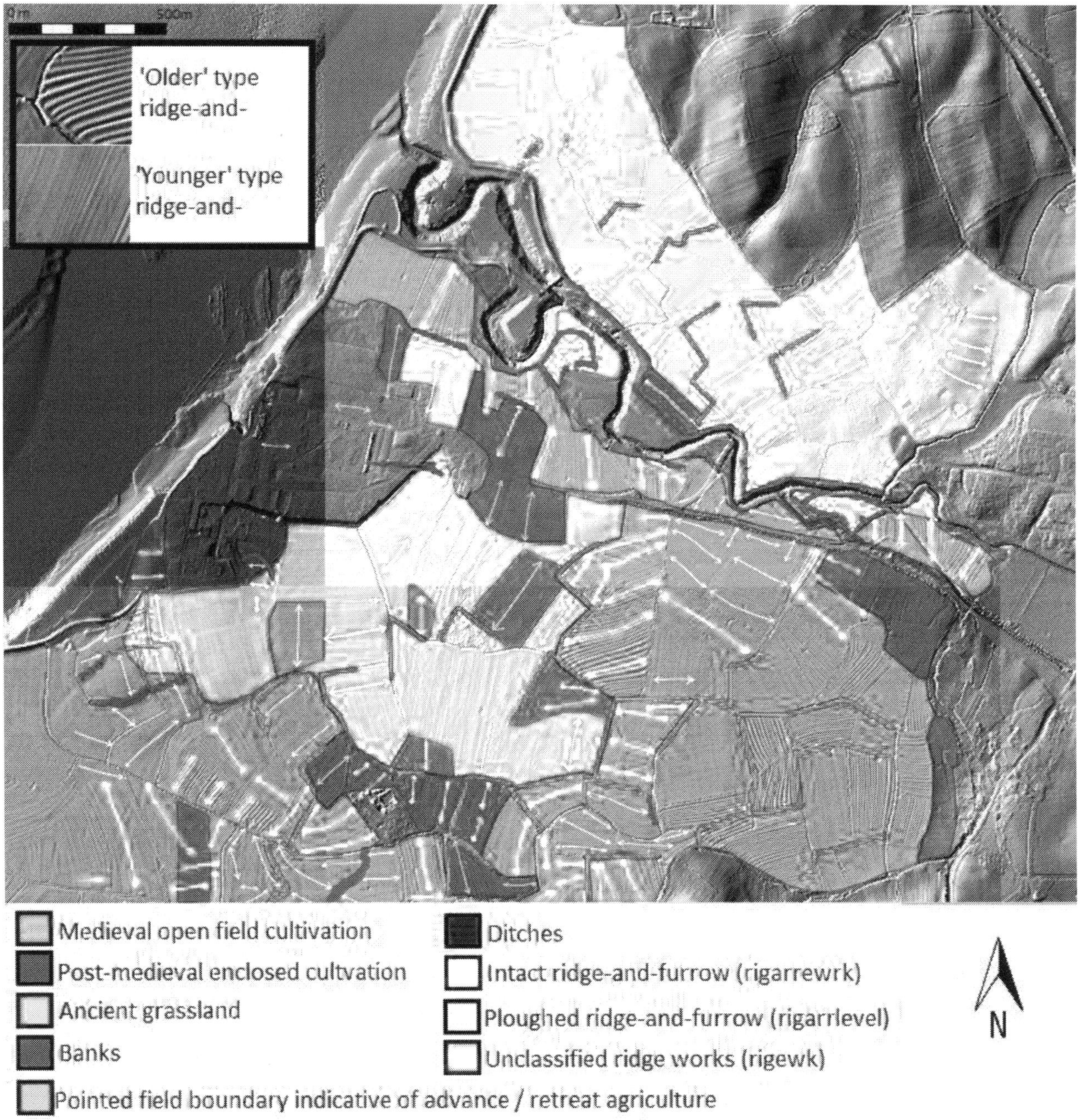

Figure 10. Map showing phased land use of the Berkeley hinterland and visible features associated with fluvioscape interaction. Partially based on (Allen, 1992, 95); 1m & 2m composite LIDAR data (Geomatics-Group © EANA, 2015); NMP data (GHER, 2015).

was also replaced in this period (Tandy 2003, 179), would have prevented tidal waters from flowing further inland and directed the waters down this channel. The drainage plan also shows new drainage channels added to the fields east of Ham. A substantial straightening of the meanders on Berkeley Pill, the Little Avon and Doverte Brook also took place throughout the 19th and 20th centuries (GRO PC1812/21/1B, PC1812/21/3; OS1880/81; OS1902/03; OS1921; OS1937; OS1971/72; OS2015). In the late 20th century a sluice gate was constructed at the mouth of Berkeley Pill effectively stopping the tidal waters from flowing inland. Previously the tidal waters could potentially flow as far inland as Newport (Tandy 2003, 179), *c.* 1.5 km further east of Berkeley.

Fluvial modifications associated with defence

The earliest defensive structure identified at Berkeley is a moat which was not concentric with later defences, offset slightly to the north-west of the present Shell Keep (Berkeley 1938, 321). Berkeley suggests that this moat was part of a Roman fort complex, a pre-Roman burial enclosure or a fortification pre-dating the Henry II Shell Keep. Two further channels were also identified by Berkeley joining the moat/ditch, one to the north-east of the ringwork and another to the south. Pimpernell (2007, 8) concluded that the channel to the north-east was part of the 12th century fortifications of Maurice [I] (1120–1190). There is no other evidence to suggest the ditch associated with the 11th century ringwork fortifications was able to be flooded using waterway modifications. The channel to the south identified by Berkeley (1938, 321) may possibly represent an outflow channel suggesting that either groundwater infiltration or more likely precipitation could fill the defensive ditch.

A grant confirmed between 1190 and 1220 made by Maurice [I] to St Augustine's Abbey, Bristol, in 'recompense for my offence committed upon the cemetery of Berkeley in cutting a ditch around my castle' (Walker 1998, 76–7) suggests the 5th Baron was engaged in constructing a moat on the north of the Shell Keep, in the present location of St Mary's church. The situation of the easternmost moat on the edge of the Shell Keep but respecting the Inner Ward, indicates that this phase of defence must pre-date the construction of the Outer Ward and Curtain Wall (1327–1361) and must therefore be associated with Maurice's modifications (Pimpernell 2007, 8). A channel was leading off the moat to the east which leads to an offshoot rivulet of the Newport Brook. This channel undoubtedly fed the northern moat with water, probably through a sluice (Prior 2005, 14) located on Newport Brook while excess water flowed down the rivulet to the south thus forming the eastern fluvial defences. The historical and landscape evidence suggests therefore that the moat would have followed the northern wall of the Shell Keep, turn north to respect the east facing elevation of the donjon and terminate somewhere to the east of St Mary's Church (Prior 2005).

The next phase of moat construction identifiable through historical accounts was carried out by Thomas [IV] (1353–1417) in 1386 where 'hee much inlarged the ditch at Berkeley Castle, by taking a part of the Church yard' (Smyth 1639, II, 12). Prior (2005) identified this phase of fortifications as those to the east of St Mary's churchyard, following the Curtain Wall of the outer ward (1327–1361), terminating west of the Thorpe Tower. An earthwork survey (Pimpernell 2007) did not identify a connecting channel between Maurice's [I] moat and those constructed by Thomas [IV] indicating that either the 14th century moat was 'dry' or connected via means which are no longer visible. Thomas [IV] also probably constructed a defensive ditch in the area of the outer gatehouse, to the west of St Mary's Church, although it is unclear how far it extended north-east, between the church and castle. Excavations carried out in 2005 (Prior 2005) indicated that a ditch in this area was of 17th century date, undoubtedly associated with Civil War defences. There is no reason to suppose that this defensive line utilised modifications to the fluvial network. It appears, therefore, that only the north, east and west sides of Berkeley were ever defended with waterfilled ditches, all of which are associated with modifications made to Newport Brook.

Roads and the fluvial network

A trackway heading to the postern gate drawbridge, identified by Berkeley (1938, 314–315) to the north of the castle possibly represents the primary route into the castle associated with the *c*. 1386 moat remodelling (Pimpernell 2007, 9).

To the south of the castle, Tandy (2003, 176) suggests that a bridge at the bottom of High Street, known today as Lockfast Bridge, was not present prior to the late 12th century fluvial modifications. This theory is potentially borne out by a possible palaeochannel seen as a mid- to low resistance feature in a resistivity and gradiometer survey of Castle Mead intersecting with Berkeley Pill at approximately the location of Lockfast Bridge and with the Little Avon at a meander *c* 200 m west of the bridge into the village of Ham.

The 12th–13th century diversion of Newport Brook therefore possibly also included a rerouting of Berkeley Pill to the west, thereby encircling the south and east of the castle ridge. The course of this proposed palaeochannel would result in a large meander, almost at a right-angle, in Berkeley Pill. As part of the same geophysical survey Rowe (2005, 20, 25; 2014, 9) identified a linear high resistance feature also visible as a bank and ditch on LIDAR images, interpreted as a bank of a fishpond or mill leat, running parallel to the palaeo-channel, to the east. This linear appears to continue north of the present course of Berkeley Pill, strongly suggesting it was created prior to the 12th century rerouting of Berkeley Pill. A re-interpretation of this feature as a causeway may represent a Romano-British or Anglo-Saxon southern road into Berkeley, with associated ditch or canal on the western side. While numerous Anglo-Saxon and medieval canals have been identified in association with monastic complexes (Bond 2001, 102–3), similar causeways were in use into the post-medieval period.

The 12th century changes would have made this causeway which followed but did not cross the earlier line of Berkeley Pill, redundant, and necessitated the construction of a new road out of Berkeley to the south. The 'new road', following the line of the present road to Ham now crossed the pill requiring the construction of Lockfast Bridge. The name 'Lockfast' may refer to Maurice's sluice system which, if closed, would have caused a back-up of the waters from Newport Brook to the west and prevented the tidal waters coming up-stream along Berkeley Pill from proceeding further. Thus, east of the 'new road' freshwater would collect behind the bridge and, to the west, tidal saltwater could flood the meads. A further high resistance feature (Rowe 2005, 20) clearly visible as two sections is located within the linear canal/ditch (Fig. 13) may indicate a sluice, suggesting that this linear feature was incorporated into Maurice's [I] new hydrological regime. It even appears on the *c*. 1800 plan of proposed drainage channels, annotated 'Old Drain' (GRO PC/401).

The presence of a wide expanse of braided wetland channels on the western route out of Berkeley may have provided the name for the Longbridge which crossed it. Today only the 17th century Longbridge and its associated causeway are visible, however, during the medieval period a wooden causeway bridge is known to have crossed this area (Smyth 1639, III, 259). This route may have been predated by a linear feature and identified on an earthwork survey of Little Park (Morris 2006, 3). A channel associated to this potential causeway is shown on the tithe map (GRO PC 1812/21/1B) possibly suggesting a combined channel similar to the proposed southern route.

Fishponds and mills

Newport Brook appears to have been a major focus for modification of Berkeley's fluvioscape during the early medieval period. Topographic evidence suggests the presence of relict palaeochannels flowing south across the marsh to the west of Berkeley ridge, along the current route of Newport Brook. While it is not known when these north–south orientated channels stopped flowing, a canalisation of Newport Brook and 'bankes of divers fishponds' (Smyth 1639, I, 69) may have been constructed in association with Trinity Hospital. Records attribute the foundation of the hospital to Maurice [I], locating it on the north of Berkeley, to the west of Longbridge (Smyth 1639 V.I 69, III, 259).

Earthwork (Morris 2006) and geophysical (Rowe 2006) surveys carried out on topographical anomalies seen on the north-east side of Castle Worthy field identified a possible candidate for the hospital, complete with a building platform and rectangular fishponds fed from a channel leading off Newport Brook. While these features appear to contradict the historical accounts, being to the east of Longbridge, the plan revealed is highly characteristic of other medieval monastic hospitals (Bond 1988, 97). However, rectangular platforms and possible ovoid fishponds, visible on LIDAR images, north-west of Longbridge, correlate better with the known historical location of the hospital.

This area was subject to a geophysical survey and archaeological evaluation in 2013 which identified features indicative of multi-period activity from Roman to post-medieval (Haines 2013, 16–19). A number of walls and robber trenches were recorded on the southernmost platform while, to the west, a hollow-way was observed running north–south along the western edge of the proposed fishponds (Haines 2013, 17–18). Numerous other ditches and pits were also identified some of which contained ceramics of the 11th–13th centuries while a fragment of 13th–14th century three-quarter moulded carved oolitic limestone, possibly from a window or door setting, was recovered from the topsoil (*ibid.*, 10, 19). The features recorded are highly indicative of a substantial building complex in this area dating from the early medieval period, possibly the Trinity Hospital or 'an ancillary hospital structure' (Haines 2013, 18).

Thus, we are left with two likely candidates for the Trinity Hospital on either side of Longbridge. Only excavation will reveal the true nature of the archaeology although it is possible that both locations represent structures and earthworks associated with the hospital. What is clear, however, is that substantial rerouting and channel excavation occurred in each of these two areas, consistent with the construction of fishponds. Smyth (1639, I, 142) states that Maurice [II] (1271–1326) modified much of the fluvial landscape of the Doverte Brook, particularly around the 'hurdpoole', altering 'courses as hee pleased' for purpose of fishponds and 'walkes and gardens'. The 'hurdpoole' was located in the present area of the Mobley Withybeds (Tandy 2003, 179) (NGR ST 6884 9858) where drainage channels still flow into the eastern channel of Doverte Brooke. Further topographic features to the south-east of the castle, interpreted as fishponds attributable to Maurice [II], were identified in a BCP earthwork survey (Prior 2005, 4). A feature of his fluvial modifications is the integration of both tidal saltwater and non-tidal freshwater systems which through 'sluices ... let in and kept out both salt and fresh waters at his [Maurice [II]] pleasure' (Smyth 1639, I, 141–2). Such fluvial modifications may be visible in the landscape as the ovoid features shown in Figure 8, which if dammed with sluices could prevent the flow of either depending on the state of the tide.

Domesday records two mills within the core of the Berkeley manor with a further eight in the outlying manors (Morris 1982, 163b). The two watermills of the 'core' may be represented by Sea Mills and Browns Mill (Tandy 2003, 175) although the fact that these are referred to as a single entity, called Upper Mill, in the muniments (Wells-Furby 2004, 133) may suggest that one of the 1086 mills is the 'watermill of Berkeley neere lockfast bridge' granted to St Augustine's Monastery by Robert [II] in the late 12th century (Smyth 1639, I, 86) which presumably refers to the mill on the quay to the south of High Street.

The linear nature of the Little Avon and scarp bank, to the east of Sea Mills, suggests a straightening of the channel for a leat (Pimpernell 2006, 4) although, as discussed, while the morphology of the fluvial system at Berkeley tends towards meandering, naturally occurring straight sections cannot be ruled out. Alternatively, it may indicate a long-standing position of the southern bank of the Little Avon, the channel of which has become narrowed over time due to morphodynamic processes. The fluvial modifications associated with Browns Mill, located on the banks of the Little Avon south-east of Ham (NGR 6832 808), include a potential millpond and straightening of the channel to the north of the mill.

Conclusions

The aim of this chapter has been to test the potential of a holistic methodology combining archaeological and historical data with comparative analysis in an attempt to reconstruct and understand the human exploitation of a fluvial landscape. The drainage and reclamation of agricultural land on the marshes appears to have been well established by the early medieval period and most likely occurred, at least in part, during Roman occupation of the Severn estuary. That said this process should not be viewed as static. The vast sums of money employed in maintaining and improving the drained agricultural landscape is amply demonstrated by the medieval and post-medieval accounts and features still visible in the landscape.

The present course of the major channels appears to have been largely established by the 13th–14th centuries with Maurice I and II playing key roles in their modification and formalisation. Many of the landscape features they created, however, such as fishponds, associated feeder channels and sluices, were already in decline by the 17th century (Smyth 1639, I, 69). While some of these systems can be more readily identified, such as the diversion of Newport Brook to feed the moat, others, particularly on the low-lying meads, are more difficult to understand. This is partly due to morphodynamic processes which have undoubtedly masked more ephemeral archaeology, although geophysical survey can overcome this problem in part. Geophysical survey cannot, however, overcome the further problem of an absence of identifiable features of known date in this area. Thus any interpretation of fluvial features as part of larger systems is purely conjectural assuming a contemporary phase of usage if not construction.

Bibliography

Allen, J.R.L. 1985. Intertidal drainage and mass movement processes in the Severn Estuary: Rills and creeks (pills). *Journal of the Geological Society* 142 (5), 849–61.

Allen, J.R.L. 1992. A reconnaissance map of the medieval alluvial ploughlands in the Vale of Berkeley, Gloucestershire and Avon. *Transactions of the Bristol and Gloucestershire Archaeological Society* 110, 87–97.

Allen, J.R.L. and Rippon, S.J. 1997. Iron Age to early modern activity and paleochannels at Magor Pill, Gwent: An exercise in lowland coastal-zone geoarchaeology. *Antiquaries Journal* 77, 327–70.

Berkeley, 8th Earl. 1938. Excavations at Berkeley Castle. *Transactions of the Bristol and Gloucestershire Archaeological Society* 60, 308–39.

Bond 1988. Monastic Water Management in Great Britain: A Review. *Monastic Archaeology: Papers on the Study of Medieval Monasteries*, edited by Graham Keevill, Mick Aston, and Teresa Hall, 88-136. Oxford: Oxbow Books, 2001.

Bond, J. 2001. Monastic water management in Great Britain. In: Keevill, G., Aston, M. and Hall, T. (eds) *Monastic Archaeology: Papers on the study of medieval monasteries*, 88–136. Oxford: Oxbow Books..

Crowther, S. and Dickson, A. 2008. *Severn Estuary Rapid Coastal Zone Assessment Survey. National Mapping Programme*. Gloucester/Swindon: Gloucestershire Council Archaeology Service.

Dickinson, G. 2015. A survey of two thousand years of human interaction with a fluvial landscape at Berkeley, Gloucestershire. Masters Dissertation.

Gaffney, C. and Gater, J. 2011. *Revealing the Buried Past: Geophysics for Archaeologists* (5th edn). Stroud: History Press.

Haines, C. 2013. Land at Berkeley Gloucestershire: Archaeological Evaluation. CA Project 4627/CA Report 13676, unpublished archaeological evaluation report.

Leech, R. 1981. *Historic Towns in Gloucestershire: Archaeology and planning.* Stroud: Sutton

Morris, J. (ed.) 1982. *Domesday Book: Gloucestershire.* Chichester: Phillimore.

Morris, N. 2006. *Earthwork Survey in Little Park and Castle Worthy, Berkeley Castle, Gloucestershire, 2006.* Unpublished earthwork survey report.

Oswin, J. 2009. *A Field Guide to Geophysics in Archaeology.* Chichester: Praxis.

Pimpernell, J. 2006. *Earthwork Survey in Quarf Mead & Home Ground, Berkeley Castle, Gloucestershire, 2006.* Unpublished earthwork survey report.

Pimpernell, J. 2007. *Berkeley Castle Project Report on Earthwork Survey 21st May to 15th June 2007.* Unpublished earthwork survey report.

Prior, S. 2005. *Archaeological Excavation & Earthwork Survey in The Butterfly Garden & Water Meadow at Berkeley Castle, Berkeley, Gloucestershire*. Bristol University: unpublished report (BC05), BCP Report 1.

Prior, S.J. 2005. *Project Design for an Archaeological Excavation in The Butterfly Garden, an Earthwork Survey in Quarf Mead & Home Ground and a Geophysical Survey in Nelme's Paddock, Berkeley Castle, Gloucestershire.* Bristol University: unpublished report (BC06), BCP Report 4.

Rowe, P.R. 2005. *Geophysical survey report for Berkeley Castle, Gloucestershire.* Unpublished report.

Rowe, P.R. 2006. *Geophysical survey report for Berkeley Castle, Gloucestershire.* Unpublished report.

Rowe, P R. 2014. *Geophysical survey report for Watermeadow, Berkeley, Gloucestershire.* Unpublished report.

Schmidt, A. 2013. *Earth Resistance for Archaeologists.* Lanham, MD: AltaMira Press.

Smith, B. and Ralph, E. 1972. *A History of Bristol and Gloucestershire.* Beaconsfield: Darwen Finlayson.

Smyth, J. (of Nibley). 1639 [1883]. The Berkeley Manuscripts: Lives of the Berkeleys = Maclean, J. (ed.) *Transaction of Bristol and Gloucestershire Archaeological Society* 8

Tandy, D. 2003. *Berkeley: A town in the marshes.* Privately Published.

Walker, D. 1998. The Cartulary of St Augustine Abbey, Bristol. Gloucester: Bristol and Gloucestershire Archaeological Society.

Wells-Furby, B. 2004. A Catalogue of the Medieval Munuments at Berkeley Castle I. Bristol: Gloucestershire Records Series 17.

Chapter 3

Tales from the Castle: A Biography of the Fortifications and the Castle in Berkeley

Rachel Morgan and Stuart J. Prior

From Motte to Shell

The biography of the Castle in Berkeley (Fig. 1) is historically well documented and follows all major events of English and British history of the early Norman period until the end of the 20th century (Fig. 2). A motte and bailey castle that was built by William FitzOsbern and listed in the Domesday Book as 'Ness' (D'Auvergne nd, 4; Platt 1982, 14; Cathcart King 1983, 180), was sighted on land specifically chosen for a castle (Pounds 1990, 68) within an estate previously held by Berkeley Minster (Finberg 1957, 39). It seems the original plan was to build the castle at 'Ness', modern Sharpness, close to the Severn rather than at the manorial centre of Oldminster, however the plan was altered and a site chosen near the centre of the Vale (*ibid.*, 68). William Fitz Osbern was killed in 1071 so the castle must have been raised between 1066 and 1071 (Pettifer 1995, 77), although ATA (2009, 11) suggest a date of 1076. Although initially likely constructed as a border castle to aid control of the Severn Estuary near the Welsh border, the Normans quickly penetrated into south Wales so that Gloucestershire was never part of the Marches and castles here are correspondingly more sparse (Pettifer 1995, 77). The original castle likely consisted of the motte in the north-west of the site with a ditch around three sides and the natural, possibly enhanced, defences of the southern slope and marsh below (Evans 1912, 152). A castle was certainly in place by 1121 as Henry I spent Easter there (Gascoigne 1975, 48).

As with many other castles during the 12th century (Cathcart King 1988, 62), the timber castle was rebuilt in stone. Berkeley was rebuilt by Henry II on behalf of Robert FitzHarding, to whom he had granted the castle in *c.* 1155, suggesting Henry may have controlled the castle indirectly (Pettifer 1995, 77). Few licences to crenellate were granted during the reign of Henry II which makes Berkeley unusual (Cathcart King 1988, 22). Constructing a castle in stone was very costly (Thompson 1987, 11) and this would have indebted FitzHarding and his son Maurice, who continued construction (ATA 2009, 12), to the king. This castle was constructed in the form of a two-storey 'shell keep', where the earlier motte was thought to be entirely encircled and revetted by a stone wall, and a bailey surrounded by a Curtain Wall (KHBC 2009, 2). Other comparable examples of shell keeps which revetted earlier mottes are found at Farnham Castle, Surrey and Carmarthen Castle. While still highly defensive in nature the Shell Keep is also indicative of the increasing residential use of castles (Pounds 1990, 22), with shell keeps generally superseded by the late 12th century by domestic buildings within the bailey (Evans 1912, 152). However, Berkeley was not so residential the king could not billet a garrison there in 1232 (*ibid.*, 122).

At Berkeley, the internal ground level within the Shell Keep is correspondingly higher than that within the bailey. Three semicircular bastions flank its east side where castles would normally have been strengthened by pilasters and buttresses (Fig. 2; D'Auvergne nd, 9). Pettifer remarks the half-round bastions were an early example of the type (1995, 77) however Cathcart King states they represent a contemporary development from square plan features to round ones as military defence became more scientific (1988, 92). The north-east bastion originally contained a Chapel to St John in the upper chamber (the windows of which could be original 12th century: KHBC 2009, 7) and a well in the basement; the

Figure 1. Aerial view of Berkeley castle as it is in 2020

south-east contained a dungeon in the basement which is extant. The original purpose of the southern bastion rooms and the upper chamber of the south-east bastion are unknown due to later remodelling. The southern external side of the Keep and the south-eastern bastion contain a series of original pilaster buttresses. Some original round-headed lancet windows survive in the Tower room and Chapel (Fig. 5), and the chancel floor includes remnants of medieval tiles although it is unknown whether these were introduced during the 1920's refurbishment.

The rectangular Forebuilding between the north-east and south-east bastions (Fig. 2), although constructed slightly later, *c.* 1170, was thought to have been part of the original design (KHBC 2009, 2) providing defended access from the inner bailey within the Curtain Wall up to the inner ground level of the Shell Keep. Elaborate forebuildings are a feature of the Angevin-era castles (D'Auvergne nd, 12), however they are less frequently found with circular keeps and Berkeley may be the only example of a shell keep with a forebuilding (Evans 1912, 16). At Berkeley the presence of a Forebuilding is likely facilitated by the revetted mound so that the internal stairs can be flush with the wall rather than perpendicular to it (Harvey 1911, 92). The Forebuilding contains a nationally important Romanesque doorway on the east side of the Keep. Built in the mid-12th century, the surviving north jamb is elaborately carved column and foliate capital supporting a carved archway of chevrons and zig-zag decoration with flat order between. The arch was partially infilled to contain a smaller doorway probably in the 14th or 15th century (KHBC 2009, 6).

The forebuilding was entered from the south into a two-storey tower, likely originally a free-standing structure, with a guardroom above, now called King Edward's Cell (*ibid.*, 31). A middle gateway is

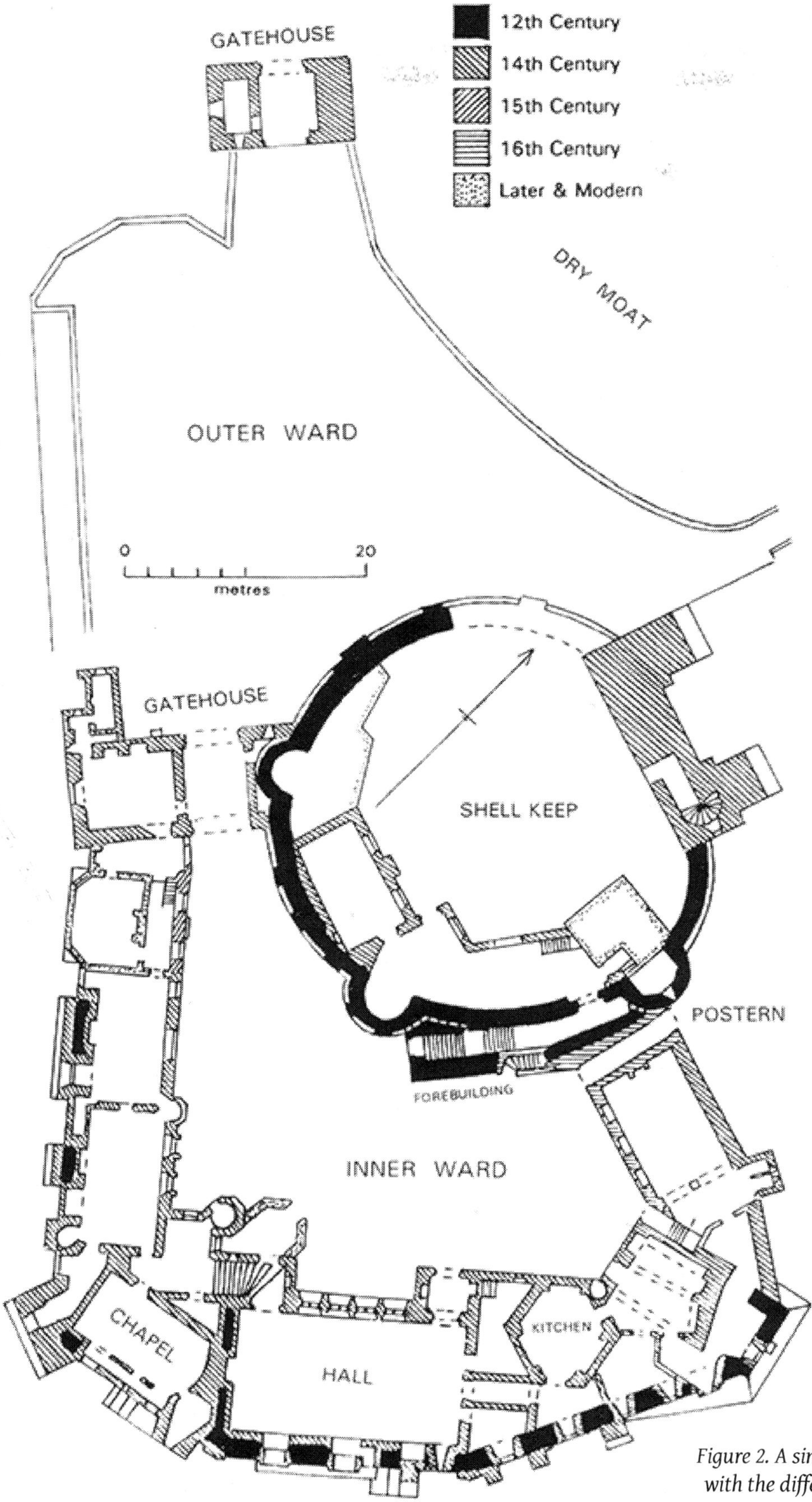

Figure 2. A simplified drawing of the castle with the different phases of development annotated.

indicated in the passage between the south entrance and the main doorway due to remaining jamb-like features, with a postulated pit and drawbridge. The ground floor stonework is 12th century with a surviving round-headed arch over the doorway.

The Curtain Wall which surrounds the inner bailey was probably constructed *c.* 1170 by Maurice de Berkeley although may have been begun in the mid-12th century (ATA 2009, 19) and maintains a terrace walk around the Inner Court (Evans 1912, 153). The outer wall to the north of the North Range may date from this time, however the remaining Curtain Wall along the east and south sides of the bailey is thought to be mainly 12th century in date (KHBC 2009, 53, 115). Pilaster buttresses survive to the north wall of the North-East Corner Range, and the outer wall of the East Range. The latter wall appears to have been constructed in two phases during the 12th century indicated by two overlapping windows suggesting a mid and late-12th century date for construction (*ibid.*, 84).

No evidence survives of the original internal structures within the Shell Keep or inner bailey. The only remnants of the original hall which remain are a shaft, base and capital of a window embrasure in the east wall of the East Range and three either 12th or 14th century external windows, two of which have sills reduced to floor level (*ibid.*). However, the hall was rebuilt *c.* 1190 (ATA 2009, 29), possibly due to the structural failure of the first building, suggested by the number of buttresses outside the Curtain Wall to the immediate north of the hall (*ibid.*). The beer cellar was also thought to have been constructed in the 12th century but rebuilt in the 14th (KHBC 2009, 104). The moats to the north and south-east were probably excavated by Maurice de Berkeley, the original moat for the Shell Keep later being built over by the Inner Gatehouse (*ibid.*, 155).

'Our native stone from English arms rebel against us'[1]

The second Thomas de Berkeley (1281–1321) and his grandson the 3rd Thomas de Berkeley (1326–1361) both undertook building work at the castle. The latter undertook an extensive programme of remodelling to create a series of high status apartments and also upgraded the defences by the construction of a defended Outer Ward west of the castle and extending the moat (ATA 2009, 21, 31). The 14th century saw a move towards bringing accommodation out of the keep and into the Inner Court of castles creating ranges of buildings around the walls which reflected changes in the nature of aristocratic society. This was due to a decline in the former itinerant nature of lords and a subsequent increase in the size of households (Liddiard 2005, 59, 61). The walls of the small Outer Ward at Berkeley appear never to have been high and the main defence would have been the moat (Oman 1926, 86). This, along with the remodelling of the initially unlicensed Beverton Castle near Tetbury, both represent the importance of the Berkeley family in the local area and show the favour the 3rd Thomas was held in by the crown (Pettifer 1995, 77, 78): he had married a daughter of Roger Mortimer who established himself in power with the queen after Edward II's capture (Finberg 1957, 149).

It was at Berkeley Castle in 1327 that King Edward II was reportedly murdered and although Thomas de Berkeley was originally arrested for the crime he was acquitted after proving he was absent from the castle at the time. However, the family papers state Thomas did not leave Berkeley until the 28 September, a full week after the murder on 21st (Finberg 1957, 149). In the late 13th century, the three knights of the Berkeley family (Thomas, Thomas Junior (son) and Maurice (other son)) were in the Low Countries with the king (Simpkin 2008, 149). The 3rd Thomas de Berkeley fought in Scotland and France and his second wife Katherine was a very rich widow. He was also noted for his sheep farming and additions to his estate (Finberg 1957, 149).

1 Shakespeare *Edward III*, Act 4, Scene 7

Berkeley Castle was extensively remodelled during this time. The inside of the southern quadrant of the Shell Keep was lined with a range of domestic buildings during the 14th century and the Forebuilding was refurbished. A series of square towers were added to the Curtain Wall and the north gate was probably rebuilt. Thorpe's Tower was added to the Shell Keep in *c.* 1342–6), possibly to position artillery towards the town where the natural defences of the castle were poor (KHBC 2009, 38). The original 12th century entrance to the Shell Keep was probably infilled in the 14th–15th century to house a smaller doorway and at least two windows were inserted in the exterior of the Shell Keep during the 14th century (*ibid.*, 6).

The south range of buildings within the Shell Keep originated in the 14th century with the construction of the recessed western end of the range. This was thought to have been service rooms accessed through a passage from the southern bastion of the Shell Keep (KHBC 2009, 9) which still retains the 14th century pointed segmental doorways. A contemporary chimney stack is present on the external wall and a narrow passage extends further west within the keep wall. The main range to the east of the recessed part appears late 15th or early 16th century in date, with mullion and transom windows from this date in the eastern and middle rooms, although the window in the ground floor of the west room in the main block is re-used. Seemingly most of the 14th century features in the main ranges were introduced here during the 1920's refurbishment although a window and doorjamb in the room over the lobby to the dungeon could be 14th century (*ibid.*, 10–11).

The Forebuilding was altered in the 14th or 15th century with a new doorway added from the inner bailey. The original 12th century doorway in the south front was partially blocked and a smaller doorway with round arch-head and chamfered surround inserted asymmetrically. A further doorway which dates from at least the 14th century leads from the platform of the Forebuilding onto the roof of the North Range. Four arrow loops in the central merlon of the tower parapet are all likely 14th century (KHBC 2009, 31–4).

Thorpe's Tower was constructed in the 14th century projecting outwards from the north side of the Shell Keep and commanded the view of the church from where an attack could be mounted, as occurred later during the Civil War (Oman 1926, 86). It was formed from two square towers joined by a thick wall and likely formed an emplacement for artillery (KHBC 2009, 38). The towers were originally constructed one storey higher than the surrounding Keep but were reduced to the current height in *c.* 1701 (*ibid.*, 38). The original entrance was through a lobby which was enlarged during the construction of the laundry in 1765–6. The eastern tower contained a newel stair with a straight branch across to the western tower, which leads to the top of the connecting wall and the western tower. Two or three 14th century cruciform arrow-loop windows are present in the east and north walls, one of which contains the remains of old plaster in the embrasure. A latrine may have been located in the buttress of the east tower which was accessed through a doorway in the north wall discovered during early 20th century excavations (KHBC 2009, 38). These excavations also uncovered stone piers and a cross wall which were interpreted as belonging to buildings in a north range.

The buildings within the Curtain Wall were rebuilt and extended. The section of Curtain Wall which extended east from the Shell Keep and forms the crenelated outer wall of the North Range is at least 14th century and could be 12th (*ibid.*, 46). A postern gateway is thought to have existed in the western part of bridge across the moat found during excavations in the 1920s. The southern exterior wall into the Inner Bailey largely dates from the late 18th century renovations, with a 14th century window as a later insert. The original use of the North Range is unknown, and the current layout reflects the 18th century renovations, although a two-bay 14th century arcade is still present in the east end of the ground floor billiard room which separates it from the (later) stairs in the North-east Services Block. In the late 17th century the North Range may have been the location of the stables with a 'great chamber' above, which was described in the early 18th century as being the steward's room but could be representative of an earlier layout (KHBC 2009, 46).

The North-east Corner block housed the services (*i.e.* scullery, still room, larders) with service accommodation above. It was built in the north-east corner of the courtyard inside the Curtain Wall in the 14th century and is two–three storeys high. A square tower was constructed in the north-west corner of the Services Block which extends out over the moat and may have been a garderobe as well as a defensive feature (*ibid.*, 54). The ground floor retains much material from this date including a vaulted stone ceiling on two large arches in the former bakehouse, now Scullery, to the north of the kitchen. This also has two original fireplaces or oven openings and a stair down under the courtyard to access the well, along with three original doorways. A further 14th century fireplace is situated in the north larder, and the east and west larders also contain 14th century chamfered beams. A small stone newel staircase built into the thickness of the wall between the kitchen and the scullery leads from the Inner Ward by now to the first floor. The rooms in the first floor are largely within the current caretaker's flat, however some 14th century chamfered beams still remain in the ceiling of the stair hall, the dining room and possibly within the long corridor. The large room over the scullery has separate access from the courtyard and was presumably a high-status chamber as it contains a large fireplace and large chamfered ceiling beams and joists, presumed to be 14th or 15th century (KHBC 2009, 53). Several windows and the south door are extant from this period.

The Hall, kitchen and services in the East Range were rebuilt in the 14th century. The kitchen is hexagonal in layout on the courtyard side of the range and rises two storeys to a lantern which projects through the roof. It contains three large fireplaces, windows to the courtyard and a large doorway to the east which may have originally lead to a lobby at the end of a passage. The passage was central to the services area and led to flanking small unheated service rooms, possibly the buttery and pantry (KHBC 2009, 70), and thence to the north end of the Hall. A small square-headed window in the Curtain Wall north of the northern buttress may be 14th century in date and all windows facing the inner courtyard date from the 14th century. Internally, two original 14th century doorways lead from the Hall to what would have been the passage and a small service room with a large central door. Further original doorways lead between the south and middle service rooms to the east and between the kitchen and scullery. The lantern roof of the kitchen was reportedly brought from Wootten Manor in the late 15th or early 16th century (Smyth 1639). It is constructed of six low-pitched roofs radiating from two perpendicular beams. The first floor was much altered in the 18th and 20th centuries, however a 14th century passage to a garderobe with a small squint window still exists and is reached from the left side of the window embrasure in what is now the Staff Room.

The Great Hall was rebuilt in the c. 1340s by the 3rd Thomas de Berkeley (KHBC 2009, 104). From the inner bailey the hall has a four-bay front with embattled parapet supported by corbels over triangular buttresses with four large close-set original mullion-and-transom windows between. Internally, the Hall is eight bays long and open to the full height of the building. The roof dates from the 14th century although it was dismantled and rebuilt in the 1920s (*ibid.*, 91). The Hall was entered to the north-west corner from the inner bailey through the porch which contains four original 14th century windows and 'Berkeley Arch' doorways at each end which consisted of a canted semi-octagonal arch-head. The roof of the porch is a lierne vault resting on King's head corbels. The Berkeley arches and the lierne vault roof may be the work of William Joy, a master mason of significance in the development of Decorated Gothic style and connected with the Berkeley tombs in Bristol Cathedral (Morris 1997). The porch led to the northern end of the Hall which also had access to the service rooms and, as such, was lower status and traditionally would have been screened off (KHBC 2009, 84). The higher status end in the south contained a dias accessed up two steps from the main body of the Hall. A large 14th century doorway led from the west of the dias to the Chapel of St Mary in the South-East corner block and to the chambers in the South Range. The first-floor chamber over the porch was accessed through a 14th century, three shoulder-headed arched doorway in the north wall which led to the lobby over the western service room in the East Range.

The South-East Corner Range was contemporary with the Hall in the East Range and originally contained the Chapel of St Mary on the first floor over a beer cellar with a 14th century lierne stone-vaulted ceiling (KHBC 2009, 104). The Chapel was licensed in 1364 (Smyth 1639) although is assumed to date to the 1340s and could also be the work of William Joy as it is stylistically similar to other works in the south-west at Wells Cathedral, Bristol Cathedral, St David's Cathedral and Palace, and Ottery St Mary Church (Morris 1997). The Chapel consists of five bays with a slightly apsidal end at the north-east with a vestry behind, and an aisle cut into the Curtain Wall. The four windows in the south-east wall of the Chapel are all 14th century, along with the timber roof which is supported on carved limestone heads. The timbers are inscribed with a 13th century translation of the Apocalypse, probably 14th century (Trotter 1990). The King's Pew, an oak-framed first floor gallery was originally located in the southern bay (KHBC 2009, 115). A triangular space at the south-west of the Chapel may have originally been a lobby to a garderobe (KHBC 2009, 105). The Chapel was accessed via a stair block in the south-west corner of the East Range which was originally 14th century but currently contains a stair dated to 1637. The 14th century stair block also allowed access to the beer cellar, via a three-storey semi-octagonal stair turret, and also gave access to both the Chapel and the parlour or dining room in the South Range.

The South Range is thought to have been constructed entirely in the 14th century as high status apartments (*ibid.*, 124), with the eastern chamber (now the Long Drawing Room) being the more important and connected to the Hall via the stairs and a landing. The original range would have extended to the end of the Middle Drawing Room. The original layout was thought to contain a solar in the Middle Drawing Room with a garderobe in the south-east corner, and a dining room or parlour in the Long Drawing Room with a large chimney stack in the room beneath suggesting this room may have originally contained a brewhouse (KHBC 2009, 124). Some of the original 14th century window openings survive, however the original entrance via the east wall was later blocked. The north-west corner of the Long Drawing Room contains a 14th century octagonal closet with original lancet windows. Several blocked 14th century doorways throughout the South Range indicate the level of remodelling the building has subsequently undergone. Remnants of a 14th century newel stair still lead from the Long Drawing Room to the services below.

The 14th century Inner Gatehouse at the south-west corner of the castle was the principal entrance from the town. Gatehouses in many castles appear to have been remodelled in line with defensive advancements during this time (Cathcart King 1988, 155) and the gatehouses at Berkeley appear in line with this development, being wide and shallow. The Inner Gatehouse was constructed to three storeys around the southern bastion of the Shell Keep and over the earlier moat (KHBC 2009, 155). There is a small Porter's Lodge to the west of the southern bastion. Entrance into the castle was via an entry way through the Inner Gatehouse to the immediate south of the Porter's Lodge. The large room over the main entrance would have housed the lifting mechanism for the portcullis and the room to the south may originally have been a steward's chamber (*ibid.*, 155). The ground floor room was originally divided into two rooms and was accessed via a doorway at the south end of the east wall from an old stair landing (KHBC 2009, 168). Much of the original 14th century ceiling structures survive on each storey. A further wide entrance was present from the inner courtyard to a large room to the south of the main entrance. At the south-west of the Inner Gatehouse the square Gatehouse Turret projected west into the outer ward. This contained narrow corridors and arrow loop embrasures throughout and would have been defensive in nature. A further Outer Tower situated to the north of the Gatehouse Turret was probably also contemporary and may have contained rooms for guards (*ibid.*, 155). A wedge-shaped tower to the south-east of the Inner Gatehouse within the inner courtyard, originally windowless apart from a slit window at second storey level, may have been a 14th century stair tower and may also have contained a garderobe in the upper storey (*ibid.*).

Early post-medieval feuding

After the 3rd Thomas de Berkeley died the family feuded for nearly 200 years over the entailment of the castle (Finberg 1957, 150), which may explain some of the lack of expenditure on the castle itself. Henry, 17th Lord Berkeley nearly bankrupted the estate trying to maintain his household in the 1550s (Rollinson 1992, 47). The castle was lost to the family in the reign of Henry VII when it was bequeathed to the King, however it came back into the family after the death of Edward VI.

The main addition which took place was the construction of the South Range Chambers between the South Range and the Inner Gatehouse in the late 15th–early 16th century, presumably while the castle was in the possession of the crown. This reflects a greater importance on privacy and specialisation within the household which developed in the later medieval period (Liddiard 2005, 61). This range is three storeys high with originally one room per storey accessed by staircases in the adjoining ranges. The two upper storeys originally contained fireplaces in the north wall and doorways towards the south ends of the east and west walls (KHBC 2009, 124). The original line of the exterior, southern wall projected slightly from that of the South Range and may have been a garderobe turret or contained a closet in the upper storey (KHBC 2009, 143; Fig. 4). It was originally accessed through a doorway from the inner ward, which was subsequently remodelled into a window.

Other parts of the castle were refurbished during this period. The south range in the Shell Keep was remodelled with the walls facing the interior of the Keep being largely late 15th or early 16th century in date, except for the 14th century westernmost section detailed above. The fireplace in the western room appears late 16th or early 17th century, showing the castle underwent small renovations throughout the period. Many of the 16th century windows and doorways within this range were introduced later, probably when the castle was extensively remodelled in the 1920s (KHBC 2009, 10–15).

The Forebuilding was partly rebuilt to include the Guardroom/King Edward's Cell on the first floor and a second stair lead down the east side of the Forebuilding to a projecting oriel porch and doorway to the first floor of the North Range. This east wall could represent the infilling of a drawbridge pit, as a stone bridge to approach from the south-west was constructed in 1587 (D'Auvergne nd, 149) which may have replaced the original drawbridge (Evans 1912, 153). A timber-framed gallery which dates from the early 16th century leads to the Guardroom doorway.

A number of small-scale refurbishments were undertaken in the domestic ranges of the inner ward. The North Range was redesigned when the second gateway at the west end was removed and replaced with a cross-passage arrangement, the doorway of which in the inner ward remains *in situ* along with a couple of windows. Also within the East Range, the roof within the Kitchen may have been brought from Wootten Manor in the late 15th or early 16th century (Smyth 1639). This roof is constructed of two main crossbeams with secondary beams jointed to them with scarf joints to create six radial low-pitched roofs. In the South-East Corner Range, the main timber stair from the Hall to the Chapel and south range dates from 1637 and is carved with faces and dragons with turned balusters and a moulded handrail and, within the Chapel, the roof has 16th century painted decoration. Externally, two buttresses to the exterior of the South-East Corner Range are also likely to date from the 16th century, with one built in 1586. The buttresses to the exterior of the South Range also likely date from the 1580s (KHBC 2009, 125).

The Inner Gatehouse was upgraded and refurbished to include high status chambers in the 16th century which would have necessitated the decommissioning of the Portcullis mechanism on the first floor (*ibid.*, 155). Some refenestration appears to have taken place at this time, with the second floor retaining a window likely dated to the second half of the 16th century. The three chimney stacks may date from this period although all were altered in the 1920s. Internally, the fireplaces on the ground floor, the Red Room on the first floor and the Great and Little State Rooms on the second floor may be original, although the ground floor one could have been introduced in the 1920s (*ibid.*, 169–78).

Civil War Period

During the Civil War (1642–1651) the castle was significantly damaged when it was attacked by artillery from the church to the north-west. The castle changed hands five times during the course of the war and was subsequently repaired and remodelled by Charles the 2nd Earl of Berkeley between 1698 and 1710 (Figs. 2 and 3). The south-west quadrant of the Shell Keep was bombarded with artillery on 24 September 1645 which created a hole in the west of the keep wall. After a three day siege the castle surrendered (Gascoigne 1975, 48). Thorpe's Tower was also badly damaged and not repaired until *c.*1700 (KHBC 2009, 183) when its height was reduced to match that of the Shell Keep. The Keep itself was not fully repaired as by then the castle was effectively a country house and the breach was made good with marlstone; a buttress was added to the south-west side (Fig. 5). Further use of marlstone in the wide western buttress against the South Range suggests this addition could be contemporary (KHBC 2009, 125). Other buttresses were also repaired or strengthened in the aftermath of the Civil War and the south Curtain Wall was also repaired. The Outer Gatehouse was modified, being reduced to a single storey from two, and the Middle Gatehouse was demolished along with the walls of the outer ward. The Inner Gatehouse was also partly remodelled although any internal renovations were largely removed in the 1920s (*ibid.*, 155). The plank and stud 'Great Gates' were inserted into the main entry way in 1701 and

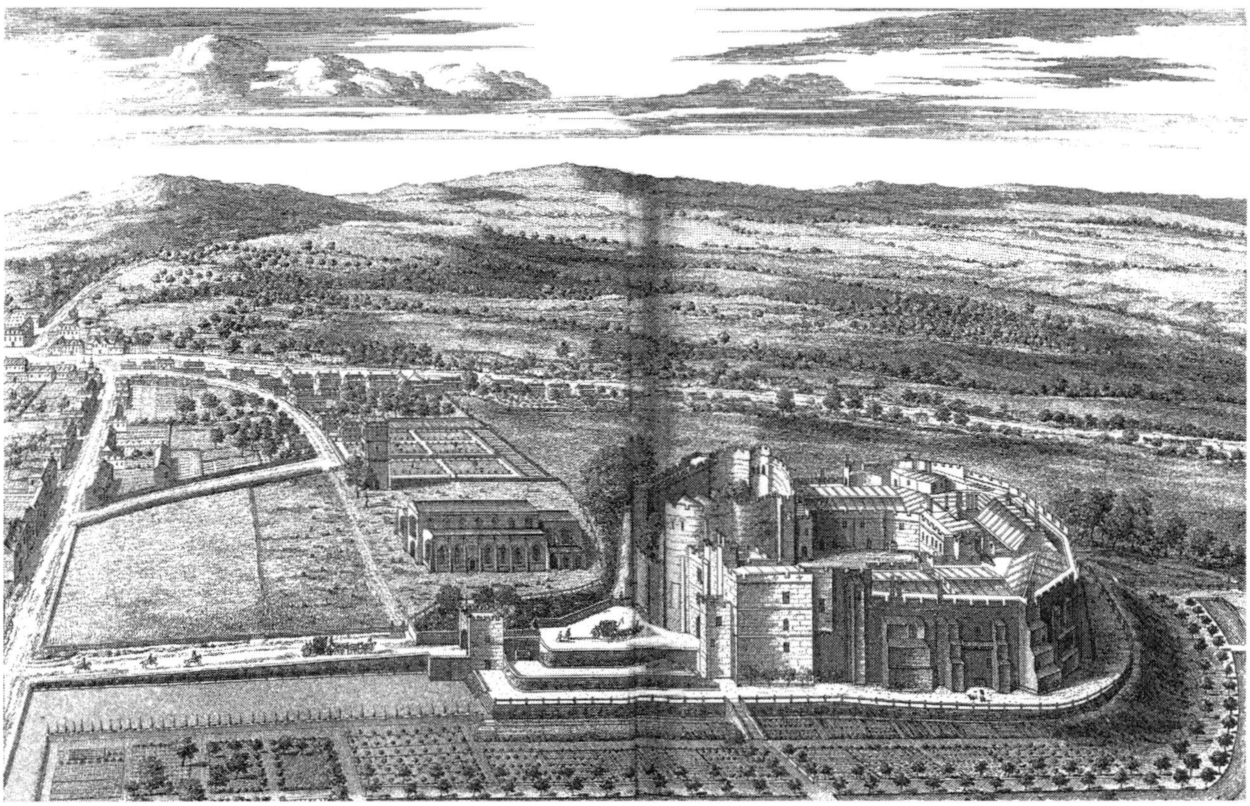

Figure 3. An engraving by Jan Kip dated in 1712. The Civil War damage to the shell keep is notable

include a small wicket door for pedestrian access. The doorway into the Outer Tower was likely blocked at this time and a window inserted (*ibid.*, 159). The remainder of the castle seems to have been largely unaffected by the Civil War bombardment, with structural work limited to small-scale repairs such as a brick repair to the south-east external ground floor window of the East Range (*ibid.*, 107). Only a few internal features date from this time including a timber chimney piece in the north wall of the Orange Bedroom in the South Range (ATA 2009). The 17th century leatherwork which currently hangs in the high-status private apartments of the Gatehouse is said to come locally from Berkeley (KHBC 2009, 171).

Regency remodelling

In the later 18th century the castle underwent a series of refurbishments although these were largely undone during the 1920s. This episode of refurbishment may have been precipitated by a fire in 1770 which partly destroyed the East Range, although alterations had already begun to the castle with the construction of the Laundry Block on the outside of Thorpe's Tower in 1765–6. There is also evidence of repairs to the fabric during the late 18th century such as a slag block in the north-east wall of the Shell Keep which may date from this time (KHBC 2009, 4). The South Range within the Shell Keep contains some 18th century features, although the building was much altered during the 1920s, but some of the internal room layouts may have originated during this period. The chimney pieces within the Darius Tent and Duke's rooms are 18th century, and the two rooms in the corridor to the south of King William's rooms could also be 18th century in date, as could some of the detailing in the remaining rooms such as doorways and ceiling cornices (*ibid.*, 17–18).

The addition of the Laundry to Thorpe's Tower enlarged the original entrance lobby into a service corridor. Two new doorways were introduced into Thorpe's Tower, one of which reconstructed a 14th century opening using a 12th century arch. The Laundry itself was a rectangular Gothic building constructed over two storeys with a slightly projecting central five-window bay with another single window to either side. Originally the ground floor was open with a fireplace at each end and contained a service corridor, also at first floor level, through the back wall and Thorpe's Tower. The first floor, which was reached via a stair in the eastern buttress of Thorpe's Tower, was originally divided into rooms by series of partitions (KHBC 2009, 38–40).

The North Range was remodelled in the 1780s when large single rooms were created on the ground and first floor levels. One window to the north wall and three to the south date from this period, and the earlier cross passage was repaired. Internally, the Billiard Room to the ground floor still retains features from this period such as the fireplace, doorway and cornice. The first floor, which had previously been a Nursery in *c.* 1750 (*ibid.*, 46), was divided into two rooms to the south with a bathroom at the west end and a corridor behind. Eighteenth century joinery and other features such as the fireplaces and built-in cupboard are still present in much of the north end and north-east corner of the North Range.

Although both casement and sash windows were inserted in the exterior wall of the North-east Range in the late 18th century, not many features appear to date from this period on the ground floor except for a timber stair to the first floor. The layout of the first floor, however, was rearranged during this period to create the Long Corridor which gave access to all the rooms. Many of the doorways and internal features such as cupboards are late 18th century in date. The Lower Maid's Chamber, with a further lobby and stair to the second floor, and the Dining Room remain largely intact.

The former service room and corridor on the ground floor in the East Range was converted to the Housekeeper's Room in the late 18th century, presumably after the fire of 1770 (KHBC 2009, 70), when it was enlarged and a Gothic fireplace inserted in the north-east corner. A basement passage to link the Kitchen and cellars of the East Range was built in the late 18th or early 19th century. The East Range otherwise appears to have been largely untouched by the renovations, although there was an 18th century fireplace in the Hall which was replaced in the 1920s, and a clock was inserted above the north end of the hall. The South-east Corner Range also appears to have had minimal alteration during the 18th century with some light fenestration and a small lobby constructed for the Beer Cellar (*ibid.*, 105).

The South Range, Inner Gatehouse and Great Hall were also refurbished, but most of the 18th century features in these areas, except possibly some of the doorways and fireplaces in the service rooms and the rainwater goods to the inner courtyard, were removed in the 1920s. The interior of the Long Drawing Room contained full-height panelling from the late 18th century refurbishment (*ibid.*, 132). Some 18th century features still exist in the Chamber Block including the full-height canted bay to the south side. Any 18th century refurbishment of the Gatehouse was undone during the 1920s except for the retention of a couple of windows. A mounting block in the inner bailey of the Shell Keep may be 18th century in date (*ibid.*, 8).

In Victorian times, Admiral Sir Maurice Berkeley (1857–1867) and his son Francis, the 1st and 2nd Baron FitzHarding (1867–96) undertook investment in the castle when the interiors were redesigned in the contemporary Arts and Crafts style. No major structural alterations appear to have taken place during the 19th century (ATA 2009, 39).

Modern remodelling

Randel, the 8th Earl of Berkeley (1916–1941) extensively remodelled the castle during the 1920s and '30s based on his antiquarian interests with the aim of creating an idealised country house (*ibid.*) (Fig. 4). Much of the later post-medieval alterations were removed and replaced with medieval features, mostly from France but also England, or moved from other parts of the castle. The remodelling was overseen by Keeble Ltd of London who recorded details of the castle during to the refurbishment so that most of the introduced features can be identified. Various modern conveniences were introduced into the castle to make the living accommodation more comfortable including a boiler room beneath the Great Hall, electricity throughout, and a lift in the stair tower of the Inner Gatehouse. *En suite* bathrooms and toilets were added to bedrooms, and double and secondary glazing was installed in the principal domestic rooms. Many of the doors within the castle also seem to date from this period.

All areas of the castle were affected to some degree by the remodelling, to the extent that some of the original or earlier features have been obscured, and it is not known whether certain features are as they appear or are early 20th century introductions. Within the Shell Keep, the 12th century chapel was rebuilt, which had not been present since at least 1712, with re-used medieval glass in one window and fragments of medieval floor tiles in the chancel (KHBC 2009, 21). Various medieval French and English windows were inserted in the ranges of the Shell Keep during the 1920s as with much of the remainder of the castle. The South Range was converted to contain domestic apartments with a stair introduced into the southern bastion to provide access while two other stairs were removed. The narrower block within the South Range was converted to bathrooms and toilets. New chimney stacks were added to the South Range and the fireplaces in the Darius Tent Room, King William's Room, Duke's Room and Willow Room/Drake's Bedroom certainly date from this period. The interior features of the Queen's Bedroom also seem to be 1920s introductions (KHBC 2009, 16). The King's Gallery was built in the 1920s and contains the original doorway to the Forebuilding along with 17th century style staircases. Within the Laundry in Thorpe's Tower, an underground service corridor was constructed through the north-east buttress leading to a doorway into the East Range, which contains doorways and windows from the 1920s, although here not all of the 18th century renovations were removed. The fireplace in the Billiard Room was also inserted in the 1920s (ibid., 50).

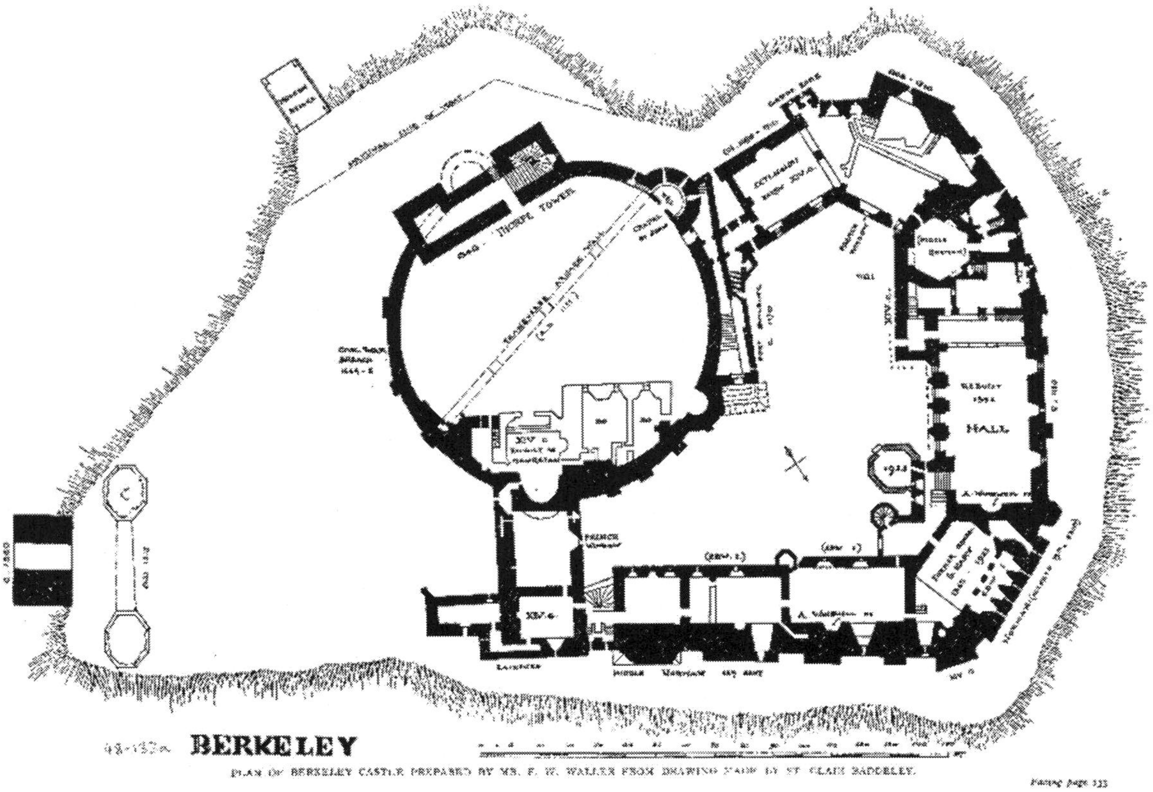

Figure 4. A 1926 plan of the Berkeley castle, after the remodelling

Some modernisation of the services in the North-east Range was undertaken in the 1920s such as the introduction of a staircase in the Scullery and tiling of the Larders. The North-east Range did not escape from partial refenestration at this time including the re-opening of external arrow loops, but the south-west elevation facing the internal courtyard had entirely new windows including a French medieval window to the ground and first floors.

The middle part of the central bay of the exterior of the East Range was rebuilt, with windows also inserted in the south bay, however the interior elevation to the inner courtyard appears to have been unaltered at this time except for the enlargement of the ground floor window (KHBC 2009, 21). Internally the China Room contains a Berkeley arch to the kitchen which was inserted in the 1920s. The servants' rooms to the first floor were altered to create a further small room with a large lobby.

The east wall of the Main Hall was straightened, work which reportedly including removing and re-inserting the late 12th century windows, and the roof was also re-erected to include a steeper pitch (*ibid.*, 84). The exterior wall of the East Range was also remodelled when a buttress between the windows was removed and both French and local windows inserted along with a French door to the garden. The elevation to the Inner Courtyard appears to have been little altered, with a small window removed and three small windows inserted into the service passage, however the 14th century windows were reglazed. Inside the Hall some detailing was repaired or inserted in the 1920s such as French doors, a 16th century screen from Caefn Mably, Pembrokeshire, and a fireplace from Wanswell Court (*ibid.*, 94).

Figure 5. The keep with Thorpe Tower and the chapel. The original round-headed lancet windows are visible.

Figure 6. The Civil War damage to the keep

Figure 7. The 8th Earl imported doorway, looking South.

The major addition to the South-east Range in the 1920s was the semi-octagonal Clock Tower built within the Inner Courtyard (Fig. 7). The late 18th century clock itself was moved from above the north end of the Hall. It contained a new stair to the Beer Cellar below and has a crenelated parapet, re-used medieval windows and an ornate imported French doorway. The Chapel on the first floor was converted to a Morning Room in the 1920s when the King's Pew was removed and re-installed in the Long Drawing Room. The elaborate fireplace was introduced where the entrance originally stood. The Apocalypse text on the roof timbers and the vestry was restored. The Treasury on the first floor was created out of the probable 14th century garderobe and lobby in order to display artefacts found during the restorations (KHBC 2009, 105). A small gallery is accessed from the Treasury via a stair.

The South Range was refurbished in the 1920s when all post-medieval fittings were removed and medieval features inserted, including an Italian balcony to the south facing window of the Long Drawing Room between the eastern and central buttresses. An additional, third, storey was added to the east bay and the ground floor elevation below the Italian balcony appears to have been rebuilt. A canted bay was added to the Middle Drawing Room section, and many of the windows in this elevation and the internal elevation were introduced. The ground floor service rooms were superficially refurbished, with some additional partitioning of the space to create the corridor and Valet's Room and the full height cupboards here date from this time.

Figure 8. The inner gatehouse

The internal layout of the Chamber Block in the South Range was reconfigured when a wide corridor, including a chimney stack, was created on each floor to connect with the state rooms in the Inner Gatehouse and a new entrance lobby was constructed on the ground floor along the north side of the block (KHBC 2009, 142). A new stair was introduced, and an extension built on the second floor to house bathroom facilities including the marble 'American Bathroom' which was imported from the Waldorf Astoria Hotel in New York (*ibid.*, 152). Stone chimney shafts were added to the chamber block of the South Range and an extension to the Inner Gatehouse was built. Many of the internal features in the South Range were introduced including French doorways, a Gothic screen and a re-used moulded timber ceiling in the Boudoir.

The Inner Gatehouse and Stair Tower were remodelled (Fig. 8), when the north side of the Stair Tower was demolished, the elevations levelled and a lift installed (KHBC 2009, 155). The upper section of the Inner Gatehouse was rebuilt to create a corridor bridge in the French Gothic style to the Shell Keep, with many of the windows inserted in the 1920s such as those on the first floor to the Inner Courtyard. The interior of the Gatehouse was extensively refurbished into high status private apartments when plans prepared by Keebles show the earlier remodelling was removed and many medieval features introduced (KHBC 2009, 167–79). In the ground floor Study all the doorways and the fireplace were either introduced or modified in the 1920s. The earlier 16th century remodelling of the first floor rooms was refurbished and further medieval features were introduced such as the doorways to both rooms and two windows of the Red Room. The leatherwork on the walls of the South Room, although 17th century Spanish, was sourced from elsewhere in the castle and erected here in the 1920s, whereas the fireplace was an introduction (*ibid*., 171). The second-floor rooms were also largely refurbished with the Great State Room and Little State Room both containing 17th century moved leatherwork and some inserted doorways although both rooms likely retain the original fireplaces (*ibid*., 175–8). A bathroom was inserted in the turret at second floor level during this refurbishment. The remodelling of the Stair Tower gave landings to all floors of the Gatehouse and also allowed room for a lift. The refurbishment included the construction of a blind arch in a medieval style to the west wall of the ground floor and a 1920s continuation of the 14th century ceiling to the second floor (KHBC 2009, 180).

Bibliography

Andrew Townsend Architects (ATA) 2009. *Berkeley Castle Conservation Management Plan.*

D'Auvergne, E.B. nd. *The English Castles.* London: T. Werner Laurie.

Cathcart King, D.J. 1983. *Castellarium Anglicanum* Vol. 1. London: Kraus International.

Cathcart King, D.J. 1988. *The Castle in England and Wales.* London and Sydney: Croom Helm.

Evans, H.A. 1912. *Castles of England and Wales.* London: Methuen.

Finberg, H.P.R. (ed.) 1957. *Gloucestershire Studies.* Leicester: Leicester University Press.

Gascoigne, C. 1975. *Castles of Britain.* London: Thames and Hudson.

Harvey, A. 1911 *The Castles and Walled Towns of England.* London: Methuen.

Keystone Historical Building Consultants (KHBC) 2009 *Gazetteer of the Buildings at Berkeley Castles, Gloucestershire.*

Liddiard, R. 2005. *Castles in Context. Power, Symbolism and Landscape 1066–1500.* Macclesfield: Windgather Press.

Morris, R.K. 1997. European prodigy or regional eccentric? The rebuilding of St. Augustine's Abbey church, Bristol', in Keen, L. (ed) *'Almost the Richest City': Bristol in the Middle Ages.*

Oman, C. 1926. *Castles.* London: Great Western Railway.

Pettifer, A., 1995. *English Castles. A Guide by Counties.* Woodbridge: Boydell.

Platt, C. 1982. *The Castle in Medieval England and Wales.* London: Secker and Warburg.

Pounds, N.J.G. 1990. *The Medieval Castle in England and Wales. A Social and Political History.* Cambridge: Cambridge University Press.

Rollinson, D. 1992. *The Local Origins of Modern Society. Gloucestershire 1500–1800.* London: Routledge.

Simpkin, D. 2008. *The English Aristocracy at War.* Woodbridge: Boydell.

Smyth, J. (of Nibley). 1639 [1883]. The Berkeley Manuscripts: Lives of the Berkeleys = Maclean, J. (ed.) *Transaction of Bristol and Gloucestershire Archaeological Society* 8.

Thompson M.W. 1987. *The Decline of the Castle.* Cambridge: Cambridge University Press.

Trotter , D.A. 1990. The Anglo-Norman Inscriptions At Berkeley Castle. *Medium Aevum* 59(1), 114-120.

Chapter 4

Tales from the Ground: Stratigraphic Narratives from the University of Bristol Research at Berkeley

Stuart J. Prior

Excavation scope and planning in Berkeley Castle grounds

Alongside the landscape and geophysical survey, archaeological excavation was the core component of the University of Bristol Berkeley Castle Project. Excavations had two-fold scope: a) to provide training on field methods to archaeology students from the Department of Anthropology and Archaeology and b) to investigate the history and archaeology of the castle and the associated settlement of Berkeley.

All archaeological work undertaken within the BCP's programme of research was carried out using appropriate methods and practices which satisfy the stated aims of the project and which comply with the 'Code of conduct, Code of approved practice for the regulation of contractual arrangements in field archaeology', and other relevant by-laws of the Chartered Institute of Field Archaeologists (CIfA). Subsequently, the methodologies have been prepared with reference to all applicable standards published by the CIfA. The decision to follow CIfA guidelines, and align the student training with them, was supported by the idea that University of Bristol graduates would be ready to be employed as field archaeologists with the completion of their degree.

For the duration of the project, each trench opened was numbered consecutively and all context numbers started with the number of the trench (*i.e.* in Trench 1 all context numbers begin with a 1, thus 101 for turf and topsoil; in Trench 2 all context numbers begin with a 2, thus 201 for turf and topsoil, etc.). Following the well-known conventions all negative archaeological features received a number in square brackets ([cuts]) while for all positive features numbers were indicated in normal brackets ((fills)). As the excavations were training excavations for undergraduate students, artefact collection was total. All artefactual and faunal remains encountered were retained, washed, weighed, sorted, analysed and recorded. Once all the finds were processed any modern material retrieved was discarded. Post-medieval material culture is considered to be of relevance to the project and therefore was retained. Artefacts/ecofacts were collected and recorded stratigraphically and therefore can be located by reference to the context in which they were discovered.

Levels were taken of all archaeological features and deposits and were related to Ordnance Datum using temporary benchmarks (TBMs). The benchmark used throughout the project is located on the west wall of the isolated church tower in St Mary's Churchyard: measuring 23.62 m AOD. Levels were entered onto site plans and context sheets and were also listed on separate Levels Sheets. The detailed progress of each excavation (or trench) was recorded in an individual Trench Notebook. The Trench Notebook included brief stage-by-stage descriptions of contexts and features encountered, a reasoned account of the excavation process and, if necessary, neat sketch plans and section drawings.

The objectives of the excavations developed through the years, from looking initially for evidence for the possible Anglo-Saxon minster in Berkeley, to creating an archaeological narrative of the development of the Castle and the associated town. As has already been mentioned in Chapter 1, excavations took place in four different sectors/areas around Berkeley Castle; the walled 'Butterfly' Garden, the Garden of the Dr Jenner Museum, the area around the castle grounds and the walled Nelme's Paddock. Test pits were also cut at the top of High Street and in the garden of the Berkeley Arms Hotel in order to prove the location of the northern edge of the minster enclosure (Fig. 1).

In this chapter, stratigraphic narratives of the main trenches excavated in Berkeley are presented, with the major finds in context. The discussion of the narratives presented here is in Chapter 9, after presentation of the pottery and the small finds.

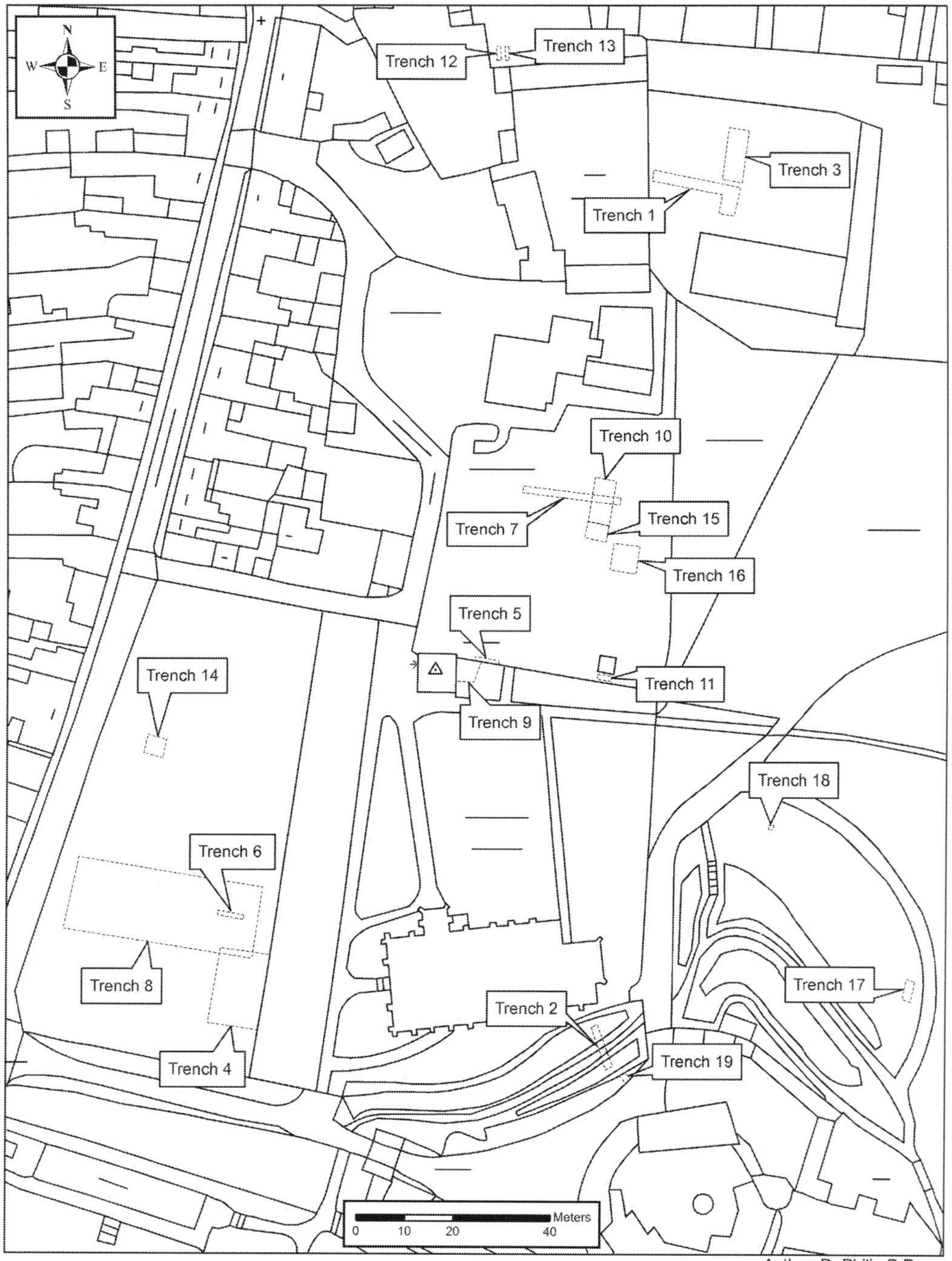

Author: Dr Philip R Rowe

Figure 1. Locations of Berkeley Castle Project trenches.

Walled Garden

Trench 1

Trench 1 was located inside the Walled Garden complex (Fig. 1) close to the medieval street frontages of Canonbury Street [ST 6850 9930]. The trench was orientated E–W initially measured 15.00 × 2.00 m and, at one point, reached a depth of 1.00 m (21.53 m AOD). During the second phase of work at the site, the east end of the trench was extended a further 3.00 m E–W × 6.00 m N–S, forming a reversed letter 'L'. At the west end, the trench abutted the garden wall and was orientated at 90° to it. To the south, it abutted the remains of the foundations of a palmhouse.

A total of 42 contexts were identified in Trench 1. The remains of the foundations of a palmhouse (105), which ran N–S and measured 6.00 m E–W, divided the trench into three sectors of roughly equal length. In the west sector, abutting the wall, the turf and topsoil (101) was divided by a modern gravel path, beneath which lay the cut for an earlier ornamental pathway [111]. The cut was filled with a moderately compact dark-brown silty loam (120) which extended into the south and north facing sections. This feature was recorded by George Nash during excavations in 2003 (Cut 403, Tr. 4), who interpreted it as a cut, probably 19th–20th century, which related in some way to a formal garden bed.

Contexts [111] and [119] cut through contexts (110) and (112), which together seem to constitute the remains of a flowerbed. Both deposits comprised moderately compact reddish or dark brown silty clay loam, and the finds from (112) suggest an 18th–20th century date for the flowerbed. Underlying these contexts was a post-medieval soil layer (114), comprising moderately compact reddish-brown sandy loam, containing 17th–18th century pottery. Beneath (114) was a heavily compacted orange to red-brown clay (138), which contained 16th–18th century pottery. Context (138) was found to fill a large linear cut [137], orientated N–S, that ran parallel with and sloped down to the base of the garden wall. The cut measured 3.00 m E–W × 2.00 m N–S (seen) × 38 cm deep (at wall). Cut [137] appeared to be a foundation trench associated with the construction of a boundary wall, and (138) the associated backfill. The foundation trench might be connected to the construction of the Walled Garden but the associated finds suggest that it may relate to an earlier wall, in the same location. Cut [137] was cut into a natural deposit (139) of heavily compacted orange-red sandy clay loam that contained occasional sandstone fragments (same as (122), (134), (135). Cutting through (114) into (138) was a large 18th–19th century oval posthole [123], 52 cm (N–S) × 35 cm (E–W) × 5 cm deep, which was filled with lightly compacted dark-brown sandy loam (124).

The centre sector of Trench 1 lay within, or beneath, the remains of a palmhouse (105), which was demolished in the 1970s. Underlying the topsoil deposit (101) and extending across the trench was a layer of garden earth (102). Below the garden earth and also extending across the trench was a deposit of moderately compact light brown sandy clay loam (106), representing a levelling deposit of imported material that formed the floor of the palmhouse. Context (106) contained 15th–20th century pottery. Below (106), and again extending across the trench, was a deposit of moderately compact dark orange-brown silty loam (117): another levelling deposit of imported material associated with the construction of the palmhouse. This contained 12th–20th century pottery along with a sherd of 2nd century Central Gaulish samian. Below (117), to the east, a fill of loosely compacted mid-brown sandy clay loam (130) sat within a cut [129] measuring 27 cm E–W × 20 cm deep. The feature continued into the south facing section. This was interpreted as the foundation trench for the east wall of the palmhouse. A similar cut must have existed for the west wall, but was not visible.

In the east sector of Trench 1, including the later extension, three deposits were found to underlie the turf and topsoil (101). Context (103), which extended across the trench, was a garden earth of loose light-brown silty loam. In the north-west corner of the trench, abutting (105) (the remains of the palmhouse foundations) and overlaying (103), was a rubble layer (104) comprising 75% brick and masonry fragments and 25% loose light brown silty loam. This was a demolition layer derived from the destruction of palmhouse in the 1970s. A similar deposit was recorded in the west sector of Trench 1 (108). At the southern end of the extension, running E–W, and underlying (101), were the remains of a gravel path (140). The cut for the path measured 3.00 m E–W (seen) × 1.80 m N–S × 16 cm deep was filled with pinkish-grey gravel and was clearly leading to the palmhouse [105].

Below (103) and extending across the trench was a deposit of moderately compact reddish-brown silty loam (113). The upper level of this deposit contained a moderate amount 18th–19th century pottery and the lower level contained occasional 17th–18th century sherds. This post-medieval soil layer appeared to be garden earth from an earlier garden pre-dating the obvious 19th century phase. Below (113), and extending across the trench, was a deposit of heavily compacted reddish-brown clay loam (115). This deposit, which included finds spanning several centuries including 12th–19th century pottery, had the appearance of 'made-up ground' comprising imported material and may be associated with the levelling of the land in this area to create a formal garden.

Beneath (115) and cut into a natural deposit (122=139), was a linear cut [133], orientated north–south. The cut was filled with heavily compacted orange-brown sandy clay loam (121), which contained numerous large stones (40–60%). This feature traversed the trench and the extension and continued into the north and south facing sections. The cut, which measured *c.*70 cm wide (E–W) × 25 cm deep, had a sharp break of slope at top and base, irregular sides that sloped down at an angle of 65° and a flat base that was inclined S–N. The fill contained 33 sherds of pottery (including seven rims and three joining body sherds) and one-quarter of a millstone. These finds are late Saxon in origin, late 9th–early 11th century. The fill also contained numerous bone fragments, a small flint blade, four sherds of Roman pottery and a possible Roman coin. The feature was interpreted as the base of a linear, flat-bottomed, ditch, that ran north–south. The ditch was probably truncated when the land in this area was levelled to form a garden. The late Saxon pottery and fragment of millstone suggest that the ditch was in use in the late 9th–early 11th century. The Roman and earlier material is residual.

In the south-east corner of the extension, against the west facing section, there was a large round posthole (141), 37 cm in diameter × 10 cm deep., It was below (115) and was cut into a natural deposit (122=139). The level of the base was 21.45 m AOD. The posthole was filled with a moderately compacted red clay that contained five medium-sized flat stones (post-packing) and frequent charcoal flecks. The position and depth of the posthole suggests that it may be associated with the Saxon ditch.

In Trench 1, a flint scraper (128), two flint blades, possibly small thumb scrapers ((115) and (121)), a struck flake (115), and two unworked fragments (106) were recovered. The flint scrapers are diagnostic of the Neolithic period and may indicate prehistoric activity on or near the site.

Five sherds of Roman pottery were recovered from Trench 1. These comprise one sherd of Central Gaulish samian (a cup Dragendorff type 33) (117), one piece of Severn Valley ware in fairly abraded condition although a reasonably sized sherd and three pieces of Oxfordshire red slipped ware (121). The latter have all lost their original surfaces but included a mortaria rim and a beaker base. The samian was probably a 2nd century import but this does not necessarily mean 2nd century occupation nearby, as such material was often curated; the remaining sherds were all typical of a late Roman site, but as no features of Romano-British date were recorded they are presumably all redeposited. As with all previous archaeological work at Berkeley, no conclusive evidence for Romano-British settlement was recorded.

The Saxon pottery, which included the three joining body and seven rim sherds, came from jars in two fabric groups. The fabric 1 jars appear to have originated from the Westgate Street kiln in Gloucester, while the fabric 2 jars may have come from south-east Wiltshire and/or southern Hampshire. The Saxon pottery assemblage was found to date, at the very earliest, to the late 9th century and, at the very latest, to the early 11th century; and probably also pre-dates the Saxon pottery sequences at Bristol and Bath, definitely pre-dates the Norman Conquest and is the only pottery of its date so far found in southern Gloucestershire (for all notes on pottery chronologies see chapter 5 of this volume).

In his report on the late Saxon pottery from trench 1, Alan Vince states 'Gloucester Westgate vessels occur on sites in Gloucester itself and on sites in the surrounding countryside, but have also been found at Winchcombe and Hereford, where they probably reflect a movement of goods and people between major urban and religious centres. The Gloucester Westgate vessels found at Berkeley Castle probably indicate a similar status for Berkeley in the late Saxon period, *i.e.* not simply a rural manor but some sort of central place.

The recording of the ditch, containing late 9th to early 11th century pottery and a Saxon millstone, clearly indicates that Berkeley was an important 'central place' in the late Saxon period. The fact that the pottery is the only pottery of its date so far found in southern Gloucestershire, and that millstones of attested Saxon date are relatively uncommon, further elevates Berkeley's status in this period, and, as it is been proved later, suggested that the ditch and its contents are in some way connected to the Saxon minster.

Trench 3

Trench 3 was located inside the Walled Garden complex (Fig. 1), close to the medieval street frontages of Canonbury Street [ST685991]. The trench was orientated north–south and was cut adjacent to, and north of Trench 1. It measured 5.00 × 11.00 m, and reached a depth of 1.63 m (20.50 m AOD).

A total of 30 contexts were identified in Trench 3. The first seven will be described in terms of their stratigraphic relationships but as the remaining 23 comprise four highly distinct groups they will be described in terms of typology and chronology. Stratigraphically, the first context noted, once the turf and topsoil (301) were removed, was a layer of garden earth (302). This deposit extended across the entire trench, with the exception of one small area in the south where it was cut by the remains of one of Nash's 2003 evaluation trenches. The terminus of Nash's trench 3, which had been backfilled with heavily compacted reddish-brown sandy clay loam (303), projected out of the west facing section and stopped *c.* 75 cm short of the east facing section cutting through a further two deposits en route. The first was a layer of garden earth (305) and the second a redeposited natural (307) both of which would also have originally extended across the whole of Trench 3. The layer of redeposited natural, which comprised heavily compacted brownish-red clay loam, contained numerous 17th–18th century finds and was doubtless associated with the construction of the formal gardens.

In the south end of Trench 3, below Nash's trench, there was a second layer of redeposited natural with a higher content of heavily compacted, natural orange-brown clay (306) which was mixed with ditchfill (310) from a 9th–11th century ditch ([311]; see below). Again, this mixed deposit probably resulted from levelling of the ground during construction of the formal gardens in the 18th or early 19th century.

The first distinctive group of contexts represented the cuts and fills of five flowerbeds which the associated finds suggest are of probable 18th century date. The largest of the flowerbeds (309)/(308) measured 2.20 m E-W × 1.40 m N-S × *c.* 10 cm deep and was located close to the north facing section; another was in the north-east corner of the trench (313)/(312) and extended into the south

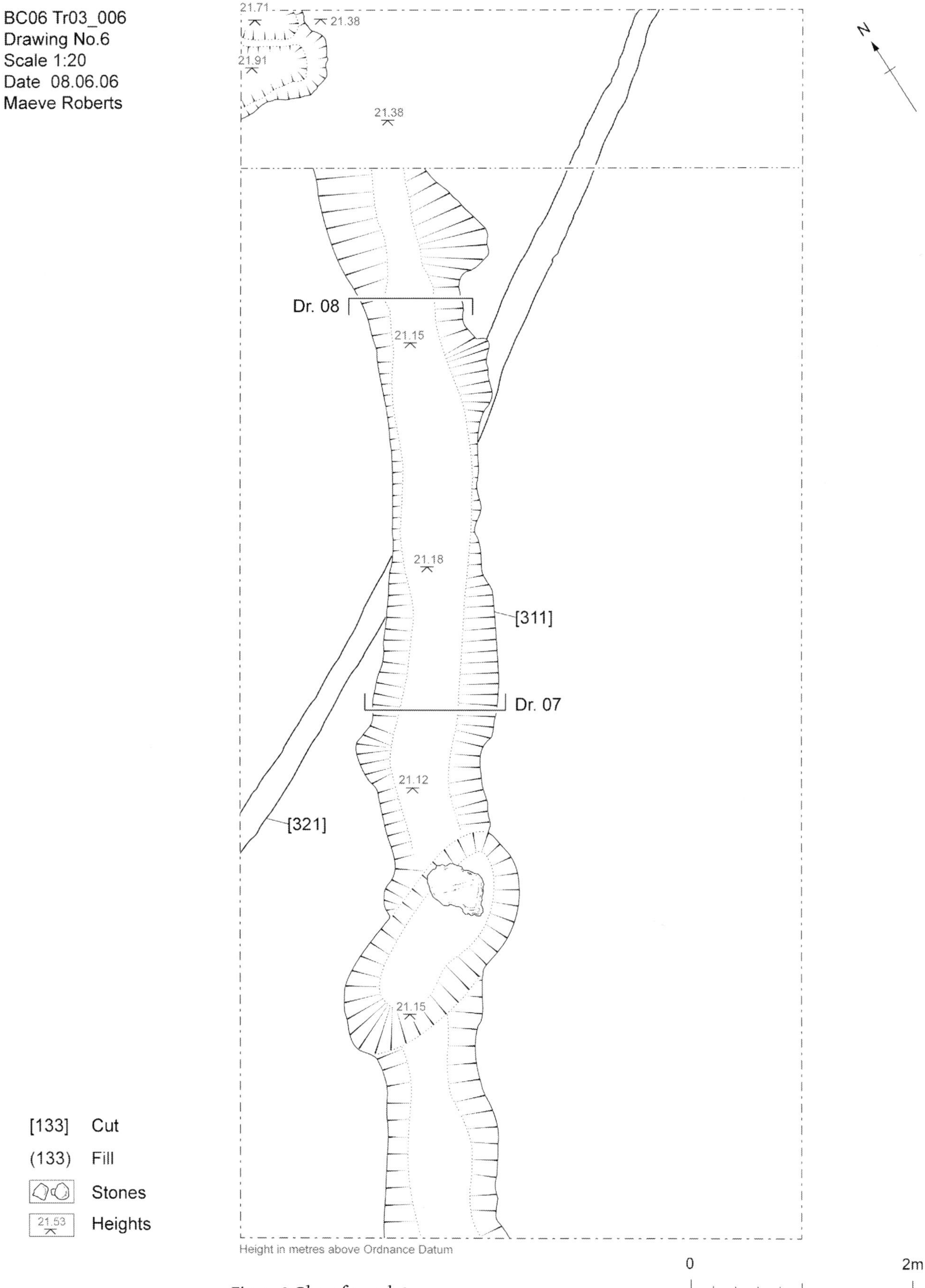

Figure 2. Plan of trench 3.

and west facing sections, whilst the final three (317)/(316), (319)/(318) and (323)/(322) formed a neat row, projecting out of the east facing section. The last four were very similar in form and comparison suggested that the average dimensions for this type of bed was 78 cm wide × 1.60 m long (2 ft 6 in × 5ft 3 in); meaning that the flowerbeds set in a row probably extend a further 68 cm into the east facing section. The large flowerbed (308)/(309) appears to be an exception and may be the remains of a single central feature of some description.

Four other contexts can be associated with the flowerbeds (321)/(320) and (326)/(325). The latter comprised tree-throw (326) – a hollow left behind when tree is blown over in a gale and/or purposefully removed – which had been backfilled with local material (325); whilst the former was an unusual bone and stone lined garden drain. The drain [321], which crossed the trench and extended into the south and east facing sections, was oriented and inclined SW–NE, and measured *c.* 16 cm wide × 28 cm deep × 8.40 m long (seen). The fill of the drain (320) was densely packed and comprised medium sized stones and an assemblage of domesticated animal bones, which consisted mainly of long bone and rib fragments of cattle (*Bos taurus* dom.) and sheep (*Ovis aries*).

Context [314], in the north-west corner of Trench 3, was at first thought to be another flowerbed as it was roughly in line with the row and projecting out of the east facing section (317)/(316), (319)/(318) and (323)/(322). On excavation it proved to be a 17th–18th century cess-pit, 1.23 m E–W × 82 cm N–S × 52 cm deep (seen), which extended into the south and east facing sections. The cess-pit almost certainly pre-dates the construction of the formal garden.

Below (306) and (307), running north–south for the full length of the trench and continuing into the sections was the truncated base of a large Anglo-Saxon ditch [311]/(310). The cut [311] measured approximately 30 cm deep × 1.10 m wide (E–W) × 11 m long (N–S; seen). The ditch, which had a concave and irregular base, was slightly inclined from south to north (21.15–21.08 m AOD). It had been cut into a natural deposit (330). The ditch fill (310) contained frequent fragments of animal bone, two sherds of Anglo-Saxon pottery, a small collection of water-worn pebbles and a large rubbing or polishing stone.

The pottery in (310) indicates that the *ditch* was in use between the late 9th and early 11th century, however, a coin from context (310), directly below, is a silver halfpenny of King Edgar the Peaceable (ruled AD959–975), great-great-grandson of Alfred the Great. It is of 'ornamental' (floral) type and the moneyer was possibly Oswine. It was issued in English Mercia/west Midlands, *c.* AD959–973.

The final four contexts recorded in Trench 3 are of great interest as they appear to be connected to the abandonment of the ditch during the late Anglo-Saxon period: indicative perhaps of a period of decline in Berkeley's fortunes. Cut [328], an oval cut into the Anglo-Saxon ditch, appears to represent re-use of the redundant or abandoned ditch for industrial purposes. The cut was designed to hold a small smelting furnace and the position in the ditch was purposely chosen as such locations provided shelter from the prevailing winds, whilst conversely enabling the smelters to control the flow of air reaching the furnace along the course of the old ditch itself.

Contexts (327) and (329), the upper and lower fills of the furnace cut, both contained frequent fragments of charcoal, large fragments of iron slag and numerous large flat stones which either formed integral components of the furnace or were used as packing to provide the structure with a firm foundation. The base of fill (329) contained a very large flat stone (*c.* 50 cm diam.) which still had (Fe) iron slag adhering. Context (324), located towards the north end of Trench 3, was of similar nature to fills (327) and (329) and was also found to contain frequent large charcoal fragments. Although virtually destroyed by the cut for the garden drain, it is highly likely that it represents the remains of a second ditch furnace.

Unfortunately, in terms of dating, none of the fills associated with the furnaces contained diagnostic finds, although the technology represented suggests an 11th–13th century date.

Trench 3 also produced one worked flint flake (307) and one flint tool fragment (316), probably of Neolithic date as were the finds from Trench 1 described above. In addition, during an earthwork survey in Castle Worthy [ST68749910] a small flint core was recovered which may be Mesolithic in origin but no archaeological features of prehistoric date have thus far been recorded.

Trench 3 was cut adjacent to Trench 1 in order to explore a longer section of the Anglo-Saxon ditch. As a result, a further 11.00 m of truncated mid-9th–early 11th century ditch was recorded. The ditch profile was wider than that recorded during the 2005 excavations, and the ditch is now estimated to have been *c.* 2.00 m wide at its top when first cut. In addition, the size and location of the ditch, the growing collection of 9th–early 11th century ceramics and the recovery of the silver Saxon coin along with one quarter of a Saxon millstone further support the theory that there was a Saxon Minster at Berkeley which appears to have gone into decline towards the end of the 10th century.

Jenner Garden

Trench 5

The exploratory Trench 5, initially 5 × 1 m, was located along the south wall of the Jenner Museum garden, against the boundary wall (Figs. 1 and 3). The area is a flowerbed in the 19th century–present day garden. Site measurements beside the separate bell tower shows that the ground level in the cemetery is 1.47 m below the ground level in the Jenner Garden on the other side of the wall. It was initially thought that this was due to the ground being made up in the garden but it seems more likely the level difference is due to a combination of regrading in the churchyard as well as a build-up of garden soil.

A total of 24 contexts were identified in Trench 5 (500–523). They comprise three distinct groups and so are described not only in terms of their stratigraphic relationships but also in terms of their typology and chronology. Stratigraphically, the first context noted was the topsoil of the garden border. The first distinct group of contexts (500, 502, 504) were above a clear cut [503] and generally comprised loosely compacted garden soil which contained a complete cross-section of finds found on the site from medieval to modern, including one musket ball thought to date from the Civil War siege of Berkeley. This group forms the upper well-worked and mixed soils of the modern garden including a tree bowl filled with redeposited material. These are probably of 19th century and later date.

The second group of contexts (505–513) all contain a well-mixed range of artefacts dating from the medieval period into the 19th century. Contexts include features associated with the wall, tree root bowls and redeposited materials. It is thought these layers formed the garden of the 16th century house known to have been in this area and later the formal gardens of the 18th century Chantry when Jenner was in occupation. Unfortunately, although layers of garden soil could be identified, no features were discovered that could help in the laying out of any restoration of the gardens in this area; which was something the Jenner Museum were hoping to learn.

All these deposits lie on context (514), a heavily compacted cobbled surface formed from grey stones in a clay matrix. Among other finds, a piece of the rim of a vessel clearly identified as Haresfield pottery dating from the late 12th or early 13th century was found embedded in the surface hence providing a *terminus ante quem* for the layer. It is suspected this was a cobbled floor, either within a building or in a yard close to a building. The layer was found to be complete over the whole area of the exploration

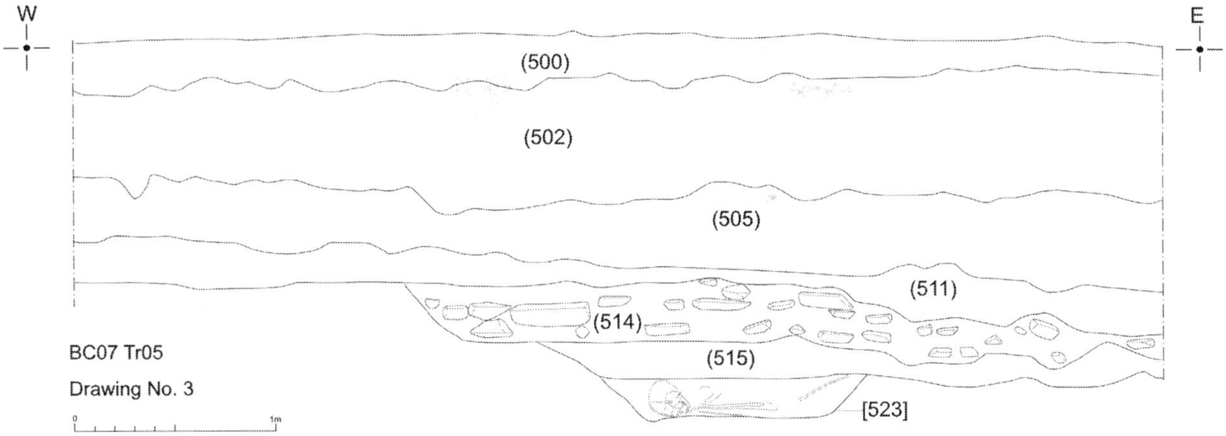

Figure 3. A section of trench 5. The paved surface (514) and the burial [523] are visible.

trench with no identified cuts or holes. This suggests that anything underlying this layer must pre-date the late 12th century.

The third distinct group of contexts (515, 522, 523) all lay beneath context (514) and hence pre-dated it. Unfortunately, no potsherds other than Roman were found from any of these contexts. This may also be significant as very little evidence for Roman occupation in or around Berkeley has been identified prior to the work of the BCP.

Two skeletons were located under the cobbled floor and, from the depth and the clean cut of context [523] (identified as a grave cut), it seems likely this area had been reduced and levelled to form the cobbled surface. Skeleton SK1 was found within the grave cut [523] unaccompanied by artefacts, the backfill being the same natural ground underlying the rest of the trench. The skeleton was not disturbed or lifted. The second skeleton was found near the centre of the trench, but no grave cut could be identified. It is thought the natural material used to backfill the grave had time to consolidate to near its natural density.

The burials discovered in Trench 5 along the south wall of the Jenner Museum garden revealed clear evidence of late Saxon or Saxo-Norman use of the site. It is tempting to attribute these burials to the Anglo-Saxon nunnery recorded historically as having been founded *c.* 883 and demolished *c.* 1043 (see chapter 9 of this volume) This nunnery appears to have formed an integral component of the Minster, whose chapel, was located adjacent to the site where the two burials were unearthed. The burial cuts appear to have been truncated when the area was levelled and a cobbled floor built over the site before the late 12th or early 13th century.

Evidence for the Jenner period garden is not clear. The ground appears to have been deep dug regularly and specific features could not be identified within the area of this small exploration trench and it is likely that the whole of Trench 5 previously lay within one of the flowerbeds of the formal garden. The upper levels are still under cultivation and make up the modern garden. The presence of refilled root bowls suggest that this area has been relatively undisturbed for some time and has probably not been modified much since at least the 19th century.

The excavation was successful in demonstrating the potential for this being the location of the Saxon monastery recorded by history, reinforcing the importance of the extended investigations into this area to throw light on what is being demonstrated to have been a previously unknown but important site, that emphasises the strategic importance of Berkeley, factors that undeniably determined the location and function of the Castle itself. Geophysical surveys carried out in the following year suggest that the Anglo-Saxon church was just over the wall from this trench (see Chapter 2, p.33).

Trench 9

During the 2008 excavation season a trench was opened in St Mary's Churchyard [ST684993] in an area adjacent to the east side of the freestanding church tower (Figs. 1 and 4). If Berkeley was indeed a double house minster it would have had two churches: one for the monks and the other for the nuns. At St Mary's there is a separate bell tower at the north end of the churchyard which was rebuilt in 1753 (GSMR 9344). This bell tower was constructed on the site of an earlier church with a tower (Fosbroke, 1821, 491; Leech 1981, 5; Tandy 2003, 108, 236–40). Early references specify that the previous church was the nunnery chapel (Fosbroke 1821, 49) and the Minster either decayed or was incorporated into the newly established parochial system sometime between 1019 and 1051. The objective of the excavation in St Mary's Churchyard was to attempt to locate the foundations of the nunnery chapel.

Before excavations could begin a number of large paving slabs had to be removed. These were found to be upturned grave stones which are thought to have been bought to the site from elsewhere as the names on the stones are not in the burial register of St Mary's. Many of the upper deposits removed during the excavations were found to be redeposited material from elsewhere. The finds recovered from these deposits were largely post-medieval based upon the pottery evidence.

A dump of domestic refuse was recorded in the north-east corner of the trench. The nature of the artefactual evidence, its date and its proximity to the Chantry all strongly suggest that the refuse came from the household of Dr Jenner. The rubbish pit was at the end of Jenner's garden against the boundary wall between his property and the churchyard. Jenner was known to be an avid user of snuff and two snuff bottles recovered from the deposit are entirely contemporary with his occupation of the house.

Below the post-medieval and modern layers, the first medieval pottery appeared in context (917). This coincides with the first of several floor layers that generally contained pottery dating to *c.* 1250–1400, which was mixed in context (940) beneath with pottery of the 10th and 11th centuries. The lowest deposit (941) contained a mix of pottery dated *c.* 850–1300 (identified by John Cotter, Oxford Archaeology, and Kurt Adams, Bristol Museum).

Abutting the floor layers was a wall which ran across the western edge of the excavated area and joined a robbed-out wall at the north side. The robbed out north wall contained material dating to the period of construction of the new church tower (1753). The lower levels contained some disarticulated human bone, indicative of the disturbance caused by the robbing of the north wall and also from disturbance due to later burials on the same plot. The later burials were largely *in situ*, the most recent recorded was clearly interred within an oak coffin.

In conclusion, the walls and floor layers encountered were clearly part of the fabric of the medieval church tower, which was subsequently robbed to provide building stone during the reconstruction of its replacement in 1753. It is clear from these excavations though, that the later church tower does not sit atop the footprint of the earlier one, it has clearly moved several meters to the west, which of course means that the nunnery chapel, or earlier church that adjoined the medieval tower, was several meters more to the east, just outside the edge of our east section, and frustratingly, the presence of a building here has now been proven via geophysics.

Trench 10

Trench 10, in the grounds of the Jenner Museum, was excavated in 2008–2010 (Fig. 1). As the trench was located in an area that has been landscaped and remodelled on a number of occasions (*e.g.* 17th–18th century formal garden; 18th–19th century kitchen garden and ornamental area; 19th–20th century tennis lawn), and doubtless planted and dug regularly, few of the upper deposits were stratigraphically sound but the trench has nevertheless yielded some surprising and significant results.

Close to the west section of Trench 10, beneath 19th and 20th century drainage features and running north–south through the trench, excavations revealed the fragmentary remains of a robbed out wall of a building and its foundation trench. In the north of the trench, on top of the layer of demolition rubble was a horse harness pendant of Norman date (*c.*1050–1150) and, nearby, a Norman hawking bell. These finds and their location strongly suggest that it was the Normans who demolished/dismantled the building and, further, that the building was of Anglo-Saxon origin. This argument was greatly strengthened by findings in the south of the trench, where a section of collapsed walling from the building, which was consequently missed by the Norman stone robbers, was found to seal Anglo-Saxon Cheddar Ware pottery and a 9th century strap-end. The argument is also supported by the historian Smyth who wrote: 'In the southeast end of this town is seated the Castle of Berkeley, a great part whereof was built out of the ruins of the (Anglo-Saxon) Nunnery which stood in the same place...' (1639, III, 91).

To the east of the wall and extending over most of the northern end of the trench, was a thin layer of dark, charcoal rich, midden material which contained numerous freshwater oyster shells, fragments of animal bone and small fragments of very denuded Roman pottery (with at least one small piece of samian ware). The make-up of this layer is characteristic of early medieval (or Dark Age) deposits found on other sites across the country and may represent evidence for occupation of the site from as early as the late 5th century.

In the closing days of the 2010 excavations, at a depth of *c.* 60 cm, the line of a curving ditch and a series of postholes were uncovered. The northern end of the ditch was somewhat disturbed due to the presence of post-medieval and early modern drainage features but the southern, deeper end contained several sherds of Roman pottery and a 3rd century AD Roman coin. The extreme southern end of the ditch, that was also located in trench 15, was found to contain a layer of burnt and blackened plaster and stone, suggestive of the presence of a nearby Roman structure. Two postholes were cut by the curving ditch and, as such, represent the earliest archaeological features so far recorded at Berkeley. The postholes were fairly substantial and may represent the remains of an early post-built Roman structure.

Trench 11

In 2010, during the 6th season of archaeological fieldwork at Berkeley, a small evaluation trench was opened behind the 'Temple of Vaccina' in the garden of the Edward Jenner Museum [ST685990] (Fig. 1). The trench measured approximately 4 m E–W × 1 m N–S, was positioned to the south of the 'Temple' and sat between the temple itself and the southern garden wall.

This evaluation trench was cut for two reasons, one practical and one academic. Practically, it was necessary to reduce the current ground level in this area prior to the proposed relandscaping of the museum garden. Academically, it was of interest to see whether there were any artefacts present, medical or otherwise, which could be linked to Edward Jenner's use of the structure during the late 18th and early 19th centuries.

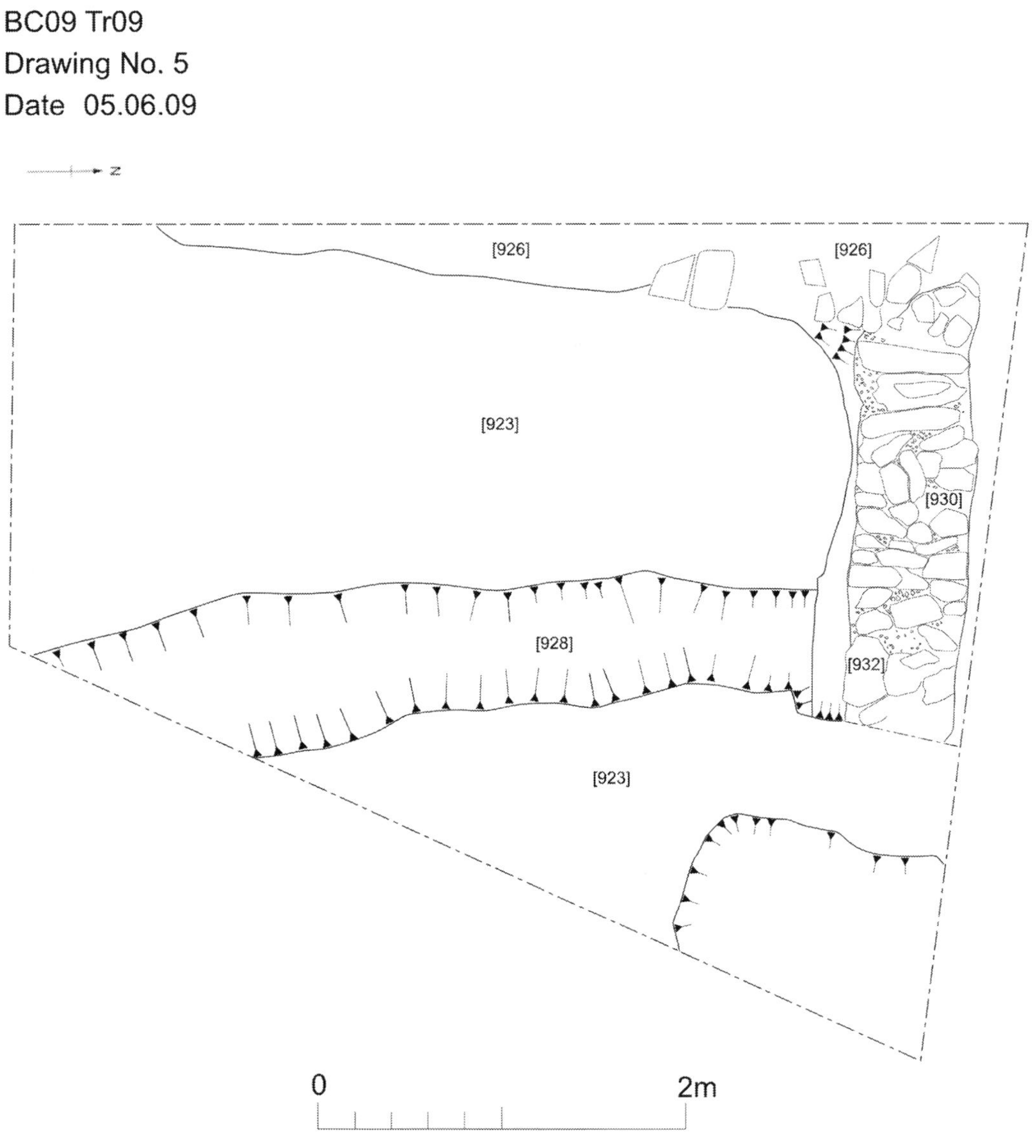

Figure 4. Plan of trench 9. The wall [930] that is abated by the church tower is visible.

Jenner's 'Temple of Vaccinia' (Grade II* listed) is an 18th century small building of stone under a thatched roof that is decorated around its doorway and inside with large sections of bark from forest trees. It contains a small fireplace. In this building Edward Jenner vaccinated the poor people of the district, without charge. It is internationally important for its historical and architectural interest and has been carefully conserved.

The trench comprised 19 contexts. The upper fills (1101–1105) were composed of reddish- brown peaty garden earth with small loose stones but contained no significant finds or features. At the west end of the trench there was an additional pile of stone, collapsed masonry and ceramic tile that had been purposefully dumped in recent times behind the temple. Adjacent to south wall of the temple itself, at a depth of *c.* 20 cm a service trench had been cut to supply the temple with electricity. This service trench – which came complete with a brown plastic flexible corrugated loom tubing conduit to protect the electrical wiring – ran the entire length of the Temple's south wall and had been backfilled with more of the same peaty garden earth that had been topped off with a small layer of sandy coloured gravel. As we did not wish to interfere with the electrical supply to the temple itself it was decided to avoid excavating this, so a gap of 50 cm was left and excavations continued adjacent to the south wall of the Jenner garden.

The lower contexts of the evaluation trench (1106–1119) – all in dark reddish-brown to dark red silty clay loam – contained a mix of detritus that one would expect to find at the bottom of a late 18th and early 19th century garden. This included glass, shell, animal bone, CBM, slate, an Fe object, charcoal, and industrial residues, as well as a mixture of 18th and early 19th century clay tobacco pipe bowls and stems. In addition, in the middle of the trench 50 cm from the southern end of the Temple, the dismembered skeleton of a small dog was uncovered at a depth of 50 cm. The skeleton had clearly been disturbed by the cutting of the electrical service trench as the skull and two legs were missing but the rest of the skeleton was present and clearly *in situ*. A clay pipe stem found next to the skeleton. provides a potential date for burial of the late 18th century.

It is very tempting to connect the dog skeleton with Edward Jenner's occupation of the house (in 1772, at the age of 23 Edward Jenner returned to Berkeley and established himself as the local practitioner and surgeon and in 1785, he bought The Chantry, and remained a resident of Berkeley for the duration of his life), and he is known to have undertaken medical experiments – either in the study that overlooks the Temple or in the Temple itself – and this would have been an ideal spot to dispose of the skeleton in a reverential fashion.

Trench 15

Trench 15 was located directly to the south of Trench 10 (excavated 2009–2010) in the grounds of the Jenner Museum within the walled garden (Figs. 1, 5 and 6). This area has been subject to numerous landscaping and remodeling efforts from the 17th–19th centuries and therefore contained the potential for its archaeological deposits to be somewhat mixed.

Trench 15 measured 4 m E–W × 3.5 m N–S. Below the topsoil, two land-drains and a large tree-throw or planting hole formed the modern deposits which cut through a mixed layer excavated in two spits (1501) and (1506). This was seen as the first significant archaeological horizon to be encountered. It was from the upper spit (1501) of this layer that a silver penny of Aethelred II (AD 978–1016) was retrieved. The lower spit (1506) yielded two Anglo-Saxon copper finger rings likely to date to the 10th century, both of which have tapering ends, shaped to butt up against each other, or overlap.

Layer (1501)/(1506) sealed a deposit of stone and dark silty clay (1507) which was later seen to lie within an irregular-shaped shallow cut or hollow [1511]. This may have been a continuation of the robbed-out wall debris seen in Trench 10 or at least denoted the remnants of a pile created during the robbing/ collapse of the (possible Anglo-Saxon) building located to the north. A slightly degraded 4th century Roman coin showing the outline of the bust of Constantine the Great was retrieved from this stony fill, but it is likely to be residual. A shallow rectangular feature [1513] and posthole [1541] were also exposed after the removal of layer 1501/1506. These cut into a generic brown layer (1508) which extended across the whole trench and contained a large amount of iron slag.

Layer (1508) also contained a 4th century Roman coin with a small hole pierced through it, possibly denoting Anglo-Saxon re-use in a necklace or bracelet. After the removal of layer (1508), a number of features were defined, most of which were filled with brownish deposits similar in composition to (1508). On the eastern side of the trench, a shallow, segmented gully with associated postholes ran directly parallel to a larger ditch *c.* 1 m to the east. It is not known if these two features are of a contemporary

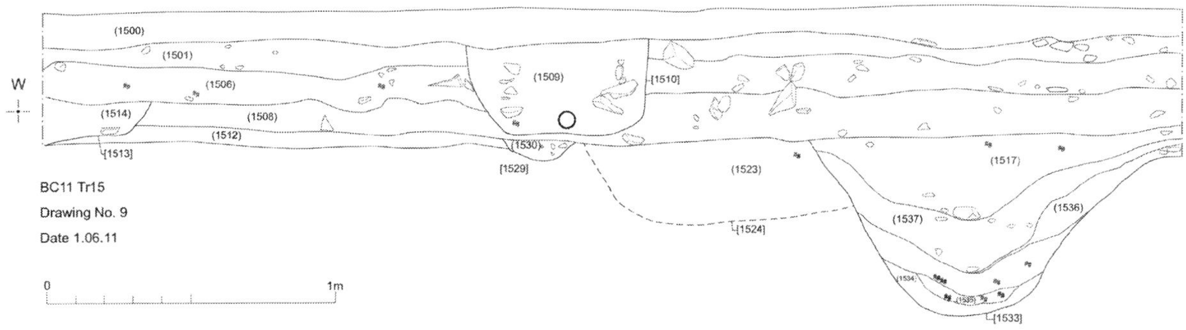

Figure 5. North facing section of trench 15.

date, perhaps a fence-line relating to the ditched boundary, or whether the gully is indicative of a beam-slot for a structure relating to the earlier postholes seen in Trench 10, forming a building. Three other postholes were excavated on the western side of the trench, some of which contained packing stones.

Ditch [1533] (Figs 5 and 6) is a southern continuation of a length of ditch excavated in Trench 10. As excavated in Trench 15, it contained six fills, the lower four of which were relatively clean and indicative of a gradual, natural deposition from the inwash of soils through the erosion of the ditch sides. These lower fills also appeared to have predominantly eroded in along the eastern edge (the section drawings and photos clearly showed evidence of a higher level of slumped deposits to the east), meaning that it is likely that this ditch had an internal bank running along its eastern side. The two uppermost fills were comprised of brown silty-/sandy clay and contained considerably more inclusions and finds than the lower four, making them distinctly different. It is possible that these uppermost fills represent the backfilling of the ditch and levelling of the area using the remaining bank material. Potentially, this was done sometime prior to the construction of the 8th/9th century Anglo-Saxon building to the north and after the boundary ditch or enclosed area denoted by the ditch went out of use (possibly the early to mid-Saxon period).

Fragments of slag were found in most of the fills; however, pottery was only retrieved from the uppermost fills and can therefore be attributed to the deliberate backfilling of the ditch. The ceramic forms are a mixed assemblage containing Black Burnished Wares and Greywares, which are likely to have been residual in nature and indicative of previous Roman activity somewhere beyond the confines of Trench 15. A very small fragment of a Roman coin dating to the 4th century was retrieved from the lowest ditch fill, however, the overall lack of dating from the more secure lower fills means that we were unable to date this ditch securely.

Ditch [1533] produced some further pieces of lime plaster to add to an assemblage which was retrieved in 2010 from Trench 10. This included some large pieces from the lower ditch fills with well-preserved wattle impression, which may point to the presence of a building of unknown function or status in the near vicinity. Unfortunately, unlike the plaster retrieved from Trench 10, there was no evidence of paint on the pieces retrieved from Trench 15.

The northernmost extent of ditch [1533] in Trench 15 truncated an earlier small pit ([1524] on fig 6), and both [1533] and [1549] cut through an east–west aligned adult burial (Sk. 1538) with the head end to the west (Fig. 6). The level of truncation meant that although the bone was in relatively good condition the skeleton was missing its left humerus and shoulder (truncated by pit 1549) and half of its lower right arm, hand, pelvis and both legs with only the feet remaining beyond the eastern side of ditch cut

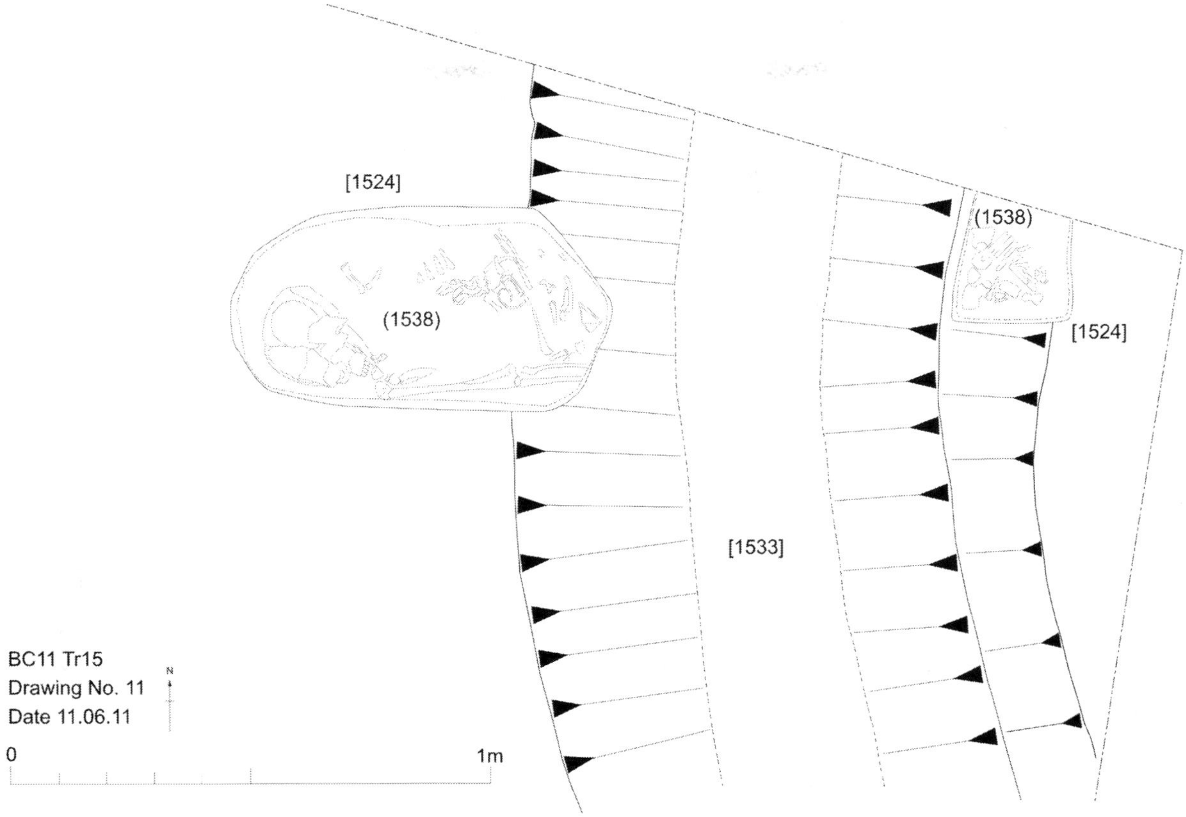

Figure 6. The truncated burial in trench 15.

1533. The burial contained no obvious dating evidence, coffin nails or grave goods and may have been interred within a shroud rather than in a coffin, as shown by the tightly-crossed nature of the feet. We can suggest that based on burial practices, this may be indicative of a 5th–7th century date. The intercutting nature of the grave, pit and ditch means that this burial is one of the earliest features seen within the trench.

The features exposed after the removal of layer (1508) were cut through a thin layer of orange-brown sandy clay (1512). This layer contained a few pieces of relatively abraded residual samian pottery and are further evidence of a background of Roman activity in the vicinity. Layer (1512) overlay the compact natural brownish-red clay layer (1545) which was ultimately exposed when all of the features encountered during the excavation had been fully excavated.

Despite the full excavation of the archaeological features it has been difficult to assign a precise chronology based on the dating of these features. Pottery ranges from Roman to Saxo-Norman and medieval and sherds were often mixed within contexts, therefore any dating assignations are currently speculative.

Trench 16

Trench 16 was initially opened in 2012 and completed in 2013. It was located to the east of Trench 15 in the grounds of the Jenner Museum walled garden (Fig. 1). The Trench measured 8 m E–W ×6 m N–S taking in *c.* 2 m of the raised bank area to the south of the lawn. The aim was to expose a further length of the ditch which turned from east–west to north–south which had been uncovered in Trenches 10 and 15 [1533] (see above).

The 2013 season of Trench 16 started where it was left off in 2012, at a brown layer of soil, excavated in two spits, which were newly numbered as (1634) and (1635). As seen in 2012, these layers continued to yield a large amount of industrial slag fragments and pottery that predominantly dated to the Roman period; however this was mixed with pottery of later periods. This mixing was further demonstrated by the range of small finds that were retrieved: four pieces of prehistoric worked flint, seven Roman coins and a fragment of a possible horseshoe. This layer may represent the abandonment of Saxon buildings and their Norman destruction by way of wall robbing to re-use the stonework. During the earliest phases of Berkeley Castle this area would have probably hosted activities such as animal processing and light industrial working creating debris and an additional soil build up in the post-conquest period.

Below this layer, numerous postholes, short gully or beam slot segments and small pits were revealed. These were similar in size and density to those seen in Trench 15. Again, these contained pottery of mixed dates and may potentially represent lean-to structures attached to the mid-late Saxon building excavated in Trench 10 (see above) or are for workshops associated with post-1066 light industrial processing.

Two main archaeological features were revealed in Trench 16 below the brown layer (1634/1635). The first was a quarter section of a circular mortar mixer (1640) in the south-east corner which comprised yellow sandy mortar shaped to form a solid base and edges into which large quantities of mortar could be mixed. Based on the stratigraphy this is likely to have been of mid-Saxon date and potentially provided the mortar for the construction of a nearby building; possibly the one partially encountered in Trench 10.

The second archaeological feature below layer (1634/1635) was a north–south running ditch [1650]. This was the continuation of the ditch that had previously been excavated in Trenches 10 and 15. The ditch appeared to have less depth in Trench 16 than was seen in Trench 15, either due to truncation after the ditch had gone out of use or because it was shallowing out prior to a terminus further south. This ditch is likely to have enclosed an area of land on the east side of the trench, however at present, the exact purpose of this land division is uncertain, as is the true date of the ditch.

The final feature of note within Trench 16 was a burial in a grave cut. The grave was orientated east–west and contained a single female skeleton with the head located at the west end. This grave was revealed after the removal of a thin layer of mortar and stone that possibly derived from the use of the mortar mixer. Therefore, this burial is likely to be later than Roman but earlier than mid-Saxon which potentially makes it contemporary with the male burial recorded *c.* 7 m to the west in Trench 15 (see above and Fig. 6).

Overall, the large quantity Roman finds seen throughout the Trench 16 deposits are indicative of Roman activity somewhere within or close to the Edward Jenner Garden. However, the high level of mixing means it may be possible that this area was heavily truncated from the mid-Saxon period (7th century onwards) as a result of landscaping for the construction of the Minster and the redevelopment that occurred in order to create a *burh*. This preparation of the land would also have included the filling in of the north–south ditch and the levelling of any bank associated with the enclosure. This could mean that any structural evidence of Roman buildings may have been lost, leaving only the associated negative archaeological features (pits and postholes) – however, the nature of these has not yet been fully identified.

Nelme's Paddock

Trench 8

Work in Trench 8 (Fig. 1) was still ongoing at the end of University of Bristol involvement in Berkeley and is planned to be completed by the Castle and new stakeholders. Thus, a definitive stratigraphic report cannot yet be provided. The earliest finds in Trench 8 dated to the late prehistoric–early Roman period and were all cut into natural clay/bedrock. The main feature was a large north–south ditch at the west end of the trench [8722] which was not fully exposed in plan or section but was at least 4.5 m wide and over 0.3 m deep with a very steep profile. This indicated a significantly sized ditch running across the full width of the trench as ditch fills were also encountered at the south side of the trench.

The second cultural phase of Trench 8 can be dated to the early to mid-Saxon period. It comprised a large wide and shallow pit [8677] that could have remained open for a considerable time. There was also a probable 'marking-out' pit for the entranceway/terminus of a large, wide and shallow NNW–SSE ditch [8555] with a terminus at the NNW end. This contained a high stone content – fill (8613). This is interpreted as part of the Saxon minster – the *Vallum Monastarium* (see Chapter 9 for further discussion).

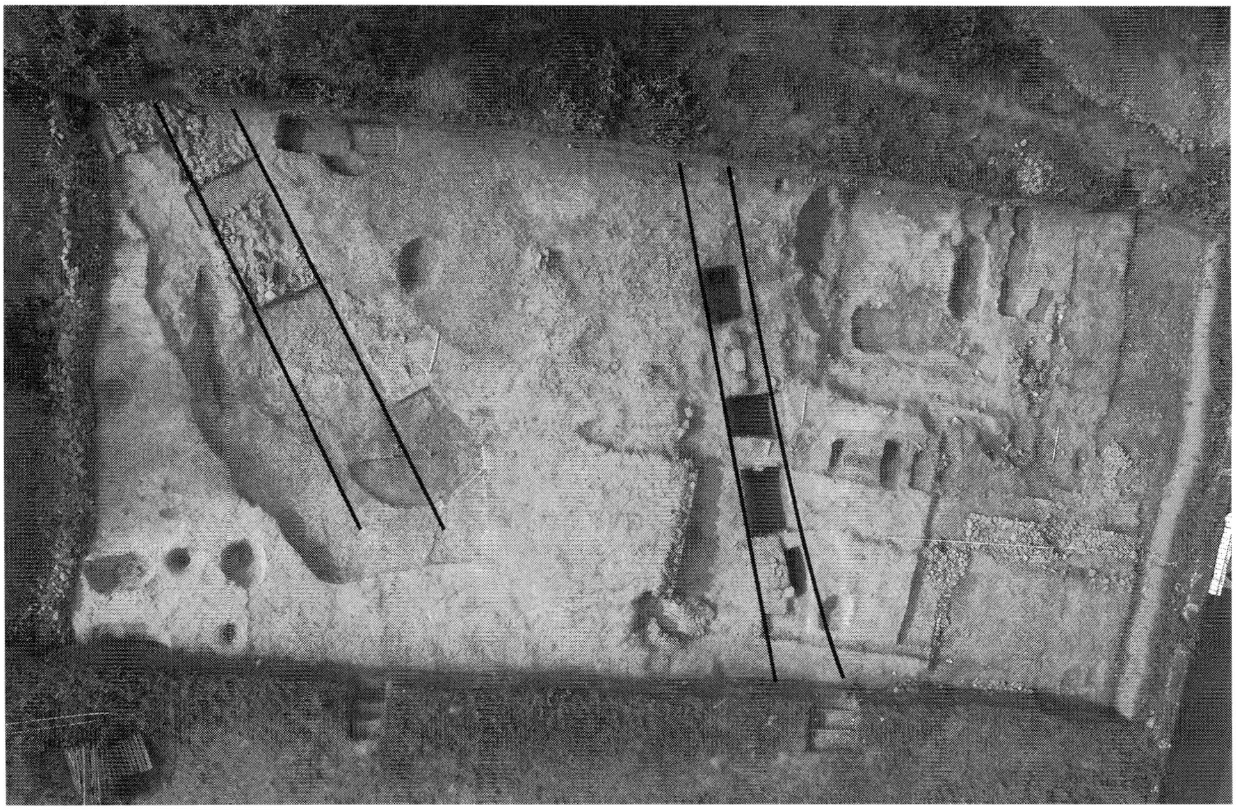

Figure 7. The Anglo-Saxon ditches in trench 8.

There was a second middle Saxon phase in the trench that was mainly characterised by a NNW–SSE Ditch [8650] with a terminus at the NNW end, near vertical sides and a flat base This was possibly a widening out of the actual minster area. Remains of a possible late Saxon building were also excavated, in the form of two wall foundations remaining on the north and west sides of the building after robbing. Some sub-flooring/stone support layers were seen along the downslope of the western side on which the building was constructed. Further to the building foundations, running remains of wall foundation, possibly stone robbed from a Saxon building were excavated in the east of the trench.

A large, wide, north–south ditch [8300], with an 'ankle-breaker' base, possibly a defensive ditch coincided with a steep break of slope at the east end of Trench 8 and was the main feature from the Saxon-Norman period. A coin of William Rufus (William II, 1087 - 1100) was found in upper backfill of this ditch. Ditch [8300] was cut by a later ditch [8310] along the western side of the trench; but as 8310 was relatively shallow in comparison to the earlier ditch it may have been for drainage.

A stone-lined water sump and associated drains excavated at the western end of Trench 8, in the north-west corner have been assigned to the post-Norman conquest phase, *c.* 12th–13th century. A robbed-out east–west wall which ran adjacent on the south side of wall 8611, can also be dated in the same phase, along with a series of rubbish pits towards eastern end of Trench 8, which cut through a ditch sequence comprising [8300], [8310] and [8220].

The next phase in Trench 8 can be dated to the 14th–early 15th century (Fig. 8). The first phase of a building in the north-west corner of the trench was represented by two walls: a north [8583] and an east wall [8586]. This building includes a succession of internal drains [8726], [8384] and [8366] all as attempts to divert natural springs below and around constructed buildings. There are also drains on the northern side of this building against the edge of the trench. This sequence of drains run up to a 15th century and may extend beyond the use life of the building. To the rear (eastern side) of this building, a pit [8337] was also excavated, from which Tudor pottery was retrieved. Associated with these features was a bread oven [8334] along with two intercutting pits truncated by later Tudor terracing (pit [8383] which cuts through pit [8362]). A dagger was found in the fill of one of these. Short segments of drains and walls seen in the south-west corner of the trench also appear to have been truncated by Tudor terracing (including [8616], [8618], [8626] and [8508]).

Figure 8. The 14th and early 15th century in trench 8.

Later in the 15th century the earliest Norman buildings were extended to the east as represented by wall construction cut [8512] for the eastern wall and [8580] for the northern wall. Internal features of this building include a paved interior entranceway plinth, an underfloor drain cut, internal wall partitions, a hearth and a south-east corner post-pad. To the south of the building, at the south-west corner of Trench 8, a Tudor terracing cut was dug for the creation of a Tudor tavern with a stabling block to the rear of building. Documentary evidence shows this to have been the *Crown Inn* (see further discussion in chapter 9). The stable block is what was visible within Trench 8, a stone edge gully was numbered as (8344), however any central flooring had been robbed away.

A hall building was constructed in the 16th century, built flush with the northern edge of St Michael's Lane (Fig. 9). Remains of three walls were present and the building had two phases. Towards the eastern end of the building there was a stone-built hearth of two phases. A series of large 'bath' shaped pits towards eastern end of Trench 8 can also be dated to the same period, with some containing large stones.

In the period of the Civil War, a further ditch was cut around the Church, running below the current church wall and bending into Trench 8 at the eastern limit of the excavation. During the Civil War demolition, levelling and burning of the remaining buildings in the Paddock was undertaken to create clear lines sight from the *Crown Inn* to the defensive trench around the Church. The ditch was dug to protect the western end of the Church, because the Church and Castle are so close together that, in order to capture the Castle the Church would need to be taken as well; as indeed happened. Local folklore states that cannons were hauled up onto the Church roof in order to capture the Castle. The possible original churchyard wall running along a similar line/position as the Saxon ditch has also been found.

Figure 9. The 16th century phase in trench 8.

The last identified phase of use in the Paddock comprised late 17th–early 18th century graves from the churchyard that were stratigraphically above the Civil War ditch but below the current churchyard wall. Later, a fallow paddock was transformed into kitchen gardens with imported topsoil for growing vegetables and glasshouses with grapevines along the churchyard wall (many vine keys were recovered). To date it is not certain when the area's use as a garden ended and the paddock for livestock was again created but this probably coincides with the construction of the walled garden in the former deer park to the north of the Castle.

Trench 12 and Test Pits 1–4

In 2009 and 2012 attempts were made to trace the northern and western extent of the Minster's boundaries. Whilst excavating in the Walled Garden to the north of the Castle the large Anglo-Saxon boundary ditch described above that was seen to run north–south in Trench 1 [133] and Trench 3 [311], was found (with further geophysical survey) to turn 90° westwards and run along the rear of the gardens of the houses that front onto the south side of Canonbury Street. To ensure this was indeed the route of the Minster's boundary ditch a further excavation and test pits were dug (Trench 12 in the *Berkeley Arms Hotel* beer garden and Test Pits 1–4 in the passageway/yard of the *Old White Hart Inn* Coachhouse).

Geophysical resistivity survey confirmed the route of the Anglo-Saxon ditch in the beer garden of the *Berkeley Arms Hotel* (Trench 12; Fig. 1). This excavation provided further evidence of the ditch which was found to continue across High Street (where the modern road has a slight but visible hump outside the *Old White Hart Inn* car park entrance, and runs down the passageway of the pub. The ditch then turning southwards, in another 90° turn, to run behind the gardens of the houses on the left-hand side of High Street before turning eastwards again to run up the Castle's private entrance driveway.

Five contexts were excavated in the beer garden. Beneath the turf and topsoil context (1201) was found to contain fairly modern finds and other detritus that would be expected of a pub's beer garden with numerous (now discarded) bottle caps, can rings and glass shards. Below this (contexts 1202–1204) were fragments of slate, coal, charcoal, glass, ceramic building material, animal bone and small finds of copper alloy, comprising a garden wall fixture and an alloy loop, along with iron fragments, *ranging* from the 14th to the 19th century. There were also 161 sherds of pottery, 34 dating from the *c.* 10/11th century and from the upper fill of the Anglo-Saxon ditch (1204).

The four test pits excavated across the road, to the rear of the *Old White Hart Inn* were positioned in response to the results of the geophysical surveys, where two longer sections, taken diagonally at 1 m intervals across the yard, seemed to indicate a backfilled ditch. All four produced finds that would be anticipated from the rear of a coaching inn, including animal bone, glass, shell, charcoal, iron and industrial residues, as well as a silver George III coin of 1817, an Elizabethan carved bone disc/gaming piece a carved bone button and a copper alloy 2nd century disc brooch. A copper alloy strap end and a very denuded Roman coin were recovered from the top of the possible ditch. Unfortunately, the presence of a considerable depth of topsoil and other overburden on the sloping ground meant that the test pits could not be dug deep enough to reach the lower fills and confirm a date for the ditch. The tentative physical and geophysical evidence, however, does point to this being the north-west corner of the Minster's enclosure.

Castle grounds

Trench 2

Trench 2 (Fig. 1) was located within the Castle moat, between St Mary's Church and the medieval Shell Keep [ST68509900]. The trench was orientated north–south, measured 12.00 × 1.00 m and reached a maximum depth of 90 cm (19.15 m AOD). At the north end the trench abutted the churchyard wall (203), and at the south end it abutted a wall that forms a boundary between the castle ward and the top of the moat (204).

A total of 27 contexts were identified in Trench 2 (Fig. 10). The uppermost context, which extended across most of the trench, was a very humic, thin, loose, dark-brown peaty deposit (201). Underlying context 202 in the northern half of the trench was a natural deposit which consisted of heavily compacted red silty clay with occasional sandstone fragments (226). A sondage, 1.00 m N–S × 1.00 m E–W × 50 cm deep, cut in the centre of the northern half of the trench, confirmed that 226 was a natural deposit and established that there was no significant archaeology in this area. A significant amount of bone (including human) was found in the northern half of the trench, but the lack of archaeology in this area suggests that the material is re-deposited; probably originating from the adjacent churchyard.

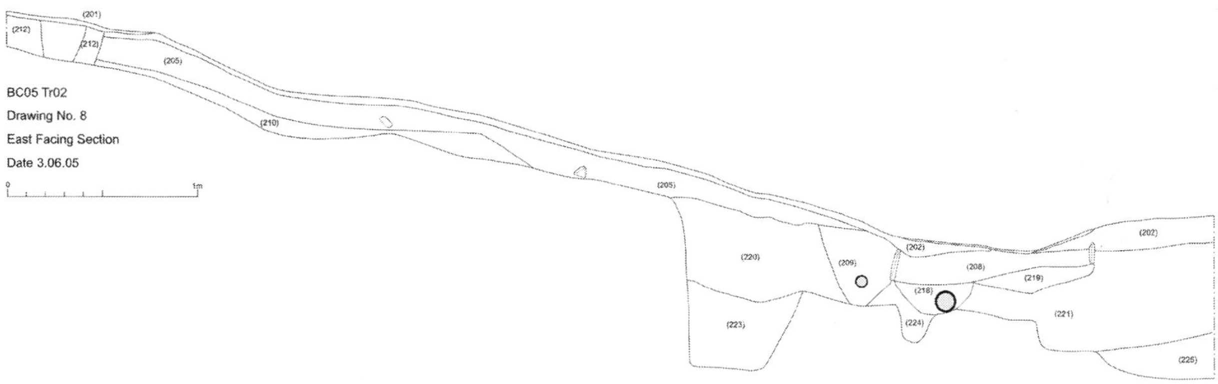

Figure 10. East facing section of trench 2.

Underlying context 202 in the southern half of the trench was ditch-fill comprising heavily compacted red clay loam (205) which contained frequent tree roots, occasional small stones and 19th–20th century pottery and glass. Below 205 was an earlier ditchfill deposit comprising loose red-brown silty loam which also contained frequent tree roots (210); the pottery however was 18th–19th century. Below 210 was a natural deposit (226). At the south end of the trench, beneath the boundary wall (204), lay a deposit of heavily compacted red silty clay that contained occasional small stones/gravel (212). The deposit was very similar to 226 (natural) and appeared to be redeposited natural. Cutting through 212 was the east–west linear cut of a pipe-trench (211/213), 34 cm N–S × 20 cm deep, running parallel to the boundary wall (204), which contained a lead water-pipe of *c.* 6 cm diameter (214). The pipe-trench also cut through contexts 202, 205 and 210, into 226. The level on top of the lead pipe, in the base of pipe-trench, was 20.57 m AOD. To verify that 226 was a natural deposit and that there was no significant archaeology in the southern half of the trench, a sondage, 50 cm N–S × 50 cm E–W × 25 cm deep, was opened 1.00 m away from the south-east corner of the trench against the boundary wall (204). Apart from the insubstantial remains of an earlier boundary wall (215), t no significant archaeological deposits were recovered.

In the centre of the trench, in the bottom of the moat were recorded an ornamental garden path and two pipe-trenches. All were 19th–20th century in date. At the break of slope on the south side of the moat was the east–west linear cut of another pipe-trench (206). The pipe-trench, which contained a metal pipe *c.* 7 cm in diameter, measured 41 cm N–S × 37 cm deep and extended into the east and west facing sections. The level in the base of the pipe-trench was 19.54 m AOD. The cut of the pipe-trench just clipped the southern edge of an ornamental pathway that ran east–west along the base of the moat. The cut for the path originally measured 1.20 m N–S × 22 cm deep and was filled with yellow gravel (some of which remained in the north side of the cut). The level in the base of the cut was 19.60 m AOD. The southern half of the pathway had been dug up and a pipe had been inserted. The level on top of the ceramic pipe, in the base of the pipe-trench, was 19.49 m AOD. After the insertion of the water-pipe the path was reinstated. Large, squared limestone slabs were set on-end to form a border for the path (207 and 216) and a layer of creamy-yellow gravel was laid down (208), up to 16 cm deep in places.

Pipe-trench 206 cut into context 220 which measured 84 cm N–S × 45 cm deep, extended into the east and west facing section and comprised loose dark red-brown silty loam that contained occasional small stones/gravel. The upper level of 220 contained occasional 19th–20th century pottery, the mid-level contained occasional 18th–19th century pottery and the lower level occasional 17th–18th century pottery. The ornamental pathway (219) cut a very similar context (221) which measured 1.80 m N–S × 50 cm deep, extended into the east and west facing sections and comprised moderately compact dark red-brown clay loam that contained occasional small stones/gravel. The upper level contained occasional 18th century pottery and the lower level a mid–late 17th century clay pipe bowl and fragments of clay pipe stem. It quickly became evident that contexts (220) and (221) were similar or the same.

Context 220 was filling the southern edge of a large east–west linear cut. The side of the cut lay 1.15 m beyond the current break of slope at the base of the moat on the south side. Below 220, context 223 which was also a fill of 222. It measured 58 cm N–S (at top) × 45 cm deep, extended into the east and west facing sections and comprised loose mustard-yellow sand. Context 223 contained frequent fragments of bone, occasional 17th and 18th century pottery (including a base and two body sherds of a 17th century North Devon ware vessel) and six sherds of a 17th–18th century sagged base bottle. With 223 removed, the north-facing side of cut of 222 was clearly visible. The side was smooth, practically vertical, had a sharp break of slope at top and bottom and dropped *c.* 90 cm to a flat base. The level of the base of cut 222 was 19.26 m AOD.

A similar scenario occurred at the break of slope in the northern half of the trench, where context (221) could be seen filling the northern edge of a large east–west linear cut. The side of the cut lay 50 cm beyond the current break of slope at the base of the moat on the north side. Below 221, context 225 was also a fill of 227. Context 225 measured 1.05 m N–S (at top) × 30 cm deep, extended into the east and west facing sections, and comprised heavily compacted red clay that contained occasional medium sized stones (5–10 cm diam.). A thin lens of loose mustard-yellow sand was seen at the base of 225 which appeared to be the same context as 223. Context 225 contained a base and three body sherds of a 17th–18th century sagged base bottle. With 225 removed, the south-facing side of cut 227 was clearly visible. The side was smooth, practically vertical, had a sharp break of slope at top and bottom, and dropped c.90 cm to a flat base. The level of the base of cut 227 was 19.15 m AOD. Cuts 227 and 222 together formed the north and south sides of a large flat-bottomed ditch which ran east–west. The finds in the lower fill (223/225) indicate that it was cut and in use in the mid–late 17th century. The ditch (222/227) was cut into a natural deposit (226). All the contexts recorded in the base of the 'moat' sat within this ditch.

Excavation suggests that the ditch would have originally measured *c.* 90 cm deep × *c.* 3 m wide (N–S) with a sharp break of slope at its top and base, along with smooth vertical sides. The ditch was cut into a natural deposit (226) and the size and shape, along with a complete lack of medieval finds, strongly suggests that this section of the 'moat' is not of medieval origin.

Trench 18

Trench 18 measured just 1.00 × 1.00 m and was excavated during the 2013 season of the Berkeley Castle Project. This was located opposite the ticket office, close to the Castle Gateway area and towards the north of the car park [ST6853499046] (Fig. 1). Human remains had previously been uncovered in this area during mid-20th century groundworks when a narrow trench was dug for pipe/cable laying along the eastern edge of the pathway leading to the Castle. It was thought that these inhumations may have been within the cemetery area of the Anglo-Saxon Minster. It is possible that this burial area was subsequently disturbed by the construction of the medieval ditch running along the north side of the Castle. In advance of the 2013 excavations a geophysical survey was undertaken over the Castle Gateway area with Trenches 17 and 18 positioned over the resulting anomalies.

In Trench 18, after the removal of topsoil (1800), context 1801 a mid-reddish-brown silty loam was revealed. This deposit contained animal bone and mortar fragments and was interpreted as redeposited earth that derived from the upcast created by the excavation of the 14th century ditch. A stone feature (1802) was found within context (1801) running east–west (Fig. 11), filled with slate, mortar and large stones and measuring *c.* 0.10 m across. This was thought to have been a stone drain/soakaway or

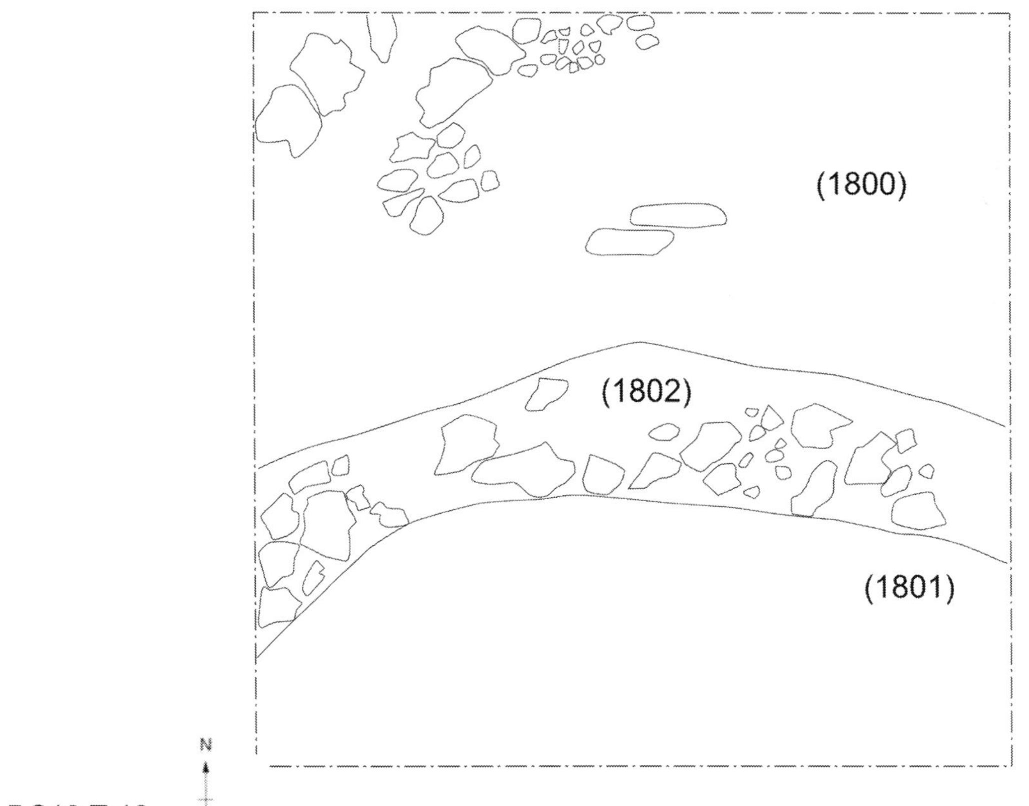

Figure 11. Plan of trench 18.

dumped patch of rubble. After removing 1802, at an approximate depth of 0.80 m, context 1803 was also seen within 1801.

Context 1803 was found to be a collection of large stones in a possible circular formation within the south corner that was completely devoid of finds. Context 1804 underlay 1801 at a depth of 0.85 m; it was a mid-brownish-red sandy clay. This was again most likely to be upcast or soil disturbed by the construction of the 14th century ditch. Due to time constraints a sondage was cut into the southern quarter of the trench. The belief that this was the natural layer was later disproved when bone fragments were found that were believed to be a mixture of human and animal. The sondage quadrant reached a maximum depth of 0.22 m, meaning it was excavated to an overall depth of 1.02 m. Excavation stopped at this limit due to the difficulties of working in such a small trench.

The current topography of the area to the east of the Castle Gateway comprises a mound sloping down to the south. From the layers excavated in Trench 18, this incline was most likely created by the dumping of upcast from the excavation of the medieval (14th century) ditch that runs along the northern side of the Castle. The presence of human bones at a depth of 1.00 m implies that if an Anglo-Saxon burial ground existed it has probably been disturbed by the ditch cutting.

Trench 17

Trench 17, measuring 3.00 m N–S × 1.00 m E–W, was located downslope and approximately 20 m to the south-east of Trench 18. It was positioned in alignment with what is suspected to be the original (northern) entrance to the Castle. The trench was oriented north–south to maximise the likelihood of encountering potential grave-cuts believed to be located in the immediate vicinity associated with the Anglo-Saxon Minster. The uppermost deposit (1700) was 0.28–0.45 cm in depth and comprised a highly disturbed, rooty mid-grey-brown silty clay loam. It contained finds of mixed date, including pottery, animal bone, a nail and a lead musket ball and was interpreted as likely upcast from the 14th century excavations of a Castle moat that ran along the northern side of the Castle. This lay above deposit 1701 which was a red-brown silty clay loam 0.70–1.0 m deep. This deposit was cleaner than 1700 and contained frequent animal bone and occasional pottery of mixed date. It was similarly interpreted as 14th century moat upcast material. Deposit 1702 was below 1701 at *c.* 1.10 m in depth. This deposit was <0.40 m deep and comprised stony deposits and rooting with patches of redeposited pale green/grey clay. This context may represent the pre-existing ground level prior to the moat's construction (or possibly another deposit of moat excavation material). Context 1703, within 1702, was a grey-yellow-greenish lens, which is likely root disturbance. Due to the depth being reached, at 1.2 m the trench was stepped in, and a central slot 0.4 m wide excavated along the length of the bottom of the trench. Layer 1704, lying at a depth of *c* 1.60 m, was the natural pink clay lying underneath 1702.

In sum, Trench 17 did not find any evidence for human burials, although it is possible that the 14th century moat construction caused severe disturbance to any earlier burials existing in the area. The uppermost deposits of the trench contained disturbed material most likely reflecting up-cast from the digging of the 14th century moat. This lay above a deposit (1702) that may have been the pre-14th century ground level prior to the moat's construction with upcast being dumped on top.

Trench 19

Trench 19 was located *c.* 6.5 m north of the east facing elevation of the Thorpe Tower (Fig. 1). The Trench was sub-trapezoid in shape and measured a maximum of 2.36 m long and 1.65 m wide. The maximum depth reached was 20.77 m AOD, approximately 0.67 m below present ground level. Natural substratum (1914) consisted of a red marl clay interbedded with narrow bands of red sandstone. The untruncated depth of this material was approximately 0.2 m below ground level (21.19 m AOD). The earliest recorded feature cutting 1914 was a natural tree bowl/bioturbation, (cut [1917]) which was filled by reddish-brown silty clay (1918).

The first feature attributed to human activity was construction cut [1916]. This cut was heavily truncated by overlying features and therefore only the base was observed which had a maximum depth of 0.55 m below the modern ground level (20.93 m AOD). [1916] was orientated north–south in line with the west facing elevation of the Thorpe Tower. The primary function of this feature was as a construction cut for foundation wall (1912), observed at a median height of 21.55 m. Wall 1912 was constructed of roughly shaped and faced limestone blocks which had a slightly sub-triangular shape in section and an average size of 53 × 31 × 15 cm. No mortar was observed in association with 1912 indicating either a drystone construction or leaching processes. A thin deposit (1913), composed of light greyish-red sandy clay with frequent greyish-white, friable mortar inclusions, was also observed in association with 1916 at a median level of 21 m AOD. The composition of this fill suggests it was deposited during a primary construction phase associated with structure 1912.

Construction cut 1916 and its associated structure and fill were truncated by robber cuts [1908] and [1907]. The earliest of these [1908], was orientated north–south, and contained a single fill (1910), of a compact reddish-brown sandy clay containing occasional limestone fragments and frequent gravel. The alignment of 1908 was comparable with 1916 and it must therefore be assumed to be a robber trench associated with the removal of structure 1912.

The northern extent of 1908 is unknown due to its removal by second robber cut 1907. This cut was aligned east–west with a maximum depth of 0.67 m below current ground level (20.77 m AOD). The eastern terminus of 1907 sat in line with masonry 1912 and can therefore be assumed to be a second phase of robbing/demolition associated with that structure. Cut 1907 was filled with a compact reddish-grey sandy clay containing moderate inclusions of small stone fragments (1909).

Overlying (1912) and (1909), although with no visible construction cut, was wall 1911. This structure was orientated north-north-east by south-south-west and was constructed from rough-hewn, unfaced, unbonded limestone blocks with an average size of 34 × 15+ × 10 cm. Overlying 1912 was the extant garden wall (1917). The north-east by south-west alignment of 1917 was slightly different to 1911 underlying it. Wall 1917 contained a variety of size stones including one which displayed a similar profile shape to those observed in structure 1912. It was bonded by a concreted mid-grey lime mortar although had almost certainly been repointed since construction.

Deposit 1906, a firm, mid-reddish-brown sandy clay, was dumped against the wall 1917. The median height of this deposit was 21.22 m AOD, *c.* 0.22 m below the current ground level. This layer contained modern 'flowerpot' ceramics and is assumed to be a levelling deposit associated with garden wall 1914. Context 1906 was cut by sub-rectangular feature [1904] which was filled with redeposited natural clay (1905). The function of this feature is unknown although it is assumed to be a 19th/20th century garden feature. Fill (1905) was overlain by cobbles (1902). The average size of these cobbles was 18 × 6 × 16 cm and they were orientated north-east to south-west. It is assumed that 1902 is part of a roadside drain dating to the 19th/20th centuries. Cobbles 1902 were overlain by subsoil 1903, a firm, mid-reddish-brown silty clay, and topsoil/turf (1901).

The archaeological remains observed in Trench 19 appear to demonstrate the presence of a heavily robbed building with structures of two later phases overlying it. The orientation of the first structural phase, (1912/1916), and the robber trench (1908) associated with them is in alignment with the south facing elevation of the Thorpe Tower. This orientation suggests that this structural phase was associated with, and presumably connected to, the Tower. It is probable, therefore, that 1912 represents a heavily robbed wall which is comparable, and most likely contemporary with, wall J3 identified by the 8th Earl in his 1938 excavations (see Fig. 5) extending from the northern elevation of Thorpe Tower. As discussed above it appears that the Shell Keep and the Thorpe Tower are of a single phase most likely dating to the mid-12th century. While there is no evidence currently that 1912/1916 and wall J3 are contemporary with this primary construction phase it must be noted that the wall 1911 overlay 1912 and re-used some of its stone.

Bibliography

Fosbroke, T.D. 1821. *Berkeley manuscripts. Abstracts and extracts of Smyth's lives of the Berkeleys, illustrative of ancient manners and the constitution; including all the pedigrees in that ancient manuscript. To which are annexed a copious history of the castle and parish of Berkeley, consisting of matter never before published; and biographical anecdotes of Dr. Jenner ....* London: J. Nichols and Son.

Leech, R. 1981. *Historic Towns in Gloucestershire.* Gloucestershire: Committee for Rescue Archaeology.

Tandy, D. 2003. *Berkeley, A Town in the Marshes.* Chippenham: Anthony Rowe Ltd.

Chapter 5

Tales from the Clay: Notes on the Pottery Fabrics from Berkeley, Gloucestershire

Paul Blinkhorn and Stuart J. Prior

Excavations in Berkeley produced a significant assemblage of more than 11,000 sherds of pottery and these sherds can be dated from Roman to modern times, providing a continuous pottery timeline for the south-west of England. All pottery from Berkeley from the 2005–2018 excavation seasons has been assessed and spot dated with the pottery assessment report deposited with the Castle and the University of Bristol library service. About 20% of the assemblage has been further analysed but very little has been sampled for scientific analysis such as petrography and lipids. In this chapter, notes regarding the most important fabrics and pottery types from the three main excavation areas (the Walled Garden, Jenner Garden and Nelme's Paddock) are presented as a concise guide for future research in the area. At the end of the chapter a quick fabrics guide, with dating is also presented.

Notes on the pottery from the Walled (Butterfly) Garden

The 2005 season of excavations in the Walled Garden produced a small collection of late Saxon pottery (see Chapter 4). The pottery was from contexts 115 and 121, fills of a single small ditch, and are likely to represent a single phase of activity. Two fabric groups were identified.

Fabric 1 contains abundant rounded voids, <2.0 mm across, sparse rounded quartz grains, <2.0 mm across and sparse rounded red clay/iron ore grains <1.0 mm across. The groundmass is fine-textured with no visible quartz inclusions and fine-grained mica. A single large fragment of shell, probably part of a fossil mollusc *Gryphaea*, was present. The quartz grains have a matt surface and high sphericity.

Fabric 2 contains abundant rounded voids, sparse rounded quartz grains <1.0 mm across, sparse white chert fragments <1.0 mm across and sparse angular white and brown flint fragments. The groundmass is fine-textured with no visible quartz inclusions and sparse fine-grained mica/sericite. In a few sherds recent breaks show that calcareous inclusions survive and some of these can be identified as calcareous algae fragments.

All the sherds come from jars. The fabric 1 jars include a vessel with a handmade body and wheel-finished, lid-seated rim. The fabric 2 jars are mainly handmade, bag-shaped vessels with everted rims and a thickened neck. The exception is a fragment of a lid-seated rim, similar to that in Fabric 1.

Fabric 1 is extremely similar to the products of the Westgate Street kiln found at 1 Westgate Street in the centre of Gloucester (Heighway *et al.* 1979). The fabric characteristics at ×20 magnification are consistent with a Gloucester source but thin-section and chemical analysis is required to confirm this identification.

Fabric 2 contains inclusion types which are inconsistent with a Severn Valley source. Polished quartz grains originate in lower Cretaceous deposits which outcrop in Wiltshire and south Somerset (*e.g.* the Blackdown Hills) and from those outcrops then occur in detrital sands in south Somerset and west Wiltshire. They occur rarely in gravels of the Bristol Avon terraces but not at all in Severn Valley gravels, and certainly not to the exclusion of matt-surfaced, spherical grains of Triassic origin which form the majority of the quartzose grains in Severn Valley sands. Chalk-tempered vessels of similar visual appearance to the Fabric 2 examples occur on sites in eastern Wiltshire and Hampshire but, whereas angular flint has been noted as a minor inclusion in their fabric, polished quartz grains have not. However, this may simply be an oversight in recording and a comparison of the Wiltshire/Hampshire and Berkeley vessels should be made before discounting a Hampshire Basin source. If the flint fragments are indeed heavily stained, as they appear at ×20 magnification, this would suggest a Tertiary source which is consistent with south-east Wiltshire and southern Hampshire.

The Gloucester Westgate pottery has been dated to the late 10th or early 11th centuries and, at the earliest, might date to the late 9th century when lid-seated jars started to be made in the east Midlands. The thickened necked, everted-rimmed jars of Fabric 2 could date to the later part of the mid-Saxon period but occur alongside wheel-finished lid-seated vessels at Westgate Street and therefore continued to be produced into the late Saxon period. By the middle of the 11th century, however, different jar types, with a squat body and sagging base, were being produced both in the Bristol area (*e.g.* Ponsford 1998), in West Wiltshire (Bath Fabric A, found in quantity at Acton Court (Vince and England 2004), and in small quantities in Gloucester, Gloucester TF48) and at Haresfield (Gloucester TF41B, 1984; Vince 1984). The Berkeley assemblage is, therefore, at the very earliest of late 9th century and, at the very latest, early 11th century date and definitely pre-dates the Norman Conquest. The Berkeley Castle late Saxon pottery probably pre-dates the sequences at Bristol and Bath. Gloucester Westgate vessels occur on sites in Gloucester itself and on sites in the surrounding countryside but have also been found at Winchcombe and Hereford, where they probably reflect a movement of goods and people between major urban and religious centres. The Berkeley find probably indicates a similar status for Berkeley in the late Saxon period, *i.e.* not simply a rural manor but some sort of central place.

Notes on the pottery from Nelme's Paddock

Pottery from Nelme's Paddock is fairly typical of sites in the region with most of the wares occurring in Bristol and/or Gloucester (*e.g.* Heighway 1983, fiche B2; Ponsford 1998). The exception is the sherds of Ipswich Ware, which are the most westerly finds of this material in England to date, and only the third from Gloucestershire. The other two find-spots are from Lechlade, at a major river crossing where the saltway from Droitwich meets the Thames (Blinkhorn 2012, 79), and Winchcombe, where a sherd occurred at Cowl Lane (Davison *et al.* 1986, 103), with a second possible sherd in the 1972 excavations (ibid., 124). Winchcombe is thought to be the site of an 8th century or earlier monastic foundation and possibly the chief seat of the rulers of the Hwicce (ibid., 95).

The presence of the sherds of Ipswich Ware make a very strong case for high status activity in Berkeley in the middle Saxon period, some time between the earlier 8th and mid-9th centuries. The two sherds, both from Trench 8, are from different vessels, both with a thickness and curvature indicating that they are from large storage jars. These, along with pitchers, are far more common at sites located beyond the boundaries of the East Anglia kingdom than they are within it and were almost certainly containers for traded goods rather than objects of desire in themselves (Blinkhorn 2012). Finds of such pottery are very rare to the west of London in southern England and, in this region, it nearly always occurs at high status sites. There is only a handful of other find-spots in Oxfordshire (Blinkhorn 2012, 85).

The late medieval and early post-medieval assemblage includes a number of continental imports which demonstrate Berkeley's role as an inland port at that time. The pottery, such as the Saintonge chafing dish fragments, Spanish tin-glazed ware, Martincamp flasks and large quantities of German stoneware are typical finds at ports such as Bristol (*e.g.* Ponsford 1998, 137) but, other than the German stonewares, are rare at inland sites. German stoneware was in use at the Castle from a least the mid-16th century, as the 1559 will of Cecily, widow of Sir Thomas Berkeley included a stone cup garnished with silver.

In Trench 4 the medieval assemblage is dominated by Minety Ware (35.9% of the whole CP assemblage) along with a lesser proportion of Bristol Redcliffe Ware (11.2%), with the rest of the material dating to the 14th century or earlier, other than six tiny sherds of 'Tudor Green' ware. Late Saxon pottery is also present in the form of two small sherds of limestone-tempered ware, as is a single Roman sherd. Two small sherds from a crucible were also noted. They are almost certainly from the same vessel but do not join. They do not appear to have been heated to a particularly high temperature in that there was no vitrification of the fabric other than the outer surface, where there were also patches of a thin, glassy green and red variegated residue. Two further sherds, almost certainly from the same vessel as this one, were noted in contexts 439 and 440, both dating to CP MOD. The fabric, a hard sandy ware, suggests that they are probably of earlier medieval date, or possibly even late Saxon. They were all body sherds.

The residual material is fairly evenly divided between medieval and earlier (2307 g) and post-medieval (2795 g) material. Apart from 21 sherds of Romano-British pottery, the earliest material present comprises six sherds of late Saxon limestone-tempered ware. Most of the medieval assemblage again comprises pottery from the 12th–14th centuries, with Minety-type the most common, and Ham Green, Bristol Redcliffe and coarse sandy ware all also represented. Given that there is some evidence of activity in the late Saxon period, it is entirely possible that last-named could date to the 11th–early 12th century. As noted above, two fragments of probably the same crucible noted in the PM2 assemblage are also present.

The composition of the residual post-medieval assemblage very much reflects that of the stratified groups, being dominated by glazed red earthenwares, with the rest being drinking pottery and fine tablewares.

Notes on the pottery from the Jenner Garden

Four sherds of residual late Saxon pottery were recovered from contexts 1506 and 1508 in Trench 15. All are from the same vessel with punched and incised decoration. A number of fragments of highly decorated pots similar to this, mainly pitchers, occurred at Mary-Le-Port East, Bristol (Watts and Rahtz 1985), although most of the stamped vessels had the impressions of dies with 'wheel' or 'grid' motifs. The vessel from Trench 15 appear to have impressions made with the end of a tool or possibly even a piece of jewellery, a technique which is known on some early Saxon vessels (Briscoe 1981).

Most of the vessels at Mary-Le-Port occurred in 12th century contexts (phase 2e) but included a large quantity of residual pottery, including a sherd of late 10th–11th century Cheddar Ware, which was thought to be the same date of most of the decorated material (Watts and Rahtz 1985, 69). Residual Roman and late Saxon material occurred throughout the sequence at that site. A number of late Saxon lamps similar an examples from Trench 16 at Berkeley also occurred in the phase 2e contexts at Mary-Le-Port (*ibid.*, fig. 79). There appear to be little doubt that there was activity in this area of Berkeley before the Norman Conquest, probably during the late 10th–11th centuries. Also in Trench 15, the only stratified pottery was two sherds of Minety Ware (28 g), which could also be residual, two of Malvernian ware (9 g), and one small sherd each of 'Tudor Green' (1 g) and Cistercian Ware (4 g). The entire assemblage comprised body sherds, other than the Saintonge base.

In Trench 16, 38 sherds can be dated in the early–mid-11th century phase. Most of the pottery from this phase comprises residual Romano-British material (32 sherds, 216 g), with the bulk of the rest consisting of fragments of four lamps in fabrics F103 and F200. The only other pottery was a single body sherd in the Saxo-Norman fabric F200 (see below). In the west of England, in the 10th–11th centuries, ceramic lamps are generally very scarce. Vince (1984) does not mention lamps as being amongst the range of vessel forms for the late Saxon and Saxo-Norman fabrics from Gloucester and the only site in Bristol that appears to have produced them is Mary-Le-Port (Watts and Rahtz 1985, fig. 79, nos 70–7), where a group of fragments from eight lamps, mainly in Bristol fabric BPT3, occurred. Most are missing their bases but the two examples which do have them have a simple, flat, pedestal foot. They were described by the excavators as 'pre-Conquest' (*ibid.*, 153). It is worthy of note that the area of that site where the lamps occurred showed a lot of evidence of industrial activity, such as iron smelting, leather and textile production and bone and horn working (*ibid.*, 67–9), and a number of ceramic crucibles also occurred (*ibid.*, fig 79, nos 81–3; fig. 81 nos 135–6). It would seem likely therefore that lamps such as these were specialised vessels used for illumination for industrial or craft activity rather than as everyday domestic lighting.

There is a general lack of pottery lamps in non-industrial, late 11th and 12th century assemblages in the region, despite, in most cases, a similar range of pottery types being present, which would appear to support a pre-conquest date for the examples from here. For example, they were entirely absent from the large assemblage from Chepstow (Vince 1991) and St Bartholomew's Hospital in Bristol (Ponsford 1998), although a fragment of a 12th century stone lamp occurred at the latter (Good 1998, 166).

Examples of Fabric types from University of Bristol work at Berkeley

Pottery from Berkeley Castle Trench 4

The assemblage comprised 1220 sherds with a total weight of 9783 g. The following fabric types were noted:

F102: Limestone-tempered Ware, late 9th–early 11th century. 8 sherds, 35 g
F110: Crucible fragments. All periods. 4 sherds, 16 g.
F200: Saxo-Norman oolitic limestone ware, 11th–12th centruy. 9 sherds, 88 g.
F300: Coarse sandy ware, mid-11th–12th century. 56 sherds, 657 g
F350: Ham Green Ware, early 12th–mid-13th century. 55 sherds, 624 g.
F351: Bristol C Ware. DATE 1 sherd, 19 g.
F352: Brill/Boarstall ware, 13th–16th century. 1 sherd, 11 g.
F353: Bristol Redcliffe ware, mid-13th–15th century. 75 sherds, 405 g.
F354: Hereford fabric A6. 13th–14th century
F355: Minety-type Ware, early 12th–16th century. 101 sherds, 1253 g.
F370: Saintonge monochrome ware, mid-13th–15th century. 1 sherd, 4 g.
F401: Oxidised glazed Malvernian ware, late 14th–early 17th century. 3 sherds, 31 g.
F402: Midland Purple ware, mid-14th–17th century. 2 sherds, 16 g.
F403: 'Tudor Green Wares', late 14th–mid-16th century. 10 sherds, 24 g.
F404: Cistercian Ware, late 15th–17th century. 10 sherds, 101 g.
F405: Frechen Stoneware, mid-16th–17th century. 10 sherds, 88 g.
F410: Anglo-Dutch tin-glazed earthenwares, 17th–18th century. 45 sherds, 157 g.
F411: Wanstrow-type iron-glazed wares, mid-16th–17th century. 1 sherd, 2 g.
F412: Donyatt-type slipwares, 17th–18th century. 1 sherd, 1 g.
F413: Westerwald/Cologne stoneware, 17th–18th century. 7 sherds, 35 g.
F414: Bristol/Staffordshire manganese wares, late 17th–18th century. 25 sherds, 105 g.
F416: Bristol slipware, mid-17th–mid-18th century. 14 sherds, 88 g.
F425: Glazed red earthenwares, mid-16th–19th century. 215 sherds, 2248 g.
F426: North Devon gravel-tempered wares, 16th–19th century. 12 sherds, 244 g.

F430: Chinese export porcelain, 17–18th century. 51 sherds, 129 g.
F433: Staffordshire white salt-glazed stoneware, 1720–1780. 45 sherds, 127 g.
F438: English stoneware. 1680+. 1 sherd, 10 g.
F1000: All modern wares, 19th century +. 427 sherds, 3043 g.
F1001: All Romano-British. 23 sherds, 157 g.

The range of fabric types indicates that there was activity at the site from the late Saxon period onwards, although most of the medieval pottery dates to the 14th century or earlier.

Pottery from Berkeley Castle Trench 6

The assemblage comprised 159 sherds with a total weight of 1376 g. The following fabric types were noted:

F200: Saxo-Norman oolitic limestone ware, 11th–12th century. 2 sherds, 21 g.
F350: Ham Green Ware, early 12th–mid-13th century. 5 sherds, 264 g.
F351: Bristol C Ware, 1 sherd, 16 g.
F353: Bristol Redcliffe Ware, mid-13th–15th century. 9 sherds, 59 g.
F355: Minety-type Ware, early 12th–16th century. 36 sherds, 561 g.
F403: 'Tudor Green' wares, late 14th–mid-16th century. 1 sherd, 1 g.
F404: Cistercian Ware, late 15th–17th century. 1 sherd, 1 g.
F405: Frechen stoneware, mid-16th–17th century. 2 sherds, 8 g.
F410: Anglo-Dutch tin-glazed earthenwares, 17th–18th century. 4 sherds, 10 g.
F411: Wanstrow-type iron-glazed wares, mid-16th–17th century. 1 sherd, 7 g.
F416: Bristol slipware, mid-17th–mid-18th century. 3 sherds, 25 g.
F425: Glazed red earthenwares, mid-16th–19th century. 20 sherds, 311 g.
F430: Chinese export porcelain, 17–18th century. 5 sherds, 9 g.
F433: Staffordshire white salt-glazed stoneware, 1720–1780. 4 sherds, 5 g.
F1000: All modern wares, 19th century+. 61 sherds, 305 g.

Pottery from Berkeley Castle Trench 7

The assemblage comprised 549 sherds with a total weight of 5653 g. The following fabric types were noted:

F102: Limestone-tempered ware, late 9th–early 11th century. 4 sherds, 35 g
F110: Crucible fragments. All periods. 2 sherds, 12 g.
F200: Saxo-Norman oolitic limestone ware, 11th–12th century. 51 sherds, 414 g.
F300: Coarse sandy ware, mid-11th–12th century. 117 sherds, 1840 g
F302: Bath 'A' Ware, 11th–14th century. 4 sherds, 56 g.
F350: Ham Green Ware, early 12th–mid-13th century. 38 sherds, 294 g.
F353: Bristol Redcliffe ware, mid-13th–15th century. 30 sherds, 206 g.
F355: Minety-type Ware, early 12th–16th century. 119 sherds, 11354 g.
F357: Hereford fabric A7b, late 13th–early 16th century. 7 sherds, 30 g.
F358: Forest of Dean Sandstone-tempered Ware, 12th–13th C. 5 sherds, 56 g.
F403: 'Tudor Green' wares, late 14th–mid-16th century. 10 sherds, 24 g.
F404: Cistercian Ware, late 15th–17th century. 1 sherd, 3 g.
F405: Frechen stoneware, mid-16th–17th century. 1 sherd, 1 g.
F410: Anglo-Dutch tin-glazed earthenwares, 17th–18th century. 4 sherds, 10 g.
F411: Wanstrow-type iron-glazed wares, mid-16th–17th century. 4 sherds, 8 g.

F412: Donyatt-type slipwares, 17th–18th century. 8 sherds, 66 g.
F413: Westerwald/Cologne stoneware, 17th–18th century. 1 sherds, 1 g.
F414: Bristol/Staffordshire manganese wares, late 17th–18th century. 3 sherds, 9 g.
F416: Bristol slipware, mid-17th–mid-18th century. 3 sherds, 4 g.
F425: Glazed red earthenwares, mid-16th–19th century. 11 sherds, 52 g.
F426: North Devon gravel-tempered wares, 16th–19th century. 1 sherd, 3 g.
F433: Staffordshire white salt-glazed stoneware, 1720–1780. 3 sherds, 8 g.
F438: English stoneware. 1680+. 2 sherds, 15 g.
F1000: All modern wares, 19th century+. 77 sherds, 765 g.
F1001: All Romano-British. 47 sherds, 397 g.

Pottery from Berkeley Castle Trench 8

The assemblage comprised 6614 sherds with a total weight of 68,227 g. The estimated vessel equivalent (EVE), by summation of surviving rimsherd circumference was 15.31. The following fabric types were noted:

F96: Ipswich Ware. 725–850. 2 sherds, 52 g, EVE = 0.05.
F102: Limestone-tempered Ware, late 9th–early 11th century? 63 sherds, 794 g, EVE = 0.87
F103: Hand-built quartz and calcareous ware, 10th century. 10 sherds, 113 g, EVE = 0.02.
F110: Crucible fragments. All periods. 2 sherds, 3 g, EVE = 0.
F200: Saxo-Norman oolitic limestone ware, 11th–12th century. 261 sherds, 2768 g, EVE = 1.39.
F205: Stamford Ware, 10th–mid-12th century. 6 sherds, 35 g, EVE = 0.13.
F300: Coarse sandy ware, mid-11th–12th century. 765 sherds, 12422 g, EVE = 4.59.
F302: Bath 'A' Ware, 11th–14th century. 3 sherds, 201 g, EVE = 0.18.
F303: Early Malvernian ware, late 12th–13th century. 17 sherds, 135 g, EVE = 0
F350: Ham Green Ware, early 12th–mid-13th century. 358 sherds, 4608 g, EVE = 0.54.
F351: Bristol C Ware. Late 11th–12th century. 25 sherds, 150 g, EVE = 0.
F352: Brill/Boarstall ware, 13th–16th century. 73 sherds, 353 g, EVE = 0.
F353: Bristol Redcliffe ware, mid-13th–15th century. 1758 sherds, 6194 g, EVE = 1.02.
F354: Hereford fabric A6, 13th–14th century. 251 sherds, 1581 g, EVE = 0.88
F355: Minety-type Ware, early 12th–16th century. 1360 sherds, 21275 g, EVE = 4.85.
F357: Hereford fabric A7b, late 13th–early 16th century. 65 sherds, 582 g, EVE = 0.30.
F358: Forest of Dean sandstone-tempered ware, 12th–13th century. 1 sherd, 5 g, EVE = 0.
F359: Hereford fabric A4, 13th–14th century
F370: Saintonge monochrome ware, mid-13th–15th century. 28 sherds, 122 g, EVE = 0
F371: Saintonge chafing dishes. 16th–17th century. 2 sherds, 89 g, EVE = 0.
F375: Spanish tin-glazed wares, 15th–17th century. 1 sherd, 20 g, EVE = 0.
F401: Oxidized glazed Malvernian ware, late 14th–early 17th century. 188 sherds, 2562 g, EVE = 0.64.
F402: Midland Purple ware, mid-14th–17th century.
F403: 'Tudor Green' wares, late 14th–mid-16th century. 82 sherds, 195 g, EVE = 0.14.
F404: Cistercian Ware, late 15th–17th century. 77 sherds, 369 g, EVE = 0.07
F405: Frechen Sstoneware, mid-16th–17th century. 63 sherds, 615 g, EVE = 0.14.
F410: Anglo-Dutch tin-glazed earthenwares, 17th–18th century. 29 sherds, 124 g, EVE = 0.
F411: Wanstrow-type iron-glazed wares, mid-16th–17th century. 18 sherds, 102 g, EVE = 0
F412: Donyatt-type slipwares, 17th–18th century. 2 sherds, 22 g.
F413: Westerwald/Cologne stoneware, 17th–18th century. 9 sherds, 40 g.
F414: Bristol/Staffordshire manganese wares, late 17th–18th century. 25 sherds, 76 g.
F416: Bristol slipware, mid-17th–mid-18th century. 24 sherds, 329 g.
F420: Martincamp ware, *c*. 1470–1700. 1 sherd, 6 g.

F425: Glazed red earthenwares, mid-16th–19th century. 569 sherds, 9326 g
F426: North Devon gravel-tempered wares, 16th–19th century. 10 sherds, 224 g
F430: Chinese export porcelain, 17–18th century. 40 sherds, 103 g.
F433: Staffordshire white salt-glazed stoneware, 1720–1780. 45 sherds, 102 g.
F438: English stoneware. 1680+. 4 sherds, 16 g.
F451: Border Ware, mid-16th–mid-18th century (Pearce 1988)
F1000: All modern wares, 19th century+. 291 sherds, 1774 g
F1001: All Romano-British. 81 sherds, 708 g.

Pottery from Berkeley Castle Trench 9

The assemblage comprised 352 sherds with a total weight of 5437 g. The following fabric types were noted:

F102: Limestone-tempered ware, late 9th–early 11th century. 2 sherds, 32 g
F103: Hand-built quartz and calcareous ware, 10th century. 1 sherd, 14 g.
F200: Saxo-Norman oolitic limestone ware, 11th–12th century. 9 sherds, 129 g.
F300: Coarse sandy ware, mid-11th–12th century. 7 sherds, 96 g
F350: Ham Green Ware, early 12th–mid-13th century. 7 sherds, 68 g.
F353: Bristol Redcliffe Ware, mid-13th–15th century. 5 sherds, 56 g.
F354: Hereford fabric A6. 13th–14th century. 1 sherd, 11 g.
F355: Minety-type Ware, early 12th–16th century. 3 sherds, 66 g.
F404: Cistercian Ware, late 15th–17th century. 1 sherd, 1 g.
F410: Anglo-Dutch tin-glazed earthenwares, 17th–18th century. 3 sherds, 28 g.
F412: Donyatt-type slipwares, 17th–18th century. 1 sherd, 2 g.
F413: Westerwald/Cologne stoneware, 17th–18th century. 1 sherd, 15 g.
F414: Bristol/Staffordshire manganese wares, late 17th–18th century. 53 sherds, 341 g.
F416: Bristol slipware, mid-17th–mid-18th century. 7 sherds, 55 g.
F425: Glazed red earthenwares, mid-16th–19th century. 57 sherds, 1501 g.
F426: North Devon gravel-tempered wares, 16th–19th century. 7 sherds, 162 g.
F438: English stoneware. 1680+. 1 sherd, 35 g.
F1000: All modern wares, 19th century+. 185 sherds, 2792 g.
F1001: All Romano-British. 1 sherd, 33 g.

Pottery from Berkeley Castle Trench 10

The following fabric types were noted:

F101: Hand-built quartz and calcareous ware. 10th century. 1 sherd, 17 g.
F102: Limestone-tempered ware, late 9th–early 11th century. 16 sherds, 125 g
F103: Hand-built quartz and calcareous ware, 10th century. 1 sherd, 30 g.
F200: Saxo-Norman oolitic limestone ware, 11th–12th century. 31 sherds, 450 g.
F300: Coarse sandy ware, mid-11th–12th century. 11 sherds, 135 g
F302: Bath 'A' Ware, 11th–14th century. 1 sherd, 19 g.
F350: Ham Green Ware, early 12th–mid-13th century. 10 sherds, 181 g.
F353: Bristol Redcliffe Ware, mid-13th–15th century. 4 sherds, 22 g.
F354: Hereford fabric A6. 13th–14th century. 1 sherd, 1 g.
F355: Minety-type Ware, early 12th–16th century. 16 sherds, 201 g.
F401: Oxidised glazed Malvernian ware, late 14th–early 17th century. 3 sherds, 16 g.
F403: 'Tudor Green' wares, late 14th–mid-16th century. 1 sherd, 1 g.

F404: Cistercian Ware, late 15th–17th century. 1 sherd, 6 g.
F405: Frechen stoneware, mid-16th–17th century. 1 sherd, 5 g.
F410: Anglo-Dutch tin-glazed earthenwares, 17th–18th century. 4 sherds, 24 g.
F412: Donyatt-type slipwares, 17th–18th century. 1 sherd, 2 g.
F413: Westerwald/Cologne stoneware, 17th–18th century. 1 sherd, 5 g.
F414: Bristol/Staffordshire manganese wares, late 17th–18th century. 10 sherds, 46 g.
F416: Bristol slipware, mid-17th–mid-18th century. 10 sherds, 32 g.
F425: Glazed red earthenwares, mid-16th–19th century. 26 sherds, 361 g.
F426: North Devon gravel-tempered wares, 16th–19th century. 3 sherds, 15 g.
F430: Chinese export porcelain, 17–18th century. 1 sherd, 1 g.
F433: Staffordshire white salt-glazed stoneware, 1720–1780. 4 sherds, 9 g.
F1000: All modern wares, 19th century+. 55 sherds, 1229 g.
F1001: All Romano-British. 68 sherds, 613 g.

Pottery from Berkeley Castle Trench 11

The assemblage comprised 88 sherds with a total weight of 1330 g. The following fabric types were noted:

F101: Hand-built quartz and calcareous ware. 10th century. 1 sherd, 18 g.
F200: Saxo-Norman oolitic limestone ware, 11th–12th century. 3 sherds, 75 g.
F300: Coarse sandy ware, mid-11th–12th century. 3 sherds, 83 g
F353: Bristol Redcliffe Ware, mid-13th–15th century. 3 sherds, 34 g.
F355: Minety-type Ware, early 12th–16th century. 2 sherds, 55 g.
F401: Oxidized glazed Malvernian ware, late 14th–early 17th century. 1 sherd, 98 g.
F403: 'Tudor Green' wares, late 14th–mid-16th century. 1 sherd, 3 g.
F404: Cistercian Ware, late 15th–17th century. 1 sherd, 2 g.
F405: Frechen stoneware, mid-16th–17th century. 2 sherds, 6 g.
F410: Anglo-Dutch tin-glazed earthenwares, 17th–18th century. 3 sherds, 29 g.
F413: Westerwald/Cologne stoneware, 17th–18th century. 1 sherd, 7 g.
F414: Bristol/Staffordshire manganese wares, late 17th–18th century. 1 sherd, 7 g.
F425: Glazed red earthenwares, mid-16th–19th century. 10 sherds, 245 g.
F426: North Devon gravel-tempered wares, 16th–19th century. 2 sherds, 40 g.
F433: Staffordshire white salt-glazed stoneware, 1720–1780. 1 sherd, 4 g.
F1000: All modern wares, 19th century+. 51 sherds, 602 g.
F1001: All Romano-British. 2 sherds, 22 g.

Pottery from Berkeley Castle Trench 12

The assemblage comprised 147 sherds with a total weight of 1077 g. The following fabric types were noted:

F200: Saxo-Norman oolitic limestone ware, 11th–12th century. 8 sherds, 75 g.
F205: Stamford Ware, 10th–mid-12th century. 1 sherd, 1 g.
F300: Coarse sandy ware, mid-11th–12th century. 15 sherds, 136 g
F350: Ham Green Ware, early 12th–mid-13th century. 3 sherds, 15 g.
F353: Bristol Redcliffe Ware, mid-13th–15th century. 3 sherds, 31 g.
F354: Hereford fabric A6. 13th–14th century. 3 sherds, 14 g.
F355: Minety-type Ware, early 12th–16th century. 14 sherds, 126 g.
F405: Frechen stoneware, mid-16th–17th century. 1 sherd, 35 g.

F410: Anglo-Dutch tin-glazed earthenwares, 17th–18th century. 9 sherds, 102 g.
F412: Donyatt-type slipwares, 17th–18th century. 1 sherd, 6 g.
F414: Bristol/Staffordshire manganese wares, late 17th–18th century. 3 sherds, 4 g.
F416: Bristol slipware, mid-17th–mid-18th century. 3 sherds, 33 g.
F425: Glazed red earthenwares, mid-16th–19th century. 13 sherds, 168 g.
F426: North Devon gravel-tempered wares, 16th–19th century. 1 sherd, 5 g.
F433: Staffordshire white salt-glazed stoneware, 1720–1780. 6 sherds, 11 g.
F438: English stoneware. 1680+. 1 sherd, 7 g.
F1000: All modern wares, 19th century+. 60 sherds, 284 g.
F1001: All Romano-British. 2 sherds, 24 g.

Pottery from Berkeley Castle Trench 14

The assemblage comprised 79 sherds with a total weight of 723 g. The following fabric types were noted:

F300: BPT6: Coarse sandy ware, mid-11th–12th century. F350: Ham Green Ware, early 12th–mid-13th century. 1 sherd, 7 g.
F353: Bristol Redcliffe Ware, mid-13th–15th century. 2 sherds, 17 g.
F354: Hereford fabric A6. 13th–14th century. 1 sherd, 3 g
F355: Minety-type Ware, early 12th–16th century. 5 sherds, 122 g.
F370: TF81. Saintonge monochrome ware, mid-13th–15th century. F375: BPT333 Spanish tin-glazed wares, 15th–17th century.
F401: TF52: Oxidised glazed Malvernian ware, 14th–early 17th century.
F402: Midland Purple ware, mid-14th–17th century. F403: 'Tudor Green' wares, late 14th–mid-16th century. 1 sherd, 2 g.
F404: Cistercian Ware, late 15th–17th century. 1 sherd, 2 g.
F410: Anglo-Dutch tin-glazed earthenwares, 17th–18th century. 3 sherds, 7 g.
F411: BPT269: Wanstrow-type iron-glazed wares, mid-16th–17th century.
F412: BPT268: Donyatt-type slipwares, 17th–18th century
F414: BPT211: Bristol/Staffordshire manganese wares, late 17th–18th century.F415: Brown Border Ware, 1580–1750
F416: Bristol slipware, mid-17th–mid-18th century. 2 sherds, 20 g.
F425: Glazed red earthenwares, mid-16th–19th century. 7 sherds, 141 g.
F426: North Devon gravel-tempered wares, 16th–19th century. 2 sherds, 5 g.
F430: TF66: Chinese export porcelain, 17–18th century.
F433: Staffordshire white salt-glazed stoneware, 1720–1780. 2 sherds, 3 g.
F1000: All modern wares, 19th century+. 51 sherds, 387 g.
F1001: All Romano-British. 1 sherd, 7 g.

Pottery from Berkeley Castle Trench 15

The assemblage comprised 192 sherds with a total weight of 1418 g. The following fabric types were noted:

F102: Limestone-tempered ware, late 9th–early 11th century. 1 sherds, 8 g
F103: Hand-built quartz and calcareous ware, 10th century. 4 sherds, 29 g.
F200: Saxo-Norman oolitic limestone ware, 11th–12th century. 42 sherds, 266 g.
F300: Coarse sandy ware, mid-11th–12th century. 16 sherds, 292 g
F350: Ham Green Ware, early 12th–mid-13th century. 3 sherds, 46 g.
F354: Hereford fabric A6. 13th–14th century. 4 sherds, 32 g.

F355: Minety-type Ware, early 12th–16th century. 5 sherds, 51 g.
F370: Saintonge monochrome ware, mid-13th–15th century. 2 sherds, 36 g.
F401: Oxidised glazed Malvernian ware, late 14th–early 17th century. 2 sherds, 9 g.
F403: 'Tudor Green' wares, late 14th–mid-16th century. 1 sherd, 1 g.
F404: Cistercian Ware, late 15th–17th century. 1 sherd, 4 g.
F1001: All Romano-British. 111 sherds, 644 g.

The range of fabric types is typical of sites in the region, although 45.4% (by weight) of the pottery is Romano-British.

Pottery from Berkeley Castle Trench 16

The assemblage comprised 248 sherds with a total weight of 2898 g. The following fabric types were noted:

F103: Hand-built quartz and calcareous ware, 10th century. 2 sherds, 106 g.
F200: Saxo-Norman oolitic limestone ware, 11th–12th century. 6 sherds, 161 g.
F300: Coarse sandy ware, mid-11th–12th century. 8 sherds, 197 g
F350: Ham Green Ware, early 12th–mid-13th century. 1 sherd, 15 g.
F353: Bristol Redcliffe Ware, mid-13th–15th century. 7 sherds, 118 g.
F354: Hereford fabric A6. 13th–14th century. 2 sherds, 4 g.
F355: Minety-type Ware, early 12th–16th century. 27 sherds, 376 g.
F375: Spanish tin-glazed wares, 15th–17th century. 1 sherd, 8 g.
F401: Oxidised glazed Malvernian ware, late 14th–early 17th century. 3 sherds, 44 g.
F404: Cistercian Ware, late 15th–17th century. 3 sherds, 6 g.
F405: Frechen stoneware, mid-16th–17th century. 2 sherds, 5 g.
F410: Anglo-Dutch tin-glazed earthenwares, 17th–18th century. 45 sherds, 157 g.
F412: Donyatt-type slipwares, 17th–18th century. 1 sherd, 9 g.
F413: Westerwald/Cologne stoneware, 17th–18th century. 1 sherd, 2 g.
F416: Bristol slipware, mid-17th–mid-18th century. 2 sherds, 4 g.
F425: Glazed red earthenwares, mid-16th–19th century. 16 sherds, 252 g.
F426: North Devon gravel-tempered wares, 16th–19th century. 3 sherds, 14 g.
F433: Staffordshire white salt-glazed stoneware, 1720–1780. 1 sherd, 5 g.
F1000: All modern wares, 19th century+. 70 sherds, 593 g.
F1001: All Romano-British. 91 sherds, 965 g.

Bibliography

Blinkhorn, P. 2012. *The Ipswich Ware Project: Ceramics, Trade and Society in Middle Saxon England.* London: Medieval Pottery Research Group Occasional Paper 7.

Briscoe, T. 1981. Anglo-Saxon pot stamps. In: Brown, D., Campbell J. and Chadwick-Hawkes, S. (eds), *Anglo-Saxon Studies in Archaeology and History*. Oxford: British Archaeological Report 92.

Davison, B.K., Hinchliffe, J. and Ellis, P.J. 1986. Excavations in Winchcombe, Gloucestershire, 1962–1972: (I) a report on excavation and fieldwork, (II) at Cowl Lane and Back Lane. *Transactions of the Bristol And Gloucestershire Archaeological Society* 104, 95–138.

Good, L 1998, Stone. In Price, R. with Ponsford, M. *St Bartholomew's Hospital, Bristol. The Excavation of a Medieval Hospital: 1976-8.* York; Council for British Archaeology Research Report 110, 164–6.

Heighway, C.M. 1983. *The East and North Gates of Gloucester.* Gloucester: Western Archaeological Trust Monograph 4.

Heighway, C.M., Garrod, A.P. and Vince, A.G. 1979. Excavations at 1 Westgate Street, Gloucester, 1975. *Medieval Archaeology*, 23, 159–213.

Ponsford, M. 1998. Pottery. In: Price, R. with Ponsford, M. *St Bartholomew's Hospital, Bristol. The Excavation of a Medieval Hospital: 1976–8.* York; Council for British Archaeology Research Report 110, 136–55.

Vince, A.G. 1984. The Medieval Ceramic Industry of the Severn Valley. Unpublished PhD thesis, University of Southampton.

Vince, A.G. 1991. The medieval pottery. In: Shoesmith, R. *Excavations at Chepstow, 1973–1974.* Cambrian Archaeology Monograph 4, 93–140.

Vince, A. and England, S. 2004 Medieval and later pottery. In Rodwell and Bell, 2004 *Acton Court: the evolution of an early Tudor Courtier's mansion.* English Heritage, London, 294-348.

Watts, L. and Rahtz, P. 1985. *Mary-le-Port, Bristol: Excavations 1962–1963.* Bristol: City of Bristol Museum and Art Gallery Monograph 7.

Chapter 6

Tales from the Objects: Small Finds from Berkeley Castle Project

Emma Firth

Introduction

This is a presentation of 993 small finds recovered during excavations undertaken by the University of Bristol from 2005 to 2019 at Berkeley Castle, Gloucestershire. It is a moderately large assemblage that can be dated to the Romano-British, early medieval (Anglo-Saxon and Viking), medieval and post-medieval periods. The assemblage includes items of copper alloy, glass, iron, worked bone and lead. Examination of an anthropomorphic terminal, small find 8/8128/457, was carried out previously by Dr Leslie Webster from the British Museum, and her observations have been included in this report.

Methodology

Catalogue records were made of 993 iron, copper alloy and worked bone small finds recovered from stratified contexts excavated at Berkeley Castle from 2007 to 2019. The detailed small finds catalogue was recorded using Microsoft Excel for Office 365. All finds were initially recorded during the post-excavation process and these records formed the basis for the detailed catalogue. Small finds found during metal detecting of unstratified contexts are noted in the original records; however, no detailed catalogue entries have been created due to the limitations of time relative to the size of the assemblage.

Small finds not included within the catalogue include the following:

- 352 small finds recovered from contexts marked as unstratified
- 18 small finds recorded as metal detector finds (unstratified)
- 30 small finds that were recorded as 'unaccounted for' in the records supplied with the assemblage (small finds not present in the assemblage)
- 46 small finds listed in the original records supplied but not present in the assemblage. This includes some of the more interesting objects including a copper alloy Viking bracelet (16/1632/25) as well as several silver objects such as the hawking bell (7/712/4). There is a note in the original records showing that these objects have been published and it is assumed they have been deposited.

The small finds catalogue was created by recording the following attributes: material type, category, object type, condition, description, decoration, comparable objects, period and broad date. Where complete dimensions were present, these were measured, and coin weights and musket balls were weighed. The small finds were catalogued and assigned to categories by broad period as listed in Table 1.

The small finds include objects of iron, copper alloy, lead, animal bone and glass. They have been grouped together by period (Romano-British, early medieval, medieval and post-medieval) and then by category. The distinction between periods sometimes is not clear: objects such as dress pins have a long currency and can span the medieval to post-medieval period, and as a rule, small finds are dated to the earliest period in which they would be found.

As no small finds have been x-rayed, identification of iron objects was hindered due to their condition. Furthermore, identification could only be made if diagnostic features were visible. No measurements have been taken of any iron small finds. Where small finds were recognisable (*e.g.* nails, knives, arrowheads) they were recorded in as much detail as allows, although assigning any typologies was often not possible. All small finds are discussed in terms of their function.

The small finds have been written up by the date of each object rather than by the period of the phased context it was recovered from, as this information was not available at the time. As a result, some objects which are more ambiguous (*e.g.* flat fragments with no diagnostic features) are currently undated. These have been summarised at the end of this report.

Category	Romano-British	Early Medieval	Medieval	Post-Medieval	Modern	Undated	Total by Category
Domestic and Household	3	2	35	8	2	21	71
Dress fittings	6	21	143	31	8	28	237
Gardens	-	-	-	8	-	-	8
Hunting	-	-	2	-	-	-	2
Literacy and learning	-	1	5	3	-	-	9
Metalworking	-	-	-	-	-	59	59
Miscellaneous	2	-	11	2	1	174	190
Personal Care	1	-	1	-	-	1	3
Recreation and gaming	-	1	4	15	-	-	20
Religion	1	-	1		-	-	2
Textiles	-	1	7	9	-	-	17
Tools and manufacturing	-	-	1	-	-	3	4
Transport	-	-	5	-	-	-	5
Arms and Armour	-	-	5	68	-	1	74
Weights and measures	-	-	3	1	-	-	4
Building and furniture fittings	1	-	65	6	-	197	269
Harness fittings	-	-	14	1	-	4	19
Total by period	**14**	**26**	**302**	**152**	**11**	**488**	**993**

Condition of the Assemblage

Much of the iron assemblage is in a very poor condition: most of the iron small finds show signs of active corrosion, such as longitudinal cracks in the corrosion layer and lamination or flaking of corrosion layers, revealing spots of bright orange powdery deposits. Iron arrowhead 8/8374/823 is one of the few iron objects that would benefit from conservation.

The copper alloy assemblage is more stable than the iron small finds, with objects generally in fair to good condition. However, some copper alloy objects are beginning to show signs of active corrosion with bright green powdery spots and flaking appearing on their surfaces.

Lead objects are all stable and show little sign of corrosion or deterioration and the worked bone objects are in good, stable condition.

Unfortunately, much of the glass is too corroded or broken down to warrant retaining. The only fragments that should be kept are those with painted surfaces and those fragments that are still stable and intact.

The BCP are currently working with the castle to repackage the finds appropriately and conserve the differing materials as far as is reasonably practical.

Romano British Small Finds

The group of Romano-British small finds are fairly limited in number and all are commonly found objects on Romano-British sites. In the absence of phase information, it is not known whether any of these objects are residual or have been curated through the early medieval and later periods.

Dress Fittings

Romano-British dress fittings include a compete brooch (8/8533/874), identified as a Colchester Derivative Polden Hill Type 1.a brooch (MacKreth 2011, 70). A similar brooch was recovered from excavations at Kingscote, Gloucestershire (Timby 1998, Fig. 66:1.30). These brooches date to the 1st century AD and have a distribution that covers Somerset, Wiltshire, Gloucestershire and into the Midlands. Other Romano-British dress accessories include a closed hoop ring (4/443/127) decorated with incised lines, a spacer bead (8/8181/815) made of antler, and an iron hob nail (8/844/183) from a shoe.

A finger ring (10/1063/55), fashioned from a Romano-British armlet and decorated with groups of incised lines, was recovered from Trench 10. Armlets are particularly suitable for re-fashioning into finger rings, and similar objects have been found on Romano-British sites elsewhere (see Crummy 1983). The recycling of these types of Romano-British objects continued during the early medieval period (Rogers 2007, 133).

Building and furniture fittings

The only small find in this category is an almost complete small, iron double-looped spike with leaf-shaped arms (8/861/270). Double-looped spikes have a multitude of uses and are often found on Romano-British sites. They were used both structurally within buildings as well as for furniture fittings and fixtures. It is probable that the latter is more likely due to the small size of this object.

Domestic and Household Objects

Three small finds associated with domestic and household activities include a fleur-de-lis key handle (8/857/309), a lead pot mend (8/857/385) with tiny sherds still in situ, and an incomplete copper alloy decorated spoon handle (8/8181/530).

Personal Care

Nail cleaner 8/815/174 is an unusual Romano-British form, with a parallel from Wilcote, Oxfordshire (Crummy 2001, 4, Fig. 3b). The form, a cylindrical body decorated with lattice and a small shaft at one end, would originally have had a bone bead similar to the Wilcote example. These nail cleaners belong to a group identified by Crummy as Early South-Western Types, and date from the 1st to 2nd century. She suggests that these types do not form part of a set.

Miscellaneous

This category includes a complete, small cast copper alloy knife (8/8224/624) that has been tentatively dated as Romano-British. The knife is small, 53 mm overall in length, which includes a thick blade measuring 8 mm along its back and with a cutting edge of 17 mm in length. The size of the knife makes it difficult to see how it could have been held comfortably for any practical use, and it is possibly a votive object. A small shard of undiagnostic glass (8/8167/52) is of potential Romano-British date.

Early Medieval Small Finds

Dress fittings

The largest category of early medieval small finds are the 22 copper alloy dress fittings. The most commonly found type of dress fittings are strap ends, used to finish the ends of straps to prevent fraying. There are a range of different types represented, including an unfinished blank (8/US/405), which unfortunately was recovered from an unstratified context. However, the presence of this blank strap end is important as it suggests such objects were being manufactured either on or very near to the site. Five strap ends could be attributed to Thomas's Type A.2, one to Type A.4, one to Type A.5, two to Type B.1, one to Type C and a single Type l.

A complete copper alloy, mid-10th century Viking kidney-ringed polyhedral-headed pin (16/1632/22), identical to a pin found at Omey Feichín, Ireland (Gibbons and Gibbons 2005), Fishamble Street, Dublin (Fanning 1994 in Gibbons and Gibbons 2005) and Lagore, Knowth and Balinderry I, was recovered from Trench 16. Examples from outside of Ireland are rare. Gibbons notes six were found in the Hebrides; whilst singular pins have been found at Chester, Bishops Gate (London), Isle of Wight and Westray in the Orkneys. A pin found in Iceland (Fanning 1994, 40) shows the extent of Dublin trading at this time. The pin would have been used as a method to attach clothing together. The kidney-ring would have been fastened with a cord threaded through the ring to secure the pin to the garment. The kidney ring would have been articulated and could be rotated forward, enabling the cord to be wrapped and tied around the protruding end of the pin.

Other early medieval pins include a bi-conical pin (8/8458/853) comparable with Hinton and Parsons Type Ca2ii from Hamwic (Hinton 1996); and a complete copper alloy globular headed pin (8/8146/681), the top of which has been slightly flattened with a collar where the shaft joins the pin. It is comparable with Type Aa2ii from Hamwic (*ibid*). Both pins have slightly swollen shafts and are large. They could have been used either to fasten clothes or they may have been used as hair pins.

An unusual copper alloy pin (8/822/47) was recovered from Trench 8. Its cast head is made up of twelve pellets (each with a diameter of 5 mm), resulting in a head resembling a blackberry. There is a groove around the middle of the head, but it is not clear whether it has been cast in two parts that have then been fitted together. The construction could be confirmed by x-raying and cleaning. Nothing comparable has been found and its date is uncertain. It has been tentatively dated as early medieval.

An incomplete, early medieval, cast copper alloy d-shape buckle frame (8/814/159), comparable with a buckle found at Hamwic, Southampton (Hinton 1996, Fig. 2, No. 13/2), dates from the 8th century. Only one corner of the buckle survives. It is decorated with intermittent incised lines around the frame like the Hamwic example.

There are three cast copper alloy finger rings – 15/1500/3, 15/1506/4 and 16/1630/17 – all of which are penannular hoops with tapering ends and with circular sections. These are identifiable as Viking finger-rings. Similar examples have been found in Thetford (Goodall in Rodgerson and Dallas 1984, Fig. 110, No. 19).

Dress fittings used for fastening clothes include a small number of hooked tags, two with circular plates and one with a triangular plate. These distinctive fasteners are found from the 7th century and were in use through the medieval period, but by the post-medieval period the plate became more complex in its shape and decoration. Only two are decorated: 8/8100/489 with a border of ring and dot motif; and 8/US/841 with an incised zigzag border.

Dress fittings		
Buckle	Cu Alloy	1
Clothes Pin	Cu Alloy	1
Finger Ring	Cu Alloy	3
Hooked Tag	Cu Alloy	3
Pin	Cu Alloy	2
Strap End	Cu Alloy	11
Total of small finds		**21**

Domestic and Household

Few domestic and household small finds could be dated as early medieval, but a tiny fragment of light green glass possibly derives from a cone beaker (8/8277/687). The glass is very thin with two self-colour trails but is otherwise undiagnostic.

A small anthropomorphic terminal (8/8128/457), possibly from a knife, was dated by Dr Leslie Webster (British Museum). The figure, draped in robes, wears a domed hat with a knop on top. The head has been described possibly as a woman wearing a head dress and dates to between the 7th and 8th centuries. The eyes are made from blue glass and are comparable with glass eye insets found on the terminal of zoomorphic strap ends (Thomas 2000, 190). She notes their occurrence on high status objects, and that glass was used from the 7th century, becoming widespread in the 9th century.

Domestic and Household		
Beaker	Glass	1
Knife Terminal	Cu Alloy	1
Total of small finds		**2**

Literacy and Learning

An incomplete, copper alloy 8th century aestel (4/439/123), decorated with a pierced, Celtic-type cross engraved on the sub-circular, flat head was recovered from Trench 4. The head is intentionally bent upwards at the neck towards a hollow shaft made from two integral flaps of metal folded into a tube that would have fitted around a worked bone or wooden handle. The head and shaft would originally have been covered with gilt; however, all that now remains are small patches on the head and a tiny trace on the shaft. Aestels were used to turn the vellum pages of books, as chemicals present on the hands of the monks could damage the vellum. The presence of this object suggests a probable scriptorium at or nearby the site. The object has no known parallels and has been described as unique (BBC).

Literacy and learning		
Aestle	Cu Alloy	1
Total of small finds		**1**

Recreation and Gaming

A worked antler or bone circular gaming counter (8/861/363) with a central perforation and decorated with cross-hatching over one surface was found. Only half of the counter survives. The central perforation would have enabled the counter to be threated onto a string with other gaming counters to prevent their loss.

Recreation and gaming		
Gaming Counter	Worked bone	1
Total of small finds		**1**

Textiles

An early medieval pin beater (4/407/207) was the only object associated with textiles that could confidently be attributed to the early medieval period. The pin beater tapers at both ends and has a highly polished surface from use. Although a simple tool, it was important for warp weighted looms. Inserted between the warp threads that hang downward and are tensioned by loom weights, the pin beater was used to lift the weft upwards towards the cloth and pack the weft threads together. This repetitive use of the pin against the threads resulted in the characteristic polishing of the pin beater's surface.

Textiles		
Pin Beater	Worked bone	1
Total of small finds		**1**

Medieval Small Finds

Dress fittings

By far the largest category of finds from the medieval period are the 148 dress fittings. There is some cross-over between harness mounts and dress fittings – many of the mounts and buckles could be easily attributed to either category, as could book fittings. Sexfoil domed mounts with central perforation and rivets on either side have been identified as strap fittings for belts but could equally have been used as decorative embellishments for books. (Howsam 2016, 47).

Dress fittings		
Annular Brooch	Cu Alloy	2
Annular Brooch Pin	Cu Alloy	1
Bar Mount	Cu Alloy	6
Bar Mount central and end lobes	Cu Alloy	4
Belt Mount	Cu Alloy	1

Dress fittings		
Buckle	Cu Alloy	1
Buckle Plate	Cu Alloy	1
Button	Cu Alloy	1
Catch-Plate	Cu Alloy	1
Circular Mount	Cu Alloy	16
Domed Stud	Cu Alloy	2
Dress Weight	Lead	1
Figurative Mount	Cu Alloy	1
Finger Ring	Cu Alloy	1
Folding Clasp	Cu Alloy	1
Forked Spacer	Cu Alloy	1
Lace Chape	Cu Alloy	21
Locking Buckle	Cu Alloy	1
Mount	Cu Alloy	1
Pin	Worked Bone	1
	Cu Alloy	39
Polygonal Mount	Cu Alloy	1
Purse Frame	Cu Alloy	1
Pyramidal Mount	Cu Alloy	1
Quatrefoil Mount	Cu Alloy	1
Repousse Mount	Cu Alloy	1
Rivet	Cu Alloy	1
Septfoil Mount	Cu Alloy	1
Sexfoil Mount	Cu Alloy	12
Sheet Spherical Bell	Cu Alloy	1
Simple Bar Mount	Cu Alloy	1
Spangle	Cu Alloy	1
	Tin – lead Alloy	1
Strap End	Cu Alloy	8
Strap Fitting	Cu Alloy	3
Strap Loop	Cu Alloy	4
Suspension Loop	Cu Alloy	1
Trefoil Mount	Cu Alloy	1
Buckle - circular	Cu Alloy	1
	Iron	1
Buckle - double oval	Cu Alloy	3

Dress fittings		
Buckle - ornate	Cu Alloy	3
Buckle - rectangular	Iron	1
Buckle - single oval	Cu Alloy	4
Buckle and plate	Cu Alloy	1
Buckled -d-shaped	Cu Alloy	1
	Iron	1
Total of small finds		**160**

Finger ring

A cast copper alloy finger ring (8/8230/742) is possibly of medieval or post-medieval date. The ring is plain, with a d-section.

Mounts

Mounts are the most prevalent type of dress fitting and include 43 small finds that can be categorised as pendant loops, bar, circular, figurative, polygonal, pyramidal, trefoil, quatrefoil, sexfoil, septfoil, and repoussé mounts. Also included in this assemblage are domed studs, although these objects could equally fall within the categories of furniture fittings or harness fittings. All the mounts are commonly found medieval types, and most have parallels with objects recorded in Egan and Pritchard (1991). Most of the mounts are made from sheet copper alloy, except for the bar and pendant loops which are cast. Many would have been held in situ with copper alloy or iron rivets (often still present). The mounts can be dated from the 13th to 15th centuries. The circular domed mounts (either with integral or separate rivets) are dated slightly earlier (12th century) but these continued in use until the 15th century.

Buttons

Only a single button (4/407/46) could be confidently dated as medieval. This button is a cast copper alloy gilt button decorated with a five-pointed wavy star with a central dot. The button is slightly domed, with half circles bordering its edge. A comparable button in Egan and Pritchard (1991, Fig. 178, No. 1381) is dated from the 13th to the 14th century.

Spangles

Medieval spangles are small tin/lead alloy discs with a perforated lug that were sewn onto garments as decoration. Stott (cited in Egan and Pritchard, 1991, 236) notes 'there is no evidence so far to suggest what situations spangles were used', but the simple perforations (either singularly or in pairs) and their small size would suggest they are more likely to be attached to clothing rather than used as mounts on harnesses or belts. Spangle 4/401/40 is in the shape of an ampulla or purse and is decorated with bands of lines forming panels within a circular border. Decoration on spangles can feature complex geometric patterns or animals or birds; but it may also be plain, as with spangle 8/804/125 which has a rectangular plate with a single perforation and an undecorated oval plate.

Pins

Pins are a common dress accessory that had a multitude of uses, from small wire-drawn shroud pins used in burials, to pins for dress making and fixing clothing or hair. Pins were mainly made of copper-alloy drawn wire with heads that could be wire-wound or globular. Commonly found from the 14th century, they continued in use throughout the post-medieval period before becoming the modern pin we are familiar with today. Worked bone pins are also found, such as pin 8/829/56 made from a pig fibula. Bone pins of this type have a wide currency; they have been found on sites from the Iron Age to the medieval period. They are often identified as either dress pins or needles; however, those with more splayed heads may have been more suitable for pinning clothing because the wide splayed head makes them secure. Cool (2011, 56) notes that pig fibulas were frequently used for these types of pins (and needles), and she also observes that splayed heads may have made these objects impractical for use as needles.

Brooches

Brooches are less common at Berkeley Castle than other dress fittings in the medieval period, with only three cast copper alloy annular brooches identified. Brooches 14/1403/9 and 8/8230/650 are complete, and the third brooch (8/865/277) only consists of the pin with two incised parallel bands before a broken attachment loop. Brooch 14/1403/9 is plain and has a small, moulded ridge between the attachment loop and pin. The second brooch (8/8230/650) has incised lines on its upper surface, although much of the decoration is obscured by corrosion products. The pin of this brooch is short, and there is probably (although this needs confirmation by x-ray) a constriction in the ring where the pin sits. It is comparable with a brooch in Egan and Pritchard (1991, Fig. 162, No. 1315). There is often a difficulty distinguishing between annular brooches and simple circular framed buckles, the difference simply being that a buckle does not have the pin constriction that is found on annular brooches (Egan and Pritchard 1991, 57). These brooches have a date range from the 13th to the 15th century.

Bells

A small rumbler bell (8/804/18) could be associated with either dress or harness fittings. The bell is made from two halves of sheet metal hammered into spheres which are soldered together, with an attachment loop (also made of sheet metal), also soldered into place at the top of the bell. The bell would have contained an iron pea (no longer present). At the base of the bell are two circular holes at either end of a slit. Comparable bells in Egan and Pritchard (1991, Fig. 221, No. 1668) have a date range from the late 13th to early 15th century. A second, smaller rumbler bell (8/US/832) has been catalogued as a hawking bell, but it could equally have been used as a dress or harness fitting.

Belt Buckles, composite frames, strap loops and strap ends

Medieval small finds associated with fittings on belts include a range of buckles, strap loops, strap ends and composite frames. Buckle forms include circular frames, double oval frames, single oval frames, d-shaped frames, ornate frames and rectangular frames. The small, circular or oval buckles, often with iron pins, would have been used for fastening shoes and purses, while the more ornate buckles may have been found on belts paired with buckle mounts and strap ends. Most of the buckles are plain, undecorated types, but there is an ornate buckle (8/839/287) with evidence of gilt on its surface. Small composite frames, often with no evidence of pins, can be mistaken for small buckles, but they may also be a frame from a book clasp; and several 'buckles' could equally be used as either a dress, harness fitting or book clasps. A composite frame from a folding clasp (8/834/317), included here with the buckles, could also fall into any of these categories of use.

An elaborate buckle with a plate (4/423/126) has evidence of enamelling both on the buckle and the oval lipped buckle frame. There is a groove cut into the buckle frame within which traces of blue/green enamel can be seen with a x20 hand lens. The recessed buckle plate comprises a folded sheet plate, with two rivet holes at the attachment end. It has a rectangular panel filled with the degraded remains of enamel surrounding a zoomorphic design. There is what appears to be a 'tail' winding above a wing, possibly of a mythical beast such as a dragon, and traces of enamel surround this zoomorphic design. There is a direct parallel for this buckle and plate in Egan and Pritchard (1991, Fig. 73, No. 530) and it can be dated to the 13th century.

A compete, cast copper alloy locking buckle (14/1403/12) has parallels from Abbots Lane, London (Egan 2005, Fig. 19, No. 117). Locking buckles are distinctive as they have a rectangular frame with an off-centred pin bar that forms the u-shaped arm which extends down below the buckle frame. The arm of this pin bar rests in a rebate against the outside edge of the buckle frame and has a twisted globular knop at its terminal. The buckle pin is triangular and wraps around the u-shaped pin bar. This form of buckle dates to the 14th century and continued in use until the 16th century. It may have been used to secure bags, purses or knives.

The strap ends were attached to girdles or belts and are all made of folded copper alloy sheet. They vary in their complexity: most would have had forked spacers lying between the rectangular folded plates (spacer now absent on 8/857/466, spacer in situ on 8/861/281,) while another is crude in its construction, being simply a rectangular folded copper alloy sheet with a single rivet hole (8/814/114). All are held in place by either iron or copper alloy rivet holes. There are several different forms present, including a tongue-shaped strap end (8/815/128) and a collared acorn type knop (8/8298/740). All of the strap ends date from the mid-13th to 15th century.

There are four types of strap loops, used for holding loose straps in place. Two examples have internal projections: 8/814/189 is sub-rectangular with a curved top frame and 8/8126/474 has knops on its corners. They are comparable with examples in Egan and Pritchard (1991, Fig. 149, Nos. 1257 and 1263). The remaining strap loops all have plain frames.

Lace Chapes

Lace chapes span the medieval to post-medieval period, changing little in form. They are commonly found on domestic sites. Used to tidy the ends of laces for both garments and shoes, lace chapes are formed from rolling a thin sheet of copper alloy and fastening at the top with a small copper alloy or iron rivet. The edges of the lace chape may be folded and butted together, or simply butted together. Most found at Berkeley are broken and incomplete at one end. None are decorated and all broadly date from the 13th to 15th century.

Building and Furniture Fittings

Building and furniture fittings are the largest group of small finds, with a total of 120 objects. Small finds that are associated with buildings include nails, window cames, wall hooks, lead flashing and window glass; while small finds that may be furniture fittings includes casket mounts, decorative strips/mounts and tacks. However, there are many objects that could have been used for either of these sub categories. Most of the objects are iron nails, but forms could not be identified due to their poor condition.

Forty-two fragments of medieval window glass were recovered during excavations from Trench 8. The composition of medieval potash glass means it corrodes very quickly, so glass that was once clear is now brown and surfaces are pitted. In some cases, the glass has corroded to such a point that it is now sand-like. This is in part due to burial conditions, but the breakdown of the glass has been exacerbated by poor packaging. Due to the condition of the glass, it is impossible to ascertain whether any of the fragments were coloured in any way. However, 20 fragments of Grisaille window glass could be identified. This type of medieval painted glass dates from the early 13th century and the best examples can be seen at Salisbury Cathedral. The characteristic iron red/brown painted surface was created using a paint of iron and lead oxides mixed with gum Arabic, which was then fired on to the glass. Cross-hatching was a popular method of decoration with borders comprising simple linear or geometric designs. Of the Grisaille glass found at Berkeley, recognisable decorative motifs are visible on 11 fragments. Nine fragments are painted with cross-hatching, while linear borders and circles are present on two others.

Building and furniture fittings		
Casket mount	Cu Alloy	1
Circular Mount	Cu Alloy	1
Decorative Strip	Cu Alloy	1
Domed Mount	Cu Alloy	1
Grisaille Window Glass	Glass	6
Nail	Iron	5
Rove	Cu Alloy	3
Staple	Iron	1
Window Came	Lead	4
Window Glass	Glass	42
Total of small finds		**65**

Domestic and Household

Small finds associated with the medieval household include a range of 35 objects, including copper alloy casket keys, candlestick, knives, weights and pot mends. One of the most interesting objects in this category is a cast copper alloy foldable/adjustable double candle holder (8/US/840). Although it has been recovered from an unstratified context, it is considered an important object. The candlestick, with its double cups for candles, appears to have no parallels, and although single candle holders of a similar form have been found in London (Egan 2010, Fig. 115, MoL accession number 84.163), the Berkeley foldable double candleholder is thought to be unique. It is decorated with an incised zigzag border around the edges of the strips, and the cups have a narrow, incised band of parallel lines with chevrons between them. The candlestick has a flange that would have rotated to enable the candle to be fixed at different angles, while the pointed end of the arm would have been inserted into a space in a wall or other surface. The cups would originally have rotated upwards and could have been folded back down in when not in use. The folding feature of this candlestick together with its small size suggests this was an object that was portable.

A small, cast copper alloy simple rotary key (4/402/8), with a rounded bow with a collar and hollow shank end with a simple bit, was recovered from Trench 4. Egan (2010, 111) suggests a date range from the 12th to the late 14th century for these small keys. This type of key would have been used for locks on caskets (*ibid*, Fig. 86, No. 294).

Six knives were noted in the assemblage, of which only three could be assigned to any type due to the poor condition of the remaining three. The three identifiable knives are all whittle tanged knives and included knife 7/743/7, which is possibly a Goodall Type B found all through the medieval period; knife 14/1405/13 identified as a Goodall Type C which dates from the 14th to 15th century; and knife 8/8352/801, identified as a Goodall Type D, most common in the 12th to 13th centuries. Two knives – 10/1029/22 and 8/8224/729 – were too corroded to attribute a type but both are scale tanged knives. Knife 8/8224/729 comprises just a bone handle with part of the scale tang still in situ. The handle is slightly curved, worn and polished through use and tapers towards where the blade would start. The final knife (8/8238/655) was in very poor, fragmentary condition.

There are five pieces of glass from vessels, including the folded base from a late medieval to post-medieval pedestal beaker and the base of a stemmed goblet, both recovered from Trench 8. The remaining pieces are too small to identify any vessel type and such small fragments might indicate that they may be redeposited from elsewhere. Other vessels include four fragments likely to originate from copper alloy cauldrons; such small fragments indicate they too are redeposited.

A paired swivel ring (8/8230/633) comparable with similar objects in Griffiths (2011, Fig. 11.7, No. J265) would have had a variety of uses in the medieval house, enabling chains and cauldrons to be attached together, whilst enabling the attached item to be freely moved.

Cast lead pendant weights are the most common small find in the household and domestic category. Several forms are present, including spherical, conical and plano-convex. They would have had a variety of uses, from fishing, spinning/craft and commercial weights. None are decorated, and most fall within the early medieval to early post-medieval date. A net sinker (8/8530/860) is the only weight associated with fishing and is distinctive because of its tubular, rectangular section with a flattened end. There is an irregular groove where a net would be inserted, and the edges pressed together to hold the net. Similar lead alloy net weights were found in York at Fishergate and Coppergate (Ottaway and Rogers 2002, 2748, Fig. 1352, Nos. 15260 to 15264).

Two lead pot mends were found and are thought to be of medieval date. The first is the more commonly found molten lead pot mend, where lead was poured onto a hole in the wall of a vessel to create a plug.

Medieval Domestic and Household		
Beaker	Glass	1
Candle Holder	Cu Alloy	2
Cauldron fragment	Cu Alloy	1
Dish or Bowl	Cu Alloy	1
Folding Candle Holder	Cu Alloy	1
Key	Cu Alloy	1
Knife	Iron	6
Knife Handle	Worked bone	1
Net Sinker	Lead	1
Pot Mend	Lead	2
Swivel Rings	Iron	1
Vessel	Cu Alloy	1
	Glass	5
Pendant weight	Lead	10
Total of small finds		**35**

Literacy and learning

Objects associated with literacy and learning include a hinged book clasp (8/890/423), similar to one in Egan and Pritchard (1991, Fig. 72, No. 502); book clasp TP4/402/3, comparable with Howsam's Type A.3 (2016); and a mount (8/811/141) that is cross shaped, each arm being flared with two notches out of the end. This mount is decorated with fine, incised zigzags around its edges and there are small circular punch marks centrally on each arm.

Book mounts with domed bosses tend to be the most common find of this type; however, at Berkeley Castle only one was found (8/8230/657). This is a cast, copper alloy, quatrefoil cruciform book mount with a central circular conical boss with four projecting arms, each having a fleur-de-lis terminal. It is comparable with Howsam's' Type B.1.2. (2016, 92). These mounts date from the late 14th to the mid-16th century and were used to protect the front of books. Often four or five mounts could be found on the front and back of books, hence why they are commonly found.

A writing lead (8/829/149), with a flattened perforated end and shaft tapering to a point, could have been used to make lines on parchment, along with similar writing leads'styli', and similar objects have been found in Billingsgate Lorry Park, London (Egan 2010, Fig. 209, No. 893) and Coppergate, Bedern and Fishergate in York (Ottaway and Rodger 2002, Fig. 1502). Egan (2010) suggests a variety of uses for leads, including for marking up stone or timber, in addition to their use on parchment. The example from Berkeley differs from both the York and London examples in that it has a suspension loop. Similar leads with these loops are recorded as pencils (PAS Pencil ID: NLM-76F3B7)

Literacy and learning		
Book Clasp	Cu Alloy	1
Hinged Book Clasp	Cu Alloy	1
Mount	Cu Alloy	1
Quatrefoil Mount	Cu Alloy	1
Writing Lead	Lead	1
Total small finds		**5**

Recreation and gaming

There are two similar dice, both small with ring and dot pips. Die 8/804/310 is an incomplete small bone dice of early medieval date. It has single ring and dot motif pips, with opposing sides adding up to prime numbers (1–2, 3–4 and 5–6). Die 8/8697/960 is well used and has worn and polished sides and corners. The opposing sides all add up to seven; this layout is known as a 'regular' layout (Egan 2014).

An octagonal gaming counter (TP3/301/1) is decorated with incised pairs of parallel lines that radiate from the centre of the disc and alternate with ring and dot motif. The counter is highly polished, suggesting much use, and it has a central perforation. The counter could be simply a gaming counter, or it could be a spinning disc, as the central perforation is 6 mm in diameter through which a spindle could be passed.

Recreation and gaming		
Dice	Worked bone	2
Gaming Counter	Worked bone	2
Total small finds		**4**

Tools and manufacturing

A punch (8/8238/654) is the only medieval tool that was recognised from the iron assemblage. It is most likely a stone working tool and is comparable to a similar object described in Griffiths (2011 Fig. 4.3, No. C24).

Tools and manufacturing		
Punch	Iron	1
Total small finds		**1**

Textiles

Worked bone objects that are associated with textiles include an awl (14/1405/17); a tapering worked bone object (8/811/244); and two bone needles (8/815/204 and 14/1405/17). Worked bone object 8/811/244 is not particularly diagnostic but it is thought to be associated with textiles due to its highly polished surfaces.

Bone needle 14/1405/17 is comparable to an object recovered from excavations at St James's Priory in Bristol. The use of these types of objects may be related to making nets or weaving. The shaft of the object is polished with fine striations; both netting and weaving may result in this type of wear. (Burchill 2006, Fig. 79).

Worked bone needle 8/815/204 has a drilled, circular eye and the head tapers to a sub-triangular shape. The surfaces of this needle are highly polished from use; this polishing is commonly seen on the surfaces of worked bone objects that have been used for textiles.

Two cast lead weights – 8/8305/776 and 8/8280/852 – were the only two of all the weights that are diagnostic enough to be identified as spindle whorls. The first spindle whorl (8/8305/776) is sub-conical and the second (8/8280/852) is bi-conical and decorated with raised triangles. The bi-conical spindle whorl could be identified as Walton Rogers Type 2c (2007, Fig. 2.18).

A small, closed form copper alloy thimble (8/8385/881) with round pits spiralling around the sides to the domed crown, dates from the medieval to post-medieval period.

Textiles		
Needle	Antler	2
	Bone	1
Spindle Whorl	Lead	2
Thimble	Cu Alloy	1
Unidentified Object	Bone	1
Total small finds		**7**

Weights and measures

All three weights of medieval date are pan weights and would have been used within pan scales, as opposed to being suspended from steelyards. At this point it is worth noting that some of the lead weights with perforations assigned to the household category may possibly have been weights used with steelyards.

A complete cup weight (8/8120/443) is possibly associated with metalworking at the site. These weights were used for weighing small objects, such as scrap pieces or coins of gold or silver, and were frequently part of a nested set of weights. A comparable weight in Egan (2010 Fig. 230, No. 976) has been dated, by its association with ceramics, to the early 13th century. The second weight is a flat, hide-shaped weight (8/8229/895), with four concave sides; it is decorated on one side with a stamped motif in each corner, comprising a ring of six dots with a central dot. The same motif is placed centrally on the reverse of the weight. This type of weight is a coin weight and is paralleled by a similar weight from Billingsgate, London (Egan 2010, Fig. 239, No. 1027). The final weight (8/839/2590) is a flat rectangular weight made from lead, unlike the other two which are copper alloy. The weight has a Crusader-type 'Latin' cross stamped centrally on one side. No comparable weight could be found for this small find.

Weights and measures		
Coin Weight	Lead	2
Cup Weight	Cu Alloy	1
Total small finds		**3**

Harness fittings

The harness fittings include clasps, pendants, mounts and suspension mounts used to embellish harnesses. All are cast copper alloy apart from an iron ring and swivel hook. Most of the pendants have traces of gilt as well as traces of enamel. Most of the harness fittings would have been attached by cast copper alloy suspension mounts that would have been secured to the harness using iron rivets.

Harness pendants appeared during the 12th century, some of which could be openwork. Pendant 8/8305/774 is a gilded, openwork circular pendant frame with a cross and roundel, while pendant 7/704/3 is a suspended, plain circular concave plate. More elaborate forms are found from the 13th century with the rectangular engraved plates featuring heraldry, which became a popular feature in the later part of the century. The shield form is thought to have appeared around the 14th century, but by the end of the century the use of pendants began to decline.

Two harness pendants with heraldry were found at Berkeley Castle. The first pendant (8/US/220) is a cast copper alloy gilded rectangular plate decorated with incised lattice and is believed to represent the family of John de Scrures (8/868/422) a shield-shape pendant with the emblem of an eagle in display mode with raised wings, outstretched legs and head turned to the left. The eagle is recessed; traces of enamel are just about visible, as are traces of gilt. This pendant has been identified previously as the de Monthermer family crest, for knights or nobles, who preferred to use covers on their horses displaying their heraldic emblems. The harness pendant would be suspended from the leather breastplate (or peytrel) that attached to the front of the saddle on either side and then passed around the front of the horse, in a similar way to a more modern breastplate. Pendants may also be found on straps that passed around the rear of the horse and may also have been attached to the browband (the strap running in front of the ears of the horse) of the bridle.

Other harness mounts include a shield-shaped mount (8/8511/844), a strap fitting (8/857/490) and a diamond shaped foil mount (8/8120/452). These would have been riveted onto the leather work.

Small finds that were used to attach pendants to the harness include a gilded clasp (4/401/79), a suspension mount (8/814/99), a swivel ring (8/814/102) and a swivel hook (8/8224/745).

Two plain circular rings (8/867/302 and 8/8224/754) may have been simple frames for buckles for harnesses, with the strap fitting directly onto the frame (Egan and Pritchard 1991, 57). They are often poorly cast, and the slightly pointed oval profile of 8/8224/754 might suggest this was from a buckle for a harness. It is worth noting that buckles recorded within the dress fitting category may equally have been used to secure harnesses.

Harness fittings		
Clasp	Cu Alloy	1
Foil Mount	Cu Alloy	1
Harness Pendant	Cu Alloy	3
	Cu Alloy/Gold Gilt	1
Ring	Cu Alloy	2
Rivet	Cu Alloy	1
Shield Mount	Cu Alloy	1
Strap fitting	Cu Alloy	1
Suspension mount	Cu Alloy	1
Swivel	Cu Alloy	1
Swivel Hook	Iron	1
Buckle - circular	Cu Alloy	1
Total small finds		**14**

Transport

A single medieval horseshoe (8/8299/731) is possibly an example of a Clarkes Type 2 (formerly Norman) shoe, which are found in London in contexts dated from AD1050 to AD1350. The example here has a slightly distorted edge. The horseshoe is in too poor condition to assign it to either type 2A or 2B. Three iron fiddle key nails (10/1026/21, 10/1037/24 and 15/1507/7) were found. They have distinctive, large flat heads which sit within a recess in the shoe. There are probably more of these nails in the iron assemblage, but without being x-rayed they can be difficult to identify if they are heavily corroded.

A medieval copper alloy spur buckle (8/8519/936) is comparable with a spur buckle found on a fragment from a rowel spur with leathers found at Baynard House, London, and is dated to the late 13th century (Ellis and Egan 2004, Fig. 91.c, No. 323).

Transport		
Fiddle Key Nail	Iron	3
Horseshoe	Iron	1
Spur Buckle	Cu Alloy	1
Total small finds		**5**

Arms and armour

Few objects associated with arms and armour were present. These include a copper alloy folded sheet scabbard chape (4/407/104) and three links (4/444/188, 8/867/308 and 8/8230/730), all of which derive from chain mail. Made of iron, each link has flattened ends that would thread through a neighbouring link and were then secured together by integral rivets.

Warfare		
Chain Mail	Cu Alloy	3
Dagger	Iron	1
Scabbard Chape	Cu Alloy	1
Total small finds		**5**

Religion

An incomplete, flattened cast lead pilgrim's ampulla (8/8540/931) that would have been on a piece of leather or cord worn around the neck. During the 12th to 14th centuries, pilgrims would purchase ampullas containing holy water or oil at the shrines of saints. The ampulla is hollow cast, possibly bag-shaped, and only the lower side of the ampulla survives. It is decorated but the decoration is difficult to distinguish.

Religion		
Ampulla	Lead	1
Total small finds		**1**

Hunting

A complete iron socketed arrowhead (8/8374/823) with a triangular head comparable with Jessop's Type MP1 indicates hunting activity.

A small tin rumbler bell (8/US/832) could have had one of several uses including a dress or harness fitting, or it may have been used as a hawking bell. The bell is sub-spherical with four cast triangular petals that would have been bent inwards to form the bell (now flattened), which would have housed a 'pea'. This bell is decorated with ribs of opposed hatch that possibly run from the suspension loop (now missing) downwards. The bell is comparable with a similar bell from Billingsgate (Egan and Pritchard 1991, Fig. 221, No. 1668) which dates from the late 13th century.

The cast lead net weight (8/8530/860) with a seam could have been attached to a net for catching rabbits flushed from artificial warrens; comparable weights have been recorded (PAS Hunting object ID: NCL-B4B542)

Hunting		
Arrowhead	Iron	1
Hawking Bell	copper alloy	1
Net weight	lead	1
Total small finds		**3**

Personal Care

The only object relating to personal care from the medieval period is a fragment that possibly derives from a bone comb (4/419/64), comprising a polished rectangular piece of worked bone with ten shallow notches cut along one edge.

Personal Care		
Comb	Bone	1
Total small finds		1

Miscellaneous

Eleven small finds from the medieval period do not fall into any category because they do not have any diagnostic features that enable identification. This category of finds includes those small finds made of sheet copper alloy, lead, and worked bone. Most of the copper alloy sheet fragments seem likely to represent off-cuts from metalworking; a rectangular piece of lead may also be related to metalworking.

Small find 8/896/500 is an incomplete copper alloy unidentified object with possible traces of gilt on its surface. The shaft splits into two fine prongs, both of which are incomplete; one arm is mostly absent and the other broken. The circular sectioned shaft extends from the prongs and 15 mm along this shaft there is a small oval plate measuring 7 mm wide by 10 mm long. The object bears similarities to netting needles used to make hairnets.

Post-Medieval Small Finds

Dress fittings

Post-medieval dress fittings include a similar range of small finds to those found in the medieval period, with buckles being the most common object and other buttons, mounts, rings and lace chapes still being used. Decorative buckles and buckles with two pins became more prevalent during the post-medieval period.

Post-medieval dress fasteners bearing resemblance to the hook and eye fasteners we have today, such as dress fastener 8/8224/689, supersede the simple hooked tag, which can still be found at this time. The hook and eye fastener sometimes had a small decorative mount covering the hook (ex. PAS Eyelet Unique ID: SF-A13D23). Other dress fasteners include twisted wire loops, created by twisting the terminals of a short piece of copper-alloy-drawn wire together to form a loop. Parallels in Crummy (1988, Fig. 16. No. 1624) suggest these loops have a date range from the late medieval, but are more commonly found in post-medieval contexts.

In the late medieval to late post-medieval period, spangles were superseded by discs with a central perforation, akin to modern sequins (8/804/162 and TP4/402/1). When viewed under a x20 microscope, the first sequin (8/804/162) shows it was constructed from c-shaped fine wire coils that that were hammered together, leaving a split running from the central perforation to the edge of the sequin. Four sequins (TP4/804/162) were formed by simply stamping out a circular form from thin copper alloy sheet which was then perforated. These post-medieval sequins would have been used to embellish the garments of the wealthy.

Dress fittings		
Buckle	Cu Alloy	7
Buckle Frame	Cu Alloy	1
Button	Bone	2
	Cu Alloy	4
	Pewter/Cu Alloy	1
Catch-Plate	Cu Alloy	1
Dress Fastener	Cu Alloy	1
Lace Chape	Cu Alloy	2
Mount	Cu Alloy	1
Ring	Cu Alloy	1
Twisted Wire Loop	Cu Alloy	4
Wire Dress Hook	Cu Alloy	1
sequin	Cu Alloy	1
	Iron	4
Total of small finds		**31**

Building and Furniture Fittings

Only a small number of building and furniture fittings were dated as post-medieval, including a domed mount that may have been used on an item of furniture, an escutcheon plate, a wall hook, a rove and window glass.

Building and furniture fittings		
Domed Mount	Cu Alloy	1
Escutcheon Plate	Cu Alloy	2
Wall Hook	Iron	1
Window Glass	Glass	2
Rove	Copper alloy	1
Total of small finds		**8**

Domestic and Household

A limited number of small finds were dated as post-medieval; most of these are fragments of glass from either vessels or bottles. A glass bottle seal embossed with a crown over a bishop's mitre (8/816/145) had a note identifying it as the Berkeley crest; however, there is no evidence available to confirm this.

An iron key (8/8332/753) with a heart-shaped bow is a common form of key found in the post-medieval period. The bit of this key is quite simple and there is a near identical key on the which has been dated to the 16th century (PAS Locking key Unique ID: PUBLIC-5F1FF7).

A folded staple copper alloy pot mend (8/814/121) for a copper alloy vessel is comparable with a form created from a lozenge-shaped piece of copper alloy sheet illustrated by Egan (2005, Fig. 87.a). This type of pot mend was in use from the early medieval period, but Egan notes they are generally found in contexts dateable to the late 15th to middle or late 16th centuries. These mends were used to repair the walls of copper alloy vessels.

Domestic and Household		
Bottle Seal	Glass	1
Flask	Glass	1
Handle	Cu Alloy	1
Key	Iron	1
Pot Mend	Cu Alloy	1
Vessel	Glass	3
Total of small finds		**8**

Literacy and learning

The book clasp and book mounts were all identified as post-medieval types and all three are copper alloy. Book mount 8/8530/862 is decorated with a floral motif.

Literacy and learning		
Book Clasp	Cu Alloy	2
Book mount	Cu Alloy	1
Total of small finds		**3**

Recreation and gaming

The assemblage of clay pipes includes several stamped bowls from Bristol clay pipe manufacturer Richard Berryman, who was producing clay pipes from 1619 until 1652 (clay pipe bowls 8/804/184, 8/8224/781, 8/8224/752 and 8/8696/957). The heels of these bowls all have an incuse stamp 'R†B' (R and B separated with a dagger) with a heart below it.

There is a single bowl (8/840/940) with a pedestal base with incuse stamp 'JOHN/LEGG'. John Legg was producing pipes in Brosley, Shropshire from 1655 to 1699.

Two bowls with an incuse stamp on the heel comprising 'IH' within a circle were possibly manufactured by John Hartshome of Broseley, Shropshire, around 1680. His mark is usually in relief, not incuse (bowls 8/8342/780 and 8/8342/782).

Bowl 8/8342/795 has a stamp on the heel comprising a circular relief stamp with a cross within a diamond that could not be attributed to any manufacturer. The remaining clay pipe fragments were either not stamped or the stamp was too abraded to identify the makers.

A lead figurine (8/8183/523) may originally have been a toy. At first glance it could almost be a piece of window came, but it is clearly a figure dressed in robes and holding a staff, with its head tipped forward. The arms are crossed over the chest and there is something at its feet. Dated as post-medieval, it is possibly earlier in date. There is a similar figurine on the that was found in York (PAS Figurine Unique ID: YORYM-8A8468).

Recreation and gaming		
Clay Pipe	Clay Pipe	13
Figurine	Lead	1
Total of small finds		**15**

Textiles

A worked bone handle (4/402/9), lace bobbins (10/1022/20 and 8/829/31), a copper alloy needle (8/815/187) and small number of thimbles make up the post-medieval textile small finds. The worked bone handle is highly polished and has a spatulate end and shaft that narrows to a short square section which is snapped at the end. The handle is very light and may originate from a needlework, lacemaking/crochet type tool. The lace bobbins with their lathe-turned heads are probably from the latter end of the post-medieval period and could date well into the modern period. The thimbles include a cast copper alloy tailor's thimble (8/8224/701), which is open-ended with spiralling line of sub-square pits and an 'R' stamped on the bottom band, which is decorated with a dot and bar motif. This maker's mark could not be identified. The remaining thimbles – 8/804/173, 16/1636/41 and 14/1400/7 – are also copper alloy and are closed forms with domes and circular pits that spiral down from the dome to the base. A complete flat lead disc, with a square central perforation and moulded decoration in the form of three parallel lines with dots on one face, is possibly an incomplete cloth seal.

Textiles		
Cloth Seal	Lead	1
Handle	Bone	1
Lace Bobbin	Bone	1
	Bone/Antler	1
Needle	Cu Alloy	1
Thimble	Cu Alloy	4
Total of small finds		**9**

Weights and measures

A complete post-medieval copper alloy coin weight (8/US/372), weighing 3 g, depicts a seated figure holding a halberd in his left hand and an orb in his right; he is flanked on each side by two sets of four pillars. Above the pillars are triangles, all set within a narrow circular border. The reverse side of the weight has no visible motif. A similar coin weight was found during the Dive into Durham project (Infray, 2018).and identifies the figure as St Ladislas on one side, while on the reverse is a hand with initials of the user. The Durham example has been dated to the 16th century and was made in Antwerp; it is possible that the Berkeley coin weight also derives from Antwerp and is of a similar date range. The reverse side of the coin weight from Berkeley is very worn. It does not appear to have the stamp of the hand of Antwerp that the Durham weight has, although it is possible that the worn condition of the weight may explain this and x-raying the reverse side could possibly reveal traces of a stamp.

Weights and measures		
Coin Weight	Cu Alloy	1
Total of small finds		**1**

Arms and armour

Most of the small finds from this category are various types of musket ball and include impacted musket balls, burr shots (where the surfaces have been roughened), and pistol shot and hammered slugs, all of which are commonly found on Civil War sites. Diagnostic features such as sprues, mould lines and paring marks are visible on many of the musket balls, and the burr shots have numerous gouges removed from their surfaces. Deformation of musket balls occurred when they hit surfaces at high velocity. The resulting impacted musket balls may have flattened surfaces, and in some cases are almost completely flatted. Several powder flask caps or measures, usually flattened or distorted, were also found.

Arms and Armour		
Burr Shot	Lead	5
Hammered Slug	Lead	3
Impacted Musket Ball	Lead	18
Musket Ball	Lead	35
Pistol Shot	Lead	4
Powder Flask Cap or Measure	Lead	5
Total of small finds		**68**

Gardens

Vine eye keys (4/401/249) are likely to be of post-medieval date and consist of cast copper alloy keys, with a flat oval head with two perforations. Twine would be threaded through the eyes and this would have provided support for vines or other wall-climbing plants.

Gardens		
Vine Eye	Lead	8
Total of small finds		**8**

Undated Objects

Objects that could not be dated, a total of 477, were either too fragmentary or undiagnostic to accurately date, and in the absence of phase information they have been grouped together as undated. They are summarised in Table 22. Time does not allow for their further consideration.

Domestic and Household		
Cauldron rim	Cu Alloy	1
Cauldron Foot	Cu Alloy	1
Handle	Cu Alloy	1
Hook	Iron	1
Knife	Iron	5
Paring Knife	Iron	1
Pot Mend	Lead	2
Ring		2
Shears	Iron	1
Terminal Knop	Cu Alloy	1
Vessel	Cu Alloy	1
	Glass	1
Weight	Cu Alloy	1
	Lead	2
Domestic and Household Total		**21**

Dress fittings		
Bar Fitting	Cu Alloy	1
Bar Mount	Cu Alloy	1
Bead	Glass	1
	Worked bone	1
Buckle Frame	Iron	2
Buckle Plate	Cu Alloy	1
Hooked Tag		1
Pin		2
Square Mount	Cu Alloy	1
Dress fittings Total		**11**
Metalworking		
Flat Fragment	Cu Alloy	1
	Lead	2
Lump	Lead	2
Off-cut	Cu Alloy	4
	Lead	35
Prill	Lead	6
Sheet	Cu Alloy	1
Strip	Cu Alloy	1
	Lead	4
Waste	Lead	3
Metalworking Total		**59**
Miscellaneous		
Ball	Iron	1
Bar	Cu Alloy	1
Cap	Cu Alloy	1
Curved Fragment	Cu Alloy	2
	Iron	1
Curved Strip	Iron	5
Ferrule	Cu Alloy	3
	Iron	1
	Lead	1
Fitting	Cu Alloy	2
Flat Fragment	Cu Alloy	5
	Iron	2
	Lead	1
Folded Fragment	Lead	1
Fragments	Iron	45

Loop	Cu Alloy	1
	Iron	2
Miscellaneous	Cu Alloy	1
Ring		4
Sheet	Cu Alloy	4
Sheet Fragment	Cu Alloy	1
Strip	Cu Alloy	8
	Iron	1
	Lead	2
Strip Fragment	Cu Alloy	3
	Lead	1
Terminal	Cu Alloy	1
Unfinished Object	Cu Alloy	1
Unidentified Object	Cu Alloy	5
	Glass	1
	Iron	57
	Lead	3
	Worked bone	4
Wire	Cu Alloy	2
Miscellaneous Total		**174**
Personal Care		
Tweezers	Cu Alloy	1
Personal Care Total		1
Recreation and gaming		
Counter	Lead	1
Recreation and gaming Total		**1**
Tools and manufacturing		
Awl	Iron	2
Socket	Iron	1
Tools and manufacturing Total		**3**
Building and furniture fittings		
Bolt	Iron	1
Domed Mount	Cu Alloy	1
Fitting	Iron	1
Flashing	Lead	2
Hinge	Cu Alloy	1
Nail	Iron	159
Rivet	Cu Alloy	1

Rod	Iron	1
Sheet	Lead	1
Staple	Cu Alloy	1
Strip	Iron	1
Stud	Iron	1
Tack	Iron	1
Window Came	Lead	1
Window Glass	Glass	24
Building and furniture fittings Total		**197**
Harness fittings		
Mount	Lead	1
Harness fittings Total		**1**
Total number of undated small finds		**468**

Conclusion

The earliest dated small finds identified were from the Romano-British period and were limited to a small number of domestic, dress, personal and miscellaneous objects.

The group of small finds that are dated as early medieval includes an interesting aestel of 8th century date, likely related to the possible scriptorium thought to be located at the site. Several book mounts and clasps, as well as objects relating to gaming and textiles are also noted, but it is dress objects such as strap ends, pins, buckles and hooked tags that make up most of the small finds from this period.

The presence of Viking objects, such as the 10th century, kidney-ringed polyhedral-headed pin, suggest trading links via Bristol to Dublin where there was a known workshop for these pins. Other small finds of Viking origin have been recorded in the original small finds records, but unfortunately these objects were not present in the assemblage for cataloguing.

Overall, most of the recorded small finds could be attributed to the medieval period. They comprise an interesting range of objects associated with dress and harness adornment, as well as the more commonly found fixtures and fittings/household objects – such as knives and weights – that would have been found in the buildings at the site throughout this period. Most are everyday objects, but there are also high-status objects such as the harness mounts and buckles. These often have gilt and enamel decoration and would have belonged to individuals associated with the nobility. While many building and furniture fittings are undiagnostic, decorative window glass from the 13th century that would have been used in ecclesiastical buildings was present in or near Trench 8.

Finally, the post-medieval period brings a change in the style and quantity of dress accessories: buckles became more ornate and often more complex, and there was a move away from the elaborate and decorative harness mounts and fittings of the previous periods. This period saw Berkeley Castle being drawn into the Civil War, reflected in a moderate quantity of musket balls and powder flask caps.

Bibliography

BBC. 8thC Anglo Saxon aestle/page turner. Accessed at http://www.bbc.co.uk/ahistoryoftheworld/objects/S5fmL_qsTeqfOtOtZjLFIA

Burchill, R. 2006. Objects of Bone and Ivory. In: Jackson, R. (ed). *Excavations at St. James's Priory, Bristol.* Bristol and Regional Archaeological Services Monograph, 135–7. Oxford: Oxbow Books.

Crummy, N. 1983. Miscellaneous items of jewellery. In P. Crummy, *The Roman Small Finds from Excavations in Colchester 1971-1979.* Colchester Archaeological Report 2.

Crummy, N. 1988. *The post-Roman small finds from excavations in Colchester 1971-85*, Colchester Archaeological Report 5.

Crummy, N. 2001. Nail-cleaners: regionality at the edge of Empire. *Lucerna Roman Finds Group Newsletter 22*, 4, Figure 3b.

Egan, G. 2005. *Material Culture in London in an Age of Transition: Tudor and Stuart Period Finds c 1450 - c. 1700, From Excavations at Riverside Sites in Southwark.* London: Museum of London Archaeology Service.

Egan, G. 2010. *The medieval household: Daily living c. 1150–c. 1450.* London: Museum of London.

Egan, G. 2014. *Dice,* Finds Research Group 700–1700, Datasheet 1–24, Datasheet 23 [this sheet originally published in 1997].

Egan, G. and Pritchard, F. 1991. *Dress accessories c.1150 - c.1450: Medieval finds from excavations in London.* London: HMSO.

Ellis, M.A. and Egan, G. 2011. Spurs and spur fittings. In: Clark, J. *The medieval horse and its equipment, c.1150–c.1450,* 124–56. Woodbridge: Boydell Press in association with Museum of London.

Gibbons, M., Gibbons, M. and Higgons, J. 2005. Hiberno-Norse Ringed Pin from Omey Feichín, Connemara: Its Historical and Cultural Setting. *Journal of the Galway Archaeological and Historical Society* 57, 151–65.

Goodall, A. 1984. Non-Ferrous Metal Objects. In: Rogerson, A. and Dallas, C. (eds). *Excavations in Thetford 1948–9 and 1973–80,* EAA 22, Norfolk Museums Service NAU.

Griffiths, N. 2011. Harness pendants and associated fittings. In: Clark, J. *The medieval horse and its equipment, c.1150–c.1450.* Woodbridge: Boydell Press in association with Museum of London.

Griffiths, N. 2014. *Horse Harness Pendants.* Finds Research Group 700–1700, Datasheet 1–24, Datasheet 23.

Hinton, D.A. 1996. *The gold, silver, and other non-ferrous alloy objects from Hamwic, and the non-ferrous metalworking evidence.* Southampton Archaeology Monographs. Stroud: Alan Sutton, in association with Southampton City Council.

Howsam, C.L. 2016. *Book fastenings and furnishings: an archaeology of late medieval books.* PhD thesis, University of Sheffield.

Infray, Martha. 2018. Square Double Face Coin Weight Researched. Dive Into Durham. Accessed at http://www.diveintodurham.uk/case_studies.htm.

John Scures. Accessed at https://www.wikitree.com/wiki/Scures-2#Manor_of_Nately_Scures.

Mackreth, D. 2011. *Brooches in late Iron Age and Roman Britain.* Oxford: Oxbow Books.

Portable Antiquities Scheme (PAS). Eyelet Unique ID: SF-A13D23. Accessed at https://finds.org.uk/database/artefacts/record/id/435228.

Portable Antiquities Scheme (PAS). Figurine Unique ID: YORYM-8A8468. Accessed at https://finds.org.uk/database/artefacts/record/id/885180.

Portable Antiquities Scheme (PAS). Hunting object ID: NCL-B4B542. Accessed at https://finds.org.uk/database/artefacts/record/id/139261.

Portable Antiquities Scheme (PAS). Locking key Unique ID: PUBLIC-5F1FF7. Accessed at https://finds.org.uk/database/artefacts/record/id/801615.

Portable Antiquities Scheme (PAS). Pencil ID: NLM-76F3B7. Accessed at https://finds.org.uk/database/artefacts/record/id/732554.

Rogers, P.W., 2007. *Cloth and clothing in early Anglo-Saxon England, AD 450–700*, CBA research report. Council for British Archaeology, York.

Timby, J., 1998. *Excavations at Kingscote and Wycomb, Gloucestershire: a Roman estate centre and small town in the Cotswolds with notes on related settlements.* Cirencester: Cotswold Archaeological Trust.

Watkinson, D. and Neal, V. 1998. *United Kingdom Institute for Conservation of Historic and Artistic Works, Rescue (Trust), Museum of London, First aid for finds, 3rd ed.* RESCUE – The British Archaeological Trust; Archaeology Section of the UKIC; The Museum of London, Hertford.

Chapter 7

Tales from the animals: a preliminary account of the zooarchaeological assemblage from Berkeley Castle Project

Sarah Gosling

Introduction

The faunal assemblage at Berkeley was collected by students, volunteers, and University of Bristol staff over 14 years. An enormous assemblage of some 30,000 fragments was created, spanning multiple time periods and spread across several different areas within the site. It is hoped that this colossal assemblage will prove useful not only to the interpretation of the Berkeley site, but also for future studies and teaching at the University. This chapter presents a first assessment of the assemblage, so as strategies for further analysis can be planned. With the large size of the Berkeley assemblage in mind, the overarching objectives for assessment of the faunal remains were kept relatively broad. Recovery and initial analysis have been carried out with the following questions in mind: Which species are present? Which bone elements are present? What evidence is there for the human exploitation of each species? And what can evidence from the faunal remains infer about the diet and lifestyle of the populations occupying the site during the different time periods excavated?

Further questions relate to the comparison of areas and contexts (and therefore different periods in time). These include: Does the volume of faunal remains differ between areas/contexts? Are there differences in the identified species between areas/contexts? Does the exploitation of animals by people change between areas/contexts? Does the evidence from faunal remains infer any differences in diet or lifestyle between areas/contexts? Although the latter questions may yield some interesting information, they are not included in this report due to the preliminary character of this stage. They will be considered as analysis of the faunal assemblage continues.

Methodology

The faunal remains included in this report were collected by hand. All remains were immediately stored in plastic bags with the year, trench number and context sited on them. All faunal remains were then cleaned and stored over the winter months following each season. Student groups were employed to wash each bone fragment with tap water, using a small brush to dislodge remaining soil. The bones were then air-dried and stored in labelled, plastic bags within larger plastic boxes.

It is the intention to fully assess (and potentially analyse further) the faunal remains from the Berkeley site in the near future. In the meantime, a bone inventory has been compiled for randomly selected bags of remains to give an early idea of the species and bone elements present. The methods stated here have been used throughout the assessment so far and will be used as data collection continues.

Criteria for inclusion

The assemblage includes a wide range of fragment sizes, from whole bones to minute fragments (credit must be given to the students who had so meticulously collected and washed fragments that were mere millimetres in length). Though a count of all fragments present is being kept, only those that are identifiable as a specific bone element are recorded, thus allowing the NISP (number of identified specimens) to be calculated. Weights are not recorded as they are time consuming and potentially superfluous, especially since there is evidence to suggest a correlation between NISP and weight exists (Lyman 2008). Any skeletal remains which are not attributed to a specific context have been removed from the assessment.

Bone element identification

Terms for skeletal elements and anatomical features are standardised, according to Hillson (1999). Each fragment is examined for identifiable characteristics (articulating surfaces, bony prominences, etc.) and the following features have been noted: 1. Bone identification 2. Side (if possible) 3. Fragment location/description: proximal, distal or shaft for long bones; and specific location on the skull, pelvis, or vertebrae. In addition, long bone and rib fragments are grouped and recorded according to size (see species identification below). Teeth have been recorded according to their type (incisor, molar, etc.), but not to their specific position in the mouth. Initially, diagnostic zones for each fragment were also recorded, according to standards written by Dobney and Reilly (1988). Although there is a clear value in this method, it became apparent that it was too time consuming for a preliminary account with very broad objectives.

Species identification

Identification of bone and species is aided by a reference collection loaned from the School of Anatomy at the University of Bristol, as well as the author's personal collection. Standardised terminology for scientific names of species are taken from Baker and Worley (2019). Other reference books and atlases are also being used, including Prehn, Feneru and Rochester (2019), and Hillson (1999). Where a mammalian species is not identifiable, usually for elements such as ribs and long bone fragments, the bones are given broader identifications according to their size (Table 1). Bird and fish remains have been recorded, though an expert may be required to identify specific species and produce a more thorough investigation of the remains in the future.

TABLE 1: SIZE KEY FOR IDENTIFICATION OF MAMMALIAN RIBS AND LONG BONES

ID	Examples
MAMMAL 1	Cattle, horses, red deer
MAMMAL 2	Sheep, goats, pigs, fallow and roe deer, large dogs
MAMMAL 3	Smaller dogs, foxes, hares
MAMMAL 4	Rabbits
MAMMAL 5	Rat, mouse, shrew

Derived data recording

The sex of an animal has not been recorded and the age at death has been recorded only in a broad manner, with skeletal elements containing open growth plates being termed 'juvenile'. Tooth identification has been restricted to the type of tooth (*e.g.* molar) noted as opposed to the specific position of that tooth (*e.g.* upper 2nd molar). These features will be looked at in further detail should the need become apparent after initial assessment. Tooth wear is recorded on a scale of 0 (no wear) to 3 (high wear). Pathologies are recorded where present, as well as taphonomies such as gnaw marks and weathering.

Evidence of post-mortem use including burning, working of the bones by humans, and butchery marks have also been noted.

Quantification methods

The number of identified specimens (NISP) will be calculated for the entire assemblage, as well as for individual trenches and contexts. The minimum number of elements (MNE) will also be calculated for different contexts, once the full assemblage has been assessed. Ideally the minimum number of individuals (MNI) would be calculated using the zoning method, but as mentioned above, time constraints have not allowed zones to be recorded. Therefore, the traditional method of White (1953) will been used. As the data available at present is limited, and a calculation of the MNI across the entire site is not immediately useful, it has not yet been calculated. MNI calculations will be included in subsequent publications focusing on particular trenches and the contexts within them.

Preliminary Results and brief discussion

Preservation and recovery of remains

The soil surrounding Berkeley Castle varies considerably between layers, but the bone preservation throughout the site seems to be generally good and the faunal remains show little sign of damage due to PH or soil type. Extensive dry sieving of the spoil was carried out during excavation, as well as flotation methods applied later, though this material will be assessed separately to the rest of the faunal assemblage. As a result, the data published here and in subsequent reports may not be representative for some species including smaller birds, fish and mammals, nor for smaller bones of the large mammals. There is a broad range of species present in the collection, ranging from large equine long bones to tiny rodent mandibles. It is interesting that no articulated animal bone groups were discovered. This suggests there were no animal burials on site, but rather the remains were deposited after butchery or brought to the site by predators (discussed further below).

Species types

Table 2 details a full list of species identified across the Berkeley site so far, alongside the NISP for each. The NISP of mammalian bones identifiable only to size, as opposed to specific species, has also been included to provide further context for discussion of the results. In addition to the 1333 bone fragments identifiable to a species (or at least attributable to a size range), a further 837 fragments have been identified to bone element, but not species. These are described later in this report.

Although there are many bones still to identify, the data collected so far gives an emerging insight into the more prevalent species in the Berkeley castle area. The species list includes a variety of wild and domestic species, though none are particularly surprising given the site has been inhabited for centuries, as well as its geographical location near to the River Severn. Although cattle bones predominate, the simple fact that cattle are larger and thus are likely to produce a higher number of fragments than sheep suggests that there are a similar number of cattle and sheep remains present. Indeed, the rib and long bone fragments attributed to mammals of sheep size (mammal 2) are more numerous than those attributed to larger, cattle sized, mammals (mammal 1). Future calculations of the MNI for these species will provide further elucidation.

Within the cervid group, fallow, roe, and red species are all present, though roe appear in significantly higher numbers, accounting for over half the cervid remains so far identified. Whilst roe and red deer are native to Britain, it is thought that fallow deer were first introduced to Britain by the Romans, and then in greater numbers by the Normans (Sykes et al. 2006). It is therefore unsurprising that only a handful of fallow deer remains have been identified, and these are sited just above an ill-defined context containing small finds from Roman, Norman, and medieval periods.

The Aves group is made up mostly of chicken long bones, though smaller wild birds are present. One fragment, located in Trench 7, has been identified as a cormorant tibiotarsus.

The large numbers of pig bones may be misleading since many of these were in fact teeth. These were grouped within a small number of contexts, and may therefore have belonged to just a few individuals.

Although only a small number of equine bones have been identified, these are spread equally across trenches and time periods. By contrast, 12 of the 16 rabbit bones are attributed to the topsoil of Trench 7. The canine remains include 4 teeth and a mandible, likely from the same animal, from the topsoil of Trench 7. The remains of other species are in very small numbers, and discussion of these may need to wait until more data has been retrieved.

TABLE 2: SPECIES IDENTIFIED TO DATE ACROSS THE ENTIRE EXCAVATION SITE AT BERKELEY CASTLE, ALONGSIDE THEIR CURRENT NISP.

Species	**NISP**
Bos	219
Ovis/Capris	172
Cervid (fallow, roe and red)	110
Sus	108
Aves (wild and domestic species included)	37
Canis	13
Lepora	16
Equus	5
Fish	4
Oyster	2
Scuirus	2
Mammal 1 (likely cow and some red deer)	226
Mammal 2 (likely sheep)	277
Mammal 3 (mostly roe deer)	133
Mammal 4 (likely rabbit)	12
Mammal 5 (likely rat)	1
TOTAL	**1333**

Bone element identification

Table 3 gives the NISP for each bone element identified so far. The elements are ordered roughly in order of their abundance in the sample relative to their number in the average animal body. For example, there are 2 femurs in the body, approximately 26 ribs, and only 1 sacrum, thus one would expect to find more rib fragments than femurs, and more femurs than sacra. This does not, of course, account for the size of individual bone elements or the likelihood of them fracturing into smaller pieces, but it at least gives a clearer picture of the relative quantities of the elements shown.

The initial data has revealed some interesting results, though further data collection will provide more illumination on the efficacy of these findings. At present, almost half the humeri identified have been from sheep. This pattern is replicated for the scapulae and, to a lesser extent, the radii, suggesting that shoulder joints of mutton and lamb were popular throughout the site over a range of time periods. Bones of the hindlimb tell a different story, where cattle and sheep bones are equally dominant. Although the number of pelvis fragments is relatively low, those fragments identified are largely from the acetabular area. Coupled with the presence of sacral fragments, it might be suggested that the Berkeley inhabitants were also eating whole leg joints from both sheep and cattle.

Deer bones were present in relatively high numbers, and, although some of these were identified as fore- and hind-limb bone fragments, many were metapodials and phalanges. It is not yet clear what these results might represent. In addition, there are a relatively large number of mandibular fragments present, mostly from sheep but also cattle and pig.

The collection of teeth identified are largely from pigs, cattle and sheep. However, as mentioned above, the large number of pig teeth may be somewhat misleading since many seem to be grouped within contexts and may be attributed to individual animals. Premolars predominate in the data collected so far, though incisors, canines and molars are all also present.

TABLE 3: BONE ELEMENTS IDENTIFIED TO DATE ACROSS THE ENTIRE EXCAVATION SITE AT BERKELEY CASTLE, ALONGSIDE THEIR NISP.

Bone element	**NISP**
Mandible	35
Skull	50
Humerus	68
Tibia	64
Femur	38
Scapula	36
Radius	31
Rib	381
Pelvis	21
Metapodial	96
Ulna	19
Calcaneus	9
Sacrum	9
Astragalus	7
Horn/Antler/Horn core	13
Vertebrae	97
Phalanges	34
Fibula	2
(Other) tarsal and carpal bones	37
TOTAL	**1047**

Pathologies and demographics

There is a notable absence of pathologies present in the bones analysed so far, there being only 4 pathologies recorded: all cases of extensive wear noted on pig teeth which are likely to have come from the same animal. Tooth wear is lower in sheep teeth as well as most of the pig teeth, suggesting these species might have been younger when slaughtered, whilst cattle teeth are split evenly across all wear stages. This may be indicative of the use of older cattle for milk production or farm work before slaughtering them for food. By contrast, sheep long bones showed a range of fusion in their growth plates, with larger numbers exhibiting fused plates as opposed to unfused growth plates attributed to juveniles. In cattle long bones, the number with fused growth plates was double that of the unfused juveniles. Thus, it seems that both sheep and cattle are present here in younger and older ages. The majority of deer long bones have fused growth plates, suggesting they were older at their time of death and may therefore have been hunted.

Evidence of gnawing by carnivores and rodents can be found throughout the collection so far, though, as might be expected, the gnaw marks are restricted to marrow-containing long bones and vertebrae. Weathering occurs rarely and across a range of bone elements and species.

Evidence of human exploitation

Butchery marks have been observed on 92 of the bone fragments identified. These include a variety of bone elements, though the ribs exhibit the highest number. A range of different cut marks are present, including scraping, sawing, filleting and chopping (presumably with a cleaver to create some very neat, extensive cuts). The latter is found in abundance on bones which are likely to be cut through during the butchery process, such as the femur, pelvis and vertebrae. Burn marks were found on a smaller number of bones, and these are largely located in Trench 14. Unfortunately, the stratigraphic information for this trench is not yet available so no inferences can be made at present.

A remarkable find

During the 2019 excavation season, sieving of the spoil in Trench 8 revealed two epiphyses belonging to the tail vertebrae of a porpoise. These finds have been reported elsewhere but may provide important evidence to suggest aristocratic families from Berkeley were either consuming porpoise meat or trading in porpoise bone artifacts (Mendl and Wright 2019).

Some preliminary conclusions

Although not fully assessed, the data presented here gives an emerging picture of the people who lived at Berkeley Castle and the surrounding areas over the past centuries. The high number of meat-bearing skeletal elements, largely from animals bred or hunted for meat, suggests that meat was being consumed on site and that the faunal remains were deposited as kitchen waste. The populations inhabiting Berkeley were likely eating shoulder joints, largely form lamb and mutton, and leg joints from both sheep and cattle. Ribs were probably attached to the shoulder joints, though cut marks on these might suggest they were also cooked separately. The advanced ages of some cattle point towards a use beyond meat consumption, such as dairy production or farm labour. In addition to beef and lamb/ mutton, venison, chicken, and pork were consumed. It may be proposed that fish and oysters were also included in diets, but the evidence for this is not yet significant. The relative lack of non-meat-bearing elements implies that full butchery was not occurring on site, but that the meat was brought in from elsewhere. This may not be the case for venison since a large number of cervid metapodials have been identified in the assemblage.

Relating to the initial objectives, we can surmise on the types of species we might expect to find as assessment continues, as well as the bone elements that are appearing frequently. Some evidence has been reported which relates to the human exploitation of these species and we can therefore make some inferences as to the diet and lifestyle of the populations occupying the site. We are not yet, however, able to do any of this with absolute clarity, and it will be interesting to discover if the patterns seen here continue to exist as more data is added. Once complete, the data will certainly be suitable to address the initial objectives and, with additional contextual information, it is hoped that the further objectives detailed in the introduction will also be met.

Acknowledgements

The author wishes to thank Konstantinos Trimmis and Christianne Fernée for their invaluable help with data collection. The preliminary assessment of the zooarchaeological assemblage from BCP has been supported by the Department of Anthropology and Archaeology and the School of Arts at the University of Bristol.

References

Baker, P and Worley, F. 2019. *Animal bones and Archaeology: Recovery to archive.* Appendix 1. Historic England [Accessed online: https://historicengland.org.uk/images-books/publications/animal-bones-and-archaeology/].

Dobney, K. and Reilly, K. 1988. A method for recording information about mammal bones: The use of diagnostic zones. *Circaea* 5(2):79–96.

Hillson, S. 1999. *Mammal bones and teeth.* London: Institute of Archaeology, UCL.

Lyman, R.L. 2008. *Quantitative paleozoology.* New York: Cambridge University Press.

Mendl, E. and Write, G. 2019. *What is the purpose of porpoise? New Berkeley discoveries.* [Accessed online: http://bristoldigberkeley.blogspot.com/2019/05/what-is-purpose-of-porpoise-new.html].

Prehn, N., Feneru, F., and Rochester, J. 2020. *Beginner's guide to identifying British mammal bones.* Natural History Museum [Accessed online: https://www.nhm.ac.uk/content/dam/nhmwww/take-part/identify-nature/british-mammal-bones-ID-guide.pdf].

Sykes, N., White, J., Hayes, T., and Palmer, M. 2006. Tracking animals using strontium isotopes in teeth: The role of the fallow deer (Dama dama) in Roman Britain. *Antiquity* 80(310), 948-59.

Chapter 8

Tales from the People: Analysis of the Articulated Human Skeletal Remains from Berkeley Castle

Christianne L. Fernée

Introduction

Human skeletal remains were uncovered from two locations within the grounds of Berkeley Castle: the Jenner Garden and Nelme's Paddock. During the 2006–2007 field season, two adult female skeletons were uncovered against the south boundary wall of the Jenner Garden, in a flowerbed within the 19th century garden (Smisson 2007). These inhumations are thought to be early medieval, due to the cobbled surface uncovered and lack of grave goods, and linked to the nunnery – founded in 883 AD and demolished 1043 AD – whose chapel was located on the site where the burials were unearthed (Smisson 2007).

The majority of skeletons uncovered at the castle were excavated during the 2006–2010 field seasons within what is today called Nelme's Paddock. It is these individuals that will be the focus of this chapter. These remains were originally located within St Mary's graveyard, buried on top of the back-fill from an English Civil War defensive ditch constructed before the start of the siege of Berkeley Castle in 1645 (Witkin and Prior 2014, 1). Following this, they were cut by the western boundary wall of St Mary's churchyard. The bricks and copper slag capping used in the construction of the wall are indicative, based on historical documentation, of a mid-18th century construction (Norris 2008; Witkin and Prior 2014, 1). Consequently, the remains are likely to date to the latter half of the 17th/early 18th century. The remains of 36 articulated individuals were uncovered. These were accompanied by a number of disarticulated remains (Witkin and Prior 2014). However, the articulated remains will be the focus of this analysis (Table A.1).

Methodology

Preservation and completeness

Skeletal preservation was scored using McKinley (2004). This system scores abrasion and erosion on a scale of 0–5, with a clearly visible surface morphology graded 0 and a heavy eroded surface masking normal surface morphology graded as 5. The completeness of each individual was scored on a three-point scale: >75% (1), 25–75% (2) and <25% (3).

Demography

Age

The assessment of age at death in the adult skeletons was based upon degenerative changes of the auricular surface (Lovejoy *et al.* 1985; Meindl and Lovejoy 1989), pubic symphysis (Brooks and Suchey 1990; Todd 1921a; 1921b) and the sternal portion of the ribs (Iscan *et al.* 1984; 1985). Cranial suture closure (Meindl and Lovejoy 1985) was also included but only as part of a multifactorial approach due to its limited value when applied to archaeological assemblages (O'Connel 2004). In adults under the age of 30, epiphyseal fusion was also used (Scheafer *et al.* 2009). Individuals were placed into broad age categories for analysis: sub-Adult (<20 years), young adult (20–34 years), middle adult (35–49 years) and old adult (50+).

For sub-adults, age was estimated using dental development (AlQahtani *et al.* 2010); epiphyseal fusion (Scheafer *et al.* 2009); diaphyseal length of individuals aged between 2 and 12 years (Hoffman 1979; Hoppa 1992; Maresh, 1970); and perinatal diaphyseal length (Fazekas and Kósa 1978; Scheuer *et al.* 1980). Sub-adults were categorised into neonate (0 months), infant (1–12 months), young child (1–5 years), middle child (6–11), and old child (12–19) categories.

Sex

Despite extensive work having been undertaken on the determination of sex in juvenile remains (Molleson *et al.* 1998; Saunder 2000; Scheuer 2002; Schutkowski 1993) there are still no standards for sex estimations in this category (Brickley 2004). Therefore, sex was not estimated for the sub-adults in the sample. Dimorphism in the human skeleton emerges post-puberty. Pelvic differences become more pronounced, with female pelvic morphology adapted for childbirth, whereas the male cranium is more robust.

The sex of the adult skeletons was estimated using the morphological characteristics of the pelvis and cranium (Buikstra and Ubelaker 1994; Phenice 1969). Various studies have illustrated that the pelvis is most reliable for sex determination (Bytheway and Ross 2010; Duric *et al.* 2005; Ubelaker and Volk 2002; Walker 2005, 385). Although the pelvis offers greater accuracy, the skull is frequently used due to better preservation (Novotny *et al.* 1993; Walrath *et al.* 2004). The composite scores from the pelvis and the cranium were then placed into categories ranging from 1 to 5: male (M), probable male (M?), Undetermined sex (U), probable female (F?), and female (F). The individuals who were scored probable male/female were pooled with those scored as male/female.

Stature

Stature estimates were calculated for sexed adults using the formula for individuals devised by Trotter (1970). The stature estimates with the smallest degree of error were selected. These largely require measurements from the lower limbs. However, due to truncation of the skeletons, most estimates were calculated using upper limb measurements.

Pathology

Pathological lesions were recorded according to Roberts and Connel (2004), with reference to Aufderheide and Rodríguez-Martín (1998), Ortner (2003) and Roberts and Manchester (2010). The crude prevalence rate was calculated for pathological lesions, which is the number of individuals within a sample with a specific pathological lesion. This provides an overall average of those affected.

The dentition

The dentition was recorded using the system of Buikstra and Ubelaker (1994). Carious lesions, abscesses, and hypoplastic defects were recorded using Buikstra and Ubelaker (1994). The size of each calculus deposit was recorded using the system created by Brothwell (1981). However, over vigorous cleaning of the teeth has reduced the size of calculus deposits and therefore may result in an under-reporting of presence and size for this assemblage (Witkin and Prior 2014). Dental wear was recorded to aid dietary inferences, using Smith (1984) for incisors, canines and premolars, and Scott (1979) for molars as recommended by Buikstra and Ubelaker (1994).

Results

Preservation and completeness

Preservation and completeness were generally good/moderate for the majority of the skeletal material. Moderate preservation scores ranged between 2 and 4 (Table 1), with a median preservation score of 2. Of the 36 skeletons recorded, 8 (22%) were graded 1; 22 were graded 2 (62%); 3 (8%) were graded 3; and 3 (8%) were graded 4. The completeness of the individuals ranged from 1–3; however, the median completeness score was 3, <25%. A total of 2 (6%) skeletons were >75%; 11 (31%) were 25–75% complete; and 23 (63%) were <25% complete. The general poor completeness of the skeletal remains was largely due to the heavy intercutting of the graves and the truncation of graves by the church boundary wall (Witkin and Prior 2014).

Demography

The amount of retrievable information, both demographic and pathological, was impeded somewhat by the overall preservation of the remains and grave truncation. In a number of instances, only tentative assessments of sex (*e.g.* probable male or probable female) and/or age (*e.g.* broad age categories 'adult') could be suggested.

Of the 36 individuals, there were 24 adults (67%) and 12 subadults (33%). For adults, 18 (75%) individuals had the characteristics present for the estimation of sex. This comprised of 9 females and 9 males, a ratio of 1:1. For 6 (25%) individuals it was not possible to assign sex.

For the 12 subadults, the majority were estimated as below the age of 6 years (young child, infant and neonate) and none were estimated as being aged between 13–19 years (Fig. 1).

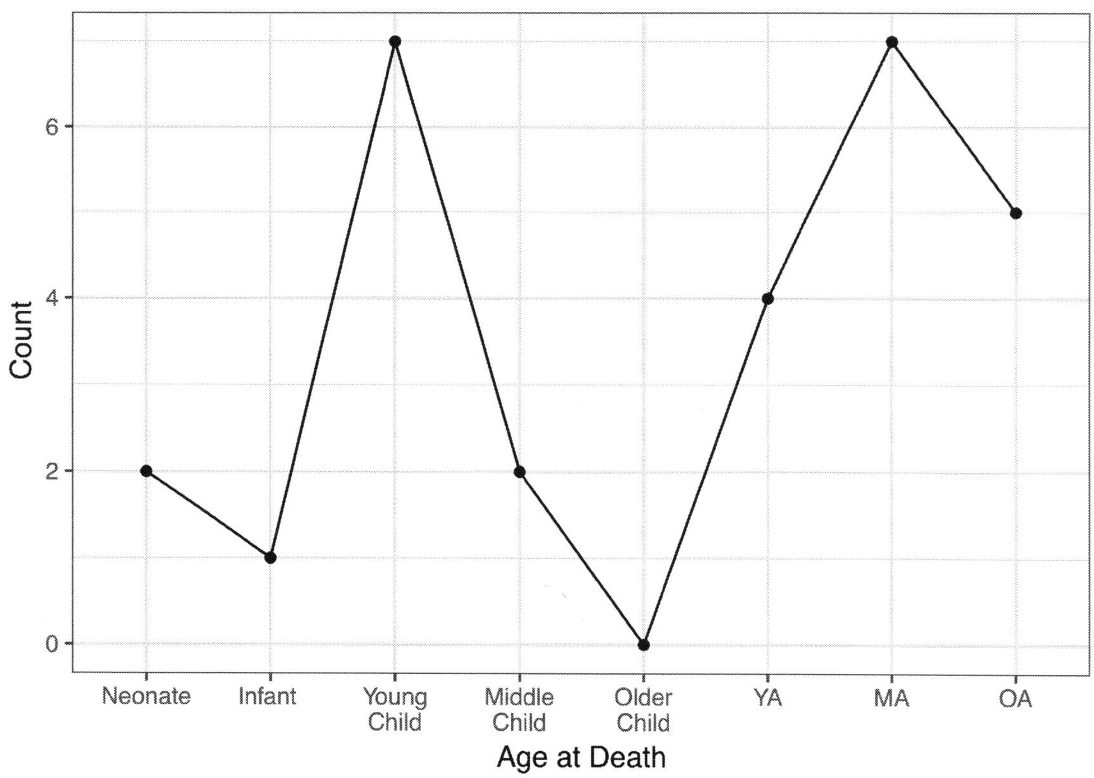

Figure 1. Distribution of aged individuals at Berkeley (n=28).

Adult age at death

Despite recent advances, the estimation of age in adult skeletal remains remains problematic (Ubelaker and Khosrowshahi 2019). Ageing adults becomes increasingly less accurate as the age increases, with particular issues with middle and old adults (Cox 2000, 75; Vodanović *et al.* 2011). Of the 24 adults, 16 individuals could be classified by age and ranged from 20 to 50+ years old. However, there was a greater proportion of middle and old adults, comprising 29% and 21% of the categorised adults, respectively (Fig. 1). A high proportion of adults could not be designated a specific age category, as the criteria necessary were either missing or damaged post-mortem, reflecting the poor preservation of individuals at the site.

The age distribution by sex differed: all old adults in the sample were estimated as male and a greater proportion of middle adults were estimated as female (Fig. 2). This may reflect a greater frequency of male old adults in this area of the cemetery. Alternatively, it may reflect, as suggested by some research, the development of more masculine cranial morphology in postmenopausal women (Walker 1995; Brickey 2004).

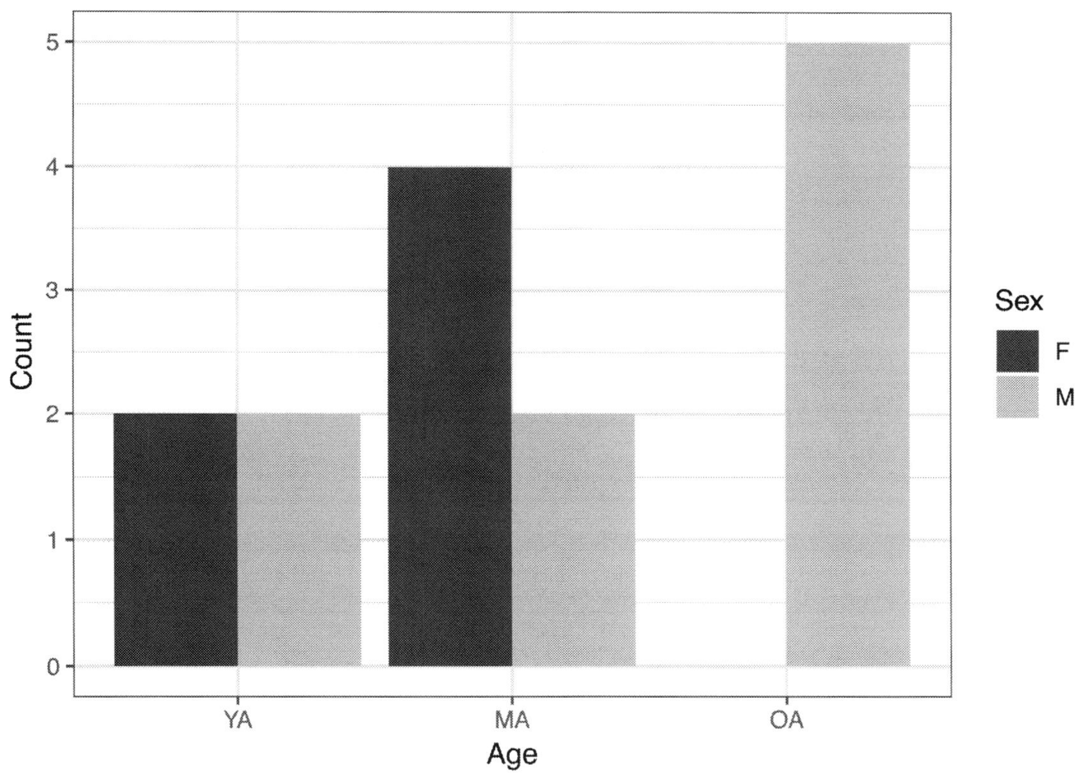

Figure 2. Age distribution of adult female (F) and male (M) individuals (n=15). Unsexed and general adult individuals not included.

Sub-adult age of death

There was one sub-adult that was categorised as infant (1–12 months). This may be an indication of problems prior to, during or just after birth (Bekvalac 2018). However, the majority of sub-adults (58%) were categorised as young children (1–6 years). Conversely, no sub-adults were categorised as older child/adolescent (Fig. 1).

Stature

Stature reflects both genetic predisposition and childhood periods of environmental and social stresses, such as childhood health and nutrition. Stature estimates can, therefore, give an insight into these factors. Stature estimates could be calculated for 11 individuals, comprising 3 females and 8 males (Fig. 3). The stature estimates for females ranged between 151 and 163 cm, with a mean of 157 cm. The stature estimates for males ranged between 156 and 179 cm, with a mean of 170 cm. Male estimates were mostly larger than female, with only a slight overlap in the ranges. However, the sample size is small.

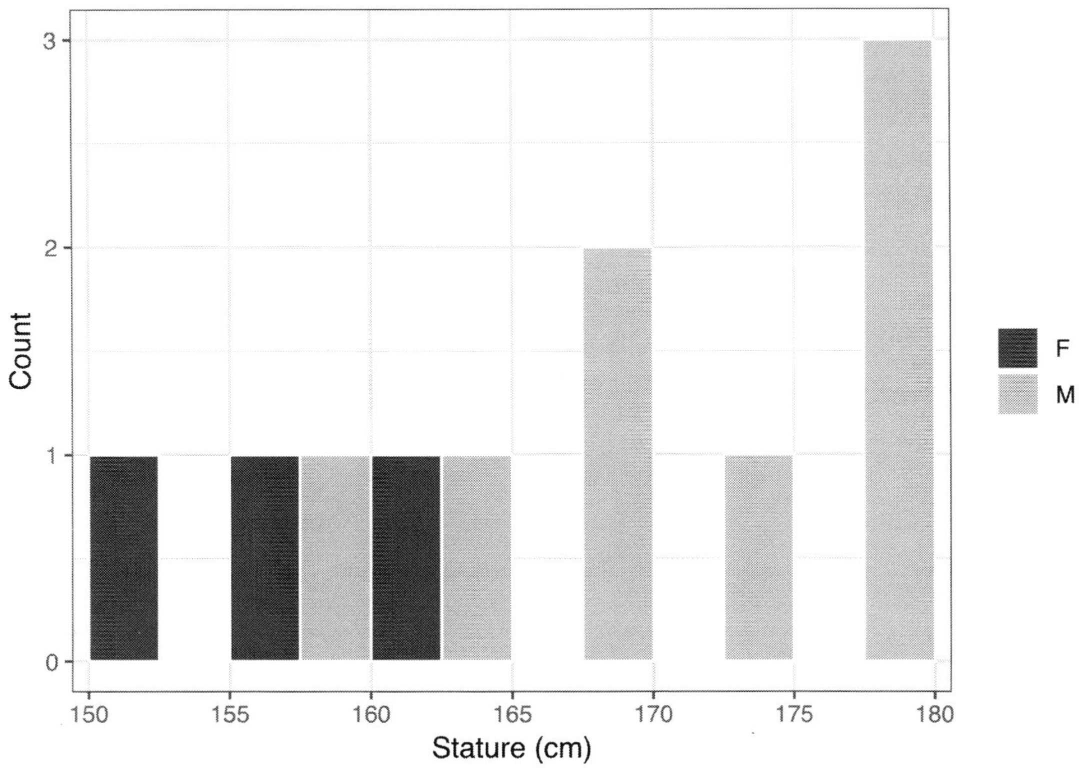

Figure 3 Stature estimate (cm) distribution for females (F) and males (M) at Berkeley.

Skeletal pathology

Twenty-four individuals showed some sort of skeletal pathological lesion: 20 (83%) adults and 4 (33%) sub-adults. Of the adult individuals, 7 (78%) were female, 9 (100%) were male and 4 (67%) unsexed.

Trauma

Skeletal trauma can give an insight into the lifestyle of an individual. For example, it can indicate their living environment, economy, occupation, material culture and availability of treatment (Roberts and Manchester 2010). Trauma can take a number of forms: for instance, accidental or purposeful fractures, such as skull deformation.

Fracture

Of all skeletal trauma, fractures are the most frequent form of trauma found in assemblages (Waldron 2009; Roberts and Manchester 2010). The crude prevalence of fractures in the sample was low. Fractures were found in 5.6% of individuals (2/36), both male old adults. SK 477 had a significant traumatic lesion to the left scapula and humerus. The healing of this fracture resulted in the ankylosis of the glenohumeral joint (Plate 1.A). This fracture was accompanied by an additional healed fracture of the distal left radius. It could not, however, be determined whether these fractures occurred at the same time. SK 462 had a colles fracture on the distal shaft of the right radius.

There was evidence of possible trauma observed in 2 further individuals. SK 498, an unsexed adult, had a possible fracture on the distal diaphysis of the right radius. Thickening of the bone here could be indicative of a healed fracture or may be due to a non-specific infection. Finally, ankylosis was observed in a distal interphalangeal joint of SK 469, a male old adult, which may be the result of a healed fracture. If these possible fractures were included this would be a fracture prevalence of 11.1% (4/36) overall and 33.3% (3/9) in males, with no fractures observed in females or subadults.

Osteochondritis Dissecans

Another frequently occurring condition found in skeletal material is osteochondritis dissecans. This involves the fragmentation and separation of part of a joint due to the death of bone tissue as a result of a lack of blood supply to the affected area (Roberts and Manchester 2010). The exact aetiology is unclear, but it is thought to result from trauma or repetitive microtrauma and is most commonly found in the knee of young males (Waldron 2009). One adult male, SK 494, had osteochondritis dissecans present on the proximal articular surface of the first right metatarsal. This represents 2.8% (1/36) of all individuals and 11.1% (1/9) of all adult males (Plate 1.B).

Congenital and developmental abnormalities

Developmental abnormalities can occur in soft tissue and the skeleton; their possible causes can be grouped into genetic, intrinsic and environmental factors (Roberts and Manchester 2010). No developmental skeletal abnormalities were observed in any of the individuals in the sample.

Degenerative diseases

Degenerative diseases are a group of diseases which involve gradual deterioration. The most common of these diseases are those affecting the joints (Roberts and Manchester 2010). Degenerative joint disease (DJD) is a progressive condition in which joint cartilage is lost and lesions subsequently form on the joint surfaces. The most common type of joint disease is osteoarthritis. Apart from dental disease, osteoarthritis is the most common condition seen in the skeleton (Waldron 2009; Roberts and Manchester 2010). New bone can be formed on the joint surface and its margins, alongside bone pitting, eburnation and joint morphology alteration (Roberts and Manchester 2010). Eburnation indicates cartilage destruction and consequential bone-on-bone contact, and is thought to be a clear indicator of osteoarthritis (Waldron and Rogers 1991). Therefore, if eburnation alone was present osteoarthritis was diagnosed. However, if eburnation was absent diagnosis was based on the presence of two of the following: osteophyte formation, surface pitting and alteration of the joint's normal morphology (Rogers and Manchester 2010). Degenerative changes can be found throughout the body and can be separated into the spine and the 'extra spine', meaning the rest of the body other than the spine.

Spinal Joint Disease

A total of 16 adult individuals had vertebrae present, of these 50% (8/16) had evidence of degenerative changes. This included, 2 females (40%, 2/5), 4 males (50% 4/8) and 2 unsexed (50% 2/4) individuals. Two of these individuals (12.5% 2/16), SK 462 and 485, also had evidence of osteoarthritic changes, one male and one female.

Schmorl's Nodes

Schmorl's nodes are lesions that result from the herniation of intervertebral disc. They present as depressions on the surface of the vertebral body (Schmorl and Junghans 1971; Pfirrman and Resnick 2001). Their exact aetiology is unknown; however, their cause is likely multifactorial. Their main contributing factors are likely genetics, developmental issues, specific disc composition and trauma (Burke 2012; Plomp *et al.* 2015). They have been found to be particularly common in those who impose great stresses on their lower spine (Waldron 2009). Eight individuals (50%, 8/16) had Schmorl's nodes present (Plate 1.C). This included 2 females (40%, 2/5), 4 males (50%, 4/8) and 2 unsexed (50%, 2/4) individuals. These were distributed predominantly over the thoracic vertebrae, a common pattern observed (see Schmorl and Junghans, 1971; Pfirrmann and Resnick, 2001).

Extra-spinal Joint Disease

A total of 5 adults (20.8%, 5/24) had osteoarthritic lesions present. This comprised of 2 females (22.2%, 2/9) and 3 males (33.3% 3/9). Osteoarthritic lesions were most prevalent on the hip joints, which was observed in SK 471, 485 and 494, 1 female and 2 males (Plate 1.D). This was followed by osteoarthritic lesions on the shoulder joint. These lesions were present in 2 individuals, SK 460 and 494, 1 female and 1 male.

Other degenerative changes were observed in 10 adults (41.6%, 10/24). This comprised of 2 females (22.2%, 2/9), 6 males (66.7%, 6/9) and 2 unsexed (22.2%, 2/9) individuals. These degenerative changes were observed most commonly in the femur (SK 460, 462, 469, 491) followed by the medial clavicle (SK 457, 470, 480).

Infectious disease

Most infectious diseases largely affect soft tissue; consequently, many show few signs on the skeleton. Therefore, the absence of lesions does not mean the absence of infection. Infectious diseases that affect the skeleton can be specific or non-specific. Specific infections are caused by agents that cause a particular disease. These include tuberculosis, syphilis, leprosy and polio (Waldron 2009). The skeletal lesions produced by these diseases have a specific distribution pattern across the skeleton, and the type of lesions produced makes it possible to differentiate between them (Ortner 2008, 192; Witkin and Prior 2014). Non-specific infections, such as periostitis and sinusitis, are those where the pathogen that causes the infection is unknown. They can result from trauma or infection and are commonly localised in their distribution.

Non-specific infection

The most commonly recorded non-specific infection is periostitis. This involves inflammation of the periosteum that covers the bone and can result in formation of new bone on the cortical surface. Periosteal new bone is found frequently in the skeleton, especially on the middle or distal tibia, as here the skin in thinner which increases risk of skin damage and low-grade infection (Waldron 2009). There can be many causes of this new bone formation; evidence has shown that periostitis may be formed by anything that breaks, stretches or even touches the periosteum (Weston 2008, 49). Periostitis may also be part of metabolic conditions such as rickets and specific infections such as syphilis (Ortner 2003, 208; Witkin and Prior 2014).

All the infectious lesions observed were non-specific. A total of 9 individuals (25%, 9/36), 8 adults (33.3%, 8/24) and 1 sub-adult (8.3%, 1/12), displayed these lesions. The most common type of non-specific infection was periostitis, present in 16.7% adults (4/24) and 8.3% older children (1/12). Of the adults, this comprised 1 (11.1%, 1/9) female and 3 (33.3%, 3/9) males. In adults, periostitis predominantly affected lower leg bones. This was healed in 2 individuals, SK 469 and 494 (Plate 2.A). In the sub-adult, SK 492, active periostitis was present on the ulna. None of these individuals, adult or sub-adults, had any other bony lesions that could be attributed to specific infections such as syphilis.

Rib lesions

New bone formation on the visceral surface of ribs is indicative of a pulmonary infection. It has been used to identify tuberculosis in an individual; however, it can also be linked to other pulmonary diseases such as bronchitis and pneumonia (Roberts *et al.* 1994, 180–181; Santos and Roberts 2006; Waldron 2009). Two adult individuals, SK 457 and 459, both unsexed adults, had active new bone formations on the pleural surface of a rib. This is a crude prevalence of 5.6% (2/36) in all individuals and 8.3% (2/24) in adults. This is indicative of a response to an inflammation such as some sort of chest infection.

Maxillary Sinusitis

Maxillary sinusitis can be caused by respiratory disease. It can be related to a range of factors related to both outdoor and indoor conditions. Outdoor factors include climate, weather, pollen, dust exposure, and smoke from fires and pollution. Indoor factors include dust mites, animals, damp housing and open fires (Roberts 2007). Fragmented crania, that allow the examination of sinus cavities, are required to detect maxillary sinusitis. Nine individuals had sinus cavities present, of which 8 could be examined. One adult, SK 464, (12.5%, 1/8) had a lesion present consistent with maxillary sinusitis.

Endocranial lesions

New bone formation on the endocranial surface has been linked to multiple diseases, such as meningitis and vascular malformation, and hematomas caused by trauma (Lewis 2004; Janovic *et al.* 2012; Sun *et al.* 2019). They are the result of tearing or inflammation of the meninges and resulting in new bone formation (Lewis 2004). One sub-adult (8.3% 1/12), SK 492, had endocranial lesions present in the form of fiberous bone on the occipital bone. In sub-adults these lesions have also been assocciated with mechanical trauma during childbirth (Isaac *et al.* 2018), as well as traumatic injuries (Coqueugniot *et al.* 2014; Kozakaitė *et al.* 2018; Sun *et al.* 2019).

Metabolic diseases

There are a number of diseases that interfere with the normal metabolism of the skeleton. Metabolic diseases cause disruption of normal bone formation, remodelling or mineralisation, or a combination of these (Mays 2007). These diseases can be an indication of stresses on the body.

Scurvy

Scurvy is caused by a deficiency in vitamin C. Humans are unable to synthesise or store vitamin C, therefore, it must be acquired through diet (Mays 2007; Brickley and Ives 2008; Ortner 2009). Prime sources of vitamin C can be found in fresh fruit and vegetables, and to a lesser extent fish and dairy. Breast milk also contains high levels of vitamin C, providing protection for breast-fed babies, whereas children who fed on cow's milk will have much lower levels (Brickley and Ives 2008; Lewis 2018).

Vitamin C is involved in the synthesis of collagen. A lack of vitamin C can produce weakness in bone and blood vessels, which can lead to haemorrhages that can provoke an osteological response (Mays 2007). Recognising scurvy in the skeleton is difficult as lesions tend to be fairly minor and non-specific (Mays 2007; Ortner 2009). They are, however, generally more prominent in sub-adults. Detailed descriptions of the distribution of lesions have been carried out by Ortner and colleagues (Ortner and Eriksen 1997; Ortner *et al.* 1999, 2001; Ortner 2003). These works describe increased bone porosity on the external surface of the cranial vault, orbits, the sphenoid greater wing, the palate, the mandible, the infra- and supraspinous fossae of the scapulae and the metaphyses of long bones (Mays 2007).

Three individuals had lesions consistent with scurvy: SK 472, 474 and 487. All these individuals were young children, aged between 1 and 6 years, which comprises 42.9% (3/7) of the age group and 8.3% (3/36) of all individuals. However, of the individuals with skeletal elements present that could be examined for scorbutic lesions – the mandible, maxilla, cranium and scapulae – all individuals in the age group had lesions. A corrected prevalence within the age group of 100% and of 60% (3/5) of sub-adult. SK 472 exhibited porosity on the left greater wing of the sphenoid (Plate 2.B). SK 487 exhibited porosity of the palate and on the right supra scapula fossa (Plate 2.C and 2.D).

Cribra Orbitalia

Cribra orbitalia are porous lesions on the superior wall of the orbit thought to be associated with similar lesions on the cranial vault known as porotic hyperstosis (Lewis 2018). It is generally thought as a sign of iron deficiency anaemia (Wapler *et al.* 2004). The most common cause of iron-deficiency anaemia is an inappropriate diet. If down to malnutrition, it is likely that the skeletal changes associated with anaemia will coexist with other changes due to rickets, scurvy, or other missing nutrients (Lewis 2018). However, there are other possible causes of iron-deficient anaemia including malaria, parasitic infection, folate deficiency and lead poisoning. It is also believed that individuals with these lesions are likely to have suffered from other nutritional deficiencies, and cribra orbitalia cannot be ascribed to a single cause (Walker *et al.* 2009). Cribra orbitalia is perhaps best viewed as a non-specific stress indicator (Witkin and Prior 2014).

Cribra Orbitalia was present in 3 individuals; of all individuals, this is a crude prevalence rate of 8.3% and a true prevalence rate, in those that had one or both obits present, of 30% (3/10). The 3 individuals comprised 2 Adults (SK 470 and 495) and 1 Young Child (SK 487). The two adults, a male and a female, had healed lesions, and the child had an active lesion. The child also displayed evidence of scurvy through active lesions.

Dental health

Dental health can be used as an indicator of general health in past populations. An individual's dental health is also very important to their overall health. Dental pathologies have been associated with systemic health problems such coronary heart disease (DeWitte and Bekvalac 2010).

Dental health of subadults

Of the 12 sub-adults, 3 had dentitions present (SK 472, 474, 487). All with dentitions had deciduous teeth only. A total of 52 teeth and 8 empty sockets were identified. All deciduous teeth present lacked pathological lesions.

Dental health of adults

A total of 149 permanent teeth were identified in the dentition of 13 adults, of which 12 had teeth present, with 72 maxillary and 77 mandibular. There was a high rate of post-mortem loss, with a total of 41 teeth lost. This was fairly evenly distributed between the maxillary 19 in the upper and 22 in the lower dentition. In addition to this there was one instance with a tooth still in its crypt. Evidence of dental diseases in the permanent dentition such as antemortem tooth loss, congenital anomalies, dental disease (*e.g.* carious lesions, calculus, abscesses and periodontal diseases), developmental defects (*e.g.* enamel hypoplasia) and unusual wear will be discussed.

Ante-mortem Tooth Loss

Teeth can be lost during the life of an individual for a number of reasons including caries, periodontal disease, abscesses and severe dental wear. In archaeological populations, high wear and caries rates can result in ante-mortem tooth loss (AMTL) in individuals at a young age (Nelson *et al.* 1999). Once the tooth is removed from the jaw, the alveolar bone, which is no longer supporting a tooth, remodels to remove the socket from the jaw as part of an age-progressive process (Nelson 2015).

A total of 10 individuals (41.6%) had a total of 55 teeth lost ante-mortem, 4 males (44.4%, 4/9), 5 females (55.6%) and 1 unsexed individual (16.7%, 1/6). There was a greater frequency of AMTL in middle adults followed by old adults, with AMTL in 1 young adult (25%, 1/4), 4 middle adults (57.1%, 4/7), 2 old adults (40%, 2/5) and 3 general adults (37.5%, 3/8). There was a greater frequency of ATML in the lower dentition, with 41 teeth lost in the lower dentition compared to 14 in the upper dentition, a prevalence of 74.5% and 25.5%, respectively.

Dental Anomalies

Dental congenital anomalies can occur throughout the dentition. Anomalies in tooth size, number, form and structure reflect the complex process under which teeth develop (Brook *et al.* 2009, 2014; Hughes and Townsend 2013). Anomalies in tooth number either involve the presence of additional (supernumerary teeth) or absence (hypodontia) of teeth. Hypodontia is the most frequent hereditary anomaly and is most prevalent in third molars (Brook *et al.* 2009, 2014).

Six teeth were observed as absent in 4 individuals, all of these were M3. Two individuals, SK 466 and 497, had two teeth absent, both the lower and upper third molars, respectively. These teeth may be congenitally absent or impacted but this could not be confirmed without the use of an x-ray. However, the absence of third molar teeth alone is consistent with the high prevalence of third molar congenital absence.

Caries

Caries is a disease process associated with the demineralisation of enamel by organic acids produced by bacteria that consume food particles in the mouth (Larsen 1997; Temple 2015). Some foods are especially cariogenic, including those with high levels of refined carbohydrates and sugars (Clarkson *et al.* 1987; Prowse *et al.* 2008; Rohnbogner and Lewis 2016). Caries formation is also dependent on an individuals' oral hygiene as well as differences in dental morphology, which affect the position and severity of carious lesions (Calcagno and Gibson 1991). Nevertheless, caries can give an insight into the diet and food processing behaviours of past populations (Kelley 1991; Meinl *et al.* 2010; Novak 2015).

A total of 7 individuals had 22 carious lesions on 22 teeth. The caries prevalence (number of carious teeth/total teeth present) was 14.8% (22/149). The prevalence in the upper dentition was greater, 19.4%

(14/72), than in the lower dentition, 10,4% (8/77). On an individual level, carious lesions were present on the teeth of 3 females (75% 3/4), 3 males (42.9% 3/7) and 1 unsexed (100% 1/1) individual.

Calculus

Dental plaque deposits form on the surfaces of teeth as a result of the accumulation of micro-organisms and extracellular material. Dental calculus is mineralised plaque which accumulates at the base of a living plaque deposit and is indicative of a long-standing accumulation of plaque (Hillson 1997, 2008). Calculus can be present above (supragingival) or below (subgingival) the gum line. Subgingival calculus occurs on the surfaces of the tooth root, at sites of periodontal disease (Hillson 2008).

Calculus deposits were present on 75 teeth from 10 individuals (83.3%, 10/12). Overall, calculus prevalence was 50.3% (75/149). The prevalence was 36.1% (26/72) in the upper dentition and 63.6% (49/77) in the lower dentition. Of individuals with one or more teeth present, calculus deposits were recorded on 4 females (100% 4/4), 5 males (71.4% 5/7) and 1 unsexed individual (100% 1/1).

Periodontal Disease

The periodontium is the supporting structure for teeth within the jaw which includes the gingivae and the alveolus. Periodontal disease results from this structure being attacked in an immune response to bacteria in dental plaque, during which inflammation causes the alveolar bone to remodel (Di Benedetto *et al.* 2013; Sima *et al.* 2014; Nelson 2015). If untreated it can lead to the destruction of the periodontium and the loss of teeth. In modern humans, periodontal infection is linked to a whole host of diseases, including diabetes, cancer and cardiovascular disease. It can, therefore, be used as an indicator of general health as well as dental health in past people (Kuo *et al.* 2008; DeWitte 2012; Nelson 2015).

Periodontal disease affected 7 individuals; of those individuals with maxillae and/or mandibles present this was a prevalence rate of 53.84% (7/13). Periodontal disease prevalence rate by sex was greatest in females, with a rate of 100% (5/5) in females, 14.3% (1/7) in males and 100% (1/1) of unsexed individuals. In individuals that could be aged, periodontal disease most prevalent in middle adults, with a prevalence rate of 33.3% (1/3) in young adults, 50% (2/4) in middle adults and 33.3% (1/3) in old adults. However, in general adults 100% (3/3) displayed evidence of periodontal disease.

Periapical Voids (Dental Abscesses)

Abscesses, or periapical voids, are infections that originate from bacteria entering the roots or cavities of teeth predisposed by heavy wear, caries or trauma. The subsequent immune response can result in puss traveling down the root, which then drains into the surrounding bone, then penetrates the alveolus, allowing the pus to escape (Nelson 2015).

Five external draining abscesses were recorded, 4 maxillary and 1 mandibular, in 4 adults. This is a prevalence rate of 30% (4/13). These individuals comprised 2 females (40%, 2/5) and 2 males (28.6%, 2/7). Of which 2 were middle adults (50%, 2/4), 1 was an old adult (33%, 1/3) and 1 a general adult (33%, 1/3). All of the individuals with abscesses, SK 464, 470, 485 and SK 495, had poor dental health. Their dentitions were also affected by dental caries, calculus, periodontal disease, ATML and enamel hypoplasia.

Enamel Hypoplasia

Enamel hypoplasias form during enamel secretion, during which insufficient formation of the enamel matrix leads to a reduction in enamel thickness (Guatelli-Steinberg 2015). A range of factors can disrupt enamel secretion and produce enamel hypoplasias, primarily associated with systemic physiological stress. These manifest as lines that record the period of stress, with a new line for each disturbance. Clinical studies indicate a link between hypoplasias and childhood infectious diseases (Sarnat and Schour 1941) as well as dietary deficiency (Sweeney *et al.* 1971; Goodman *et al.* 1991). The presence of enamel hypoplasia may indicate systemic physiological stress, but the exact nature of the stress that produced it is difficult to ascertain. However, the link between them and systemic stress makes them useful as a general indicator of physiological stress in childhood in past populations.

Hypoplastic defects were recorded on 48 teeth: 26 upper (59%) and 22 lower (41%) from 5 individuals. Of the individuals with some dentition present, this is a prevalence rate of 41.7% (5/12). By sex, this is a prevalence rate of 50% (2/4) of females and 57.1% (4/7) of males.

Dental Wear

The majority of dental wear was moderate. However, heavy dental wear was recorded in 5 individuals (41.7% 5/12) (SK 457, 460, 461, 470 and 485). These individuals comprised 1 female (25%, 1/4) and 4 males (57.1%, 4/7), of which 2 were middle adults (50%, 2/4), 1 was an old adult (33.3%, 1/3) and 1 was a general adult (50%, 1/2).

Discussion

The individuals excavated from Berkeley castle, although a relatively small sample size, offer an insight into late 17th century Berkeley. The individuals provide a palaeodemographic and pathological profile of individuals from a small window of time in post-medieval Britain which has generally been underreported osteologically. The following century was marked by rapid industrialisation and urbanisation, the effects of which have been evidenced by extensive osteological material from the 18th and 19th centuries (DeWitte *et al.* 2015; Lewis 2002; Mays *et al.* 2008; Newman *et al.* 2019; Western and Bekvalac 2019). The changes that these societies underwent make them unsuitable for direct comparison with the Berkeley material. Therefore, comparisons are limited by the sample size as well as lack of comparative material.

The available comparative material comprises three London cemetery sites: St Benet Sherehog (n=231) (WORD 2020) and St Boltoph Billingsgate (n=69) (Bekvalac 2018), cemeteries both destroyed in 1666 by the Great Fire of London; and Broadgate or 'New Churchyard' cemetery (n=682), which was founded in 1569 and in use until 1714 (Hartle *et al.* 2018). The burial profile of these cemeteries varies. Opened to relieve congestion in existing churchyards, New Churchyard became a burial place for poorer individuals (Harding 2002Sherehog was used for both the wealthy and the poor (WORD 2020). Finally, osteological evidence suggests that St Boltoph was used for middle to high status individuals (Bekvalac 2018,406).

The mortality profile of the Berkeley individuals is largely consistent with contemporaneous sites (Bekvalac 2018; Hartle *et al.* 2018; WORD 2020). The individuals fall within all age and both sex categories, apart from old child/adolescent. However, this absence is not consistent with contemporaneous sites, such as St Benet Sherehog, St Boltoph and New Churchyard, in which adolescents comprise between 2.9% and 7.8% of the sample (Bekvalac 2018; Hartle *et al.* 2018; WORD 2020). In fact, at New Churchyard adolescent individuals comprised the highest proportion of the sub-adult sample. This percentage was attributed to a high proportion of vulnerable and poor interred at New Churchyard, including migrants from rural areas that lacked immunity to common urban infections (Hartle *et al.* 2018). The absence of adolescents in the Berkeley sample may reflect higher survival rates in adolescence/young adulthood in rural sites or may be the result of the small sample size.

The majority of sub-adults at Berkeley fell within the 1 – 5 years old category, comprising 58.3% of subadults and 19.4% of the whole sample. This peak in the subadult mortality profile is also seen at the sites of St Benet Sherehog and St Boltoph. This age category covers the age at which weaning would take place and is a vulnerable period in which mortality rates increase (Bekvalac 2018). Children under the age of 5 have been highlighted as being more susceptible to stresses within the societal environment. They are also an indicator of the population's health and its ability to fight disease in adulthood (Goodman and Armelagos 1989; Lewis 2007). In 1662, John Graunt approximated that in London, during non-plague years, 36% of children died under the age of 6 years, and that urban deaths exceeded rural ones (Graunt 1662; Lewis 2007). Infant mortality figures for many past populations are uncertain, but in sixteenth-century England it was estimated that around 27% of children died before the age of 1 year (Orme 2001; Lewis 2007).

The possible impact of weaning is also highlighted by the high incidence of scurvy within the sample. Three young children, aged between 1.5 and 2 years, displayed lesions consistent with scurvy. This represented a crude prevalence of 42.9% of the age category and 25% of subadults, and a true prevalence of 100% and 60%. This prevalence rate is higher than those observed at contemporaneous sites. At St Benet Sherehog, scurvy was present in 2.4% of individuals and 17.2% of subadults (WORD 2020). The prevalence rate was even lower at New Churchyard, a crude prevalence of 0.9% of individuals and 3.4% of subadults (Hartle *et al.* 2018). Finally, bone changes associated with scurvy were not observed in any individuals at St Boltoph (Bekvalac 2018). This absence at St Boltoph may be due the higher socio-economic status of the individuals at this site compared to at St Benet Sherehog and New Churchyard.

Scurvy is caused by inadequate nutritional intake of vitamin C. Vitamin C is available from a wide range of fresh fruit and vegetables, and to a lesser extent from milk, meat and fish (Brickley and Ives 2008; Fain, 2005). However, the processing of food resources, particularly heating, can affect the availability of vitamin C in food products. In the absence of vitamin C, symptoms of scurvy can become apparent as early as 29 days after its last consumption (Brickley and Ives 2008; Pimentel, 2003). However, scurvy can be remedied or avoided by including foods rich in vitamin C into an individual's diet. The introduction of the potato, which is rich in vitamin C, in the 17th century was particularly important for the post-medieval working class of Britain. Its introduction coincided with a decline in deaths attributed to scurvy in the London Bills of Mortality by the 1720s (Roberts and Cox 2003).

Another rich source of vitamin C is human milk. Human milk produced by a nutritionally healthy mother will provide an infant with an adequate amount of vitamin C. However, its withdrawal and replacement with an inadequate diet, during weaning, will result in its deficiency. The similar age of Berkeley sub-adults that displayed signs of scurvy may reflect a similar age of weaning and the replacement of a nutritionally unsuitable diet. The inadequacy of the replacement diet may be connected to dietary seasonality, with vitamin C rich foods such as turnips becoming scarce at the end of winter (Witkin and Prior 2014).

The consequences of these individuals being low in vitamin C are linked to its numerous important roles. It has been linked to blood formation and the metabolism of iron (Cheung *et al.* 2003; Pangan and Robinson 2001), and consequently individuals with a vitamin C deficiency are more likely to develop anaemia (Brickley and Ives 2008). Evidence of this was found in one young child from Berkeley, SK 487, who displayed active cribra orbitalia, lesions associated with anaemia, alongside scurvy. Vitamin C also plays an important role in maintaining immune function; individuals deficient in vitamin C are more prone to infection with impaired rates of recovery (Brickley and Ives 2008; Jacob and Sotoudeh 2002). It is likely that this susceptibility infection, not the deficiency itself, caused the death of these subadults from Berkeley.

Inferences can also be made regarding other environmental and dietary factors that played a role in the lives of the individuals excavated from Berkeley by considering features such as stature and non-specific stress indicators such as cribra orbitalia and enamel hypoplasia. Variation in stature can reflect genetic and nutritional factors. Specifically, disease, poor diet, inefficient absorption of nutrients and a weakened immune system have all been associated with adult height (Hartle *et al.* 2018). The mean stature of both females and males excavated at Berkeley falls within the range of contemporaneous sites (Bekvalac 2018; Hayes *et al.* 2018; WORD 2020), with mean female and male measurements most similar to the site of St Boltoph (Table 1).

Sex	Berkeley	St Benet Sherehog	St Boltoph	New Churchyard
Female	157 (151.0-163.0)	160.2 (155.7-165.2)	155.3 (152-155.5)	160.9 (145.7-171.8)
Male	170 (156.0-179.0)	169.4 (158.8-177.1)	175 (168.5-182.3)	169.1 (155.9-184.2)

Other pathological indicators of stress, nutritional or otherwise, include cribra orbitalia and enamel hypoplasia. Cribia orbitalia is thought to be a sign of iron deficient anaemia, which is often attributed to an inappropriate diet, but can also result from a number of other deficiencies. A total of 3 individuals from Berkeley had cribra orbitalia present (8.3% crude prevalence/30% true prevalence). As mentioned previously, one of these individuals, SK 487, a sub-adult, also exhibited signs of scurvy. The coexistence of these pathologies is indicative of malnutrition in this sub-adult. However, the remaining two individuals, 2 adults, did not exhibit signs of any other metabolic diseases. Therefore, the cause of their lesions could not be attributed to malnutrition alone. The prevalence rate of cribra orbitalia at Berkeley was similar to that found at St Boltoph, which had a crude prevalence of 8.7% (Bekvalac 2018). However, it was lower than the prevalence observed at New Churchyard, where cribra orbitalia had a crude prevalence of 14.5%.

Enamel Hypoplasias are primarily associated with systemic physiological stress, such as childhood disease and nutritional deficiency. A compromised immune system during dental development is a key cause of enamel hypoplasia (Hillson 2014, 190–1). At Berkeley, there were 5 individuals with hypoplastic bands present on one or more teeth. Two of these individuals, SK 470 and SK 495, also had healed cribra orbitalia. Several factors, such as impaired health status, growth demands and diet, have been found to influence the development of enamel hypoplasia and cribra orbitalia in a particular population (Obertová and Thurzo 2008). Any of these could be the cause of their coexistence in these two individuals. The prevalence rate of enamel hypoplasia was considerably lower than that observed at other contemporaneous sites (Bekvalac 2018; Hartle *et al.* 2018; WORD 2020). This may reflect differences in the number of non-specific stressors between urban and rural sites, with less occurring at rural Berkeley. However, it may be the result of the small sample size.

A further insight into the diet and health of individuals at Berkeley can be obtained from their dental health. During the 16th and 17th centuries dental hygiene was rarely practiced in Britain (Hartle *et al.* 2018). This coincided with the increasing availability of sugar in the 17th century. As a consequence, the post-medieval period saw an increase in the prevalence of dental pathologies such as caries, AMTL, dental abscesses and calculus compared to earlier periods. The dental health profile of the individuals at Berkeley is typical of individuals transitioning from late medieval to post-medieval periods.

The prevalence rate of caries at Berkeley, 19.4%, was lower than contemporaneous sites, with the prevalence of caries at New Churchyard being considerably higher (56.4%). A similar pattern is observed in prevalence rates of AMTL, dental abscesses and calculus. This pattern may suggest a greater consumption of sugar and other cariogenic foods at London sites. However, it appears that the individuals at Berkeley were consuming a diet that included cariogenic foods, such as starchy carbohydrates like bread and potatoes.

Information regarding the lifestyle of the individuals at Berkeley may be gleaned from specific pathological lesions, such as osteoarthritis. There was a crude prevalence of osteoarthritis of 20.8% in adults, which was higher than that observed at contemporaneous sites such as St Boltoph (10.3%, 6/58) and New Churchyard (16.9%, 85/503). At Berkeley, there was a greater prevalence of osteoarthritis in males and at the hip joint. It is possible that this distribution pattern of osteoarthritis may be activity related. Various epidemiological studies have supported the link between farming and osteoarthritis of the hip (Croft *et al.* 1992; Sulsky *et al.* 2012; Thelin and Holmberg 2007; Walker-Bone and Palmer 2002). This is a possibility at Berkeley due to its rural location and its higher prevalence in males. However, osteoarthritis is multifactorial in origin and cannot be conclusively linked to specific activities. In addition to this, differences between sexes may often be a consequence of hormones, body size and anatomy, rather than activity related (Weiss and Jurmain 2007). However, research has indicated that osteoarthritis can be more likely to develop is some populations, particularly those where biomechanical stresses on joints are high and begin early in life (Weiss and Jurmain 2007).

Conclusions

At Berkeley, the small sample size means that generalisations about the population are not possible. However, insights can be gained into the lives of the individuals uncovered. These individuals appear to have had an active lifestyle which included less stressors than those experienced by individuals in urban London. Their diet likely comprised of starchy foods such as bread and potatoes, which in some cases did not provide sufficient nutrition and caused problems for children of weaning age.

Skeleton Number	Age Category	Sex	Pathology
454	Middle Adult	Probable Female	No visible pathology
454	Young Child	Subadult	No visible pathology
455	Adult	Unsexed	No visible pathology
457	Adult	Unsexed	Vertebral Pathology, Extraspinal Joint Disease, Infection and Dental Pathology**
458	Young Adult	Probable Male	Vertebral Pathology, Extraspinal Joint Disease Infection and Dental Pathology
459	Adult	Unsexed	Infection and Dental Pathology*
460	Middle Adult	Probable Female	Vertebral Pathology, Extra Spinal Joint Disease and Dental Pathology*
461	Middle Adult	Male	Extraspinal Joint Disease and Dental Pathology*
462	Old Adult	Male	Trauma, Vertebral Pathology, Extra Spinal Joint Disease and Dental Pathology*
463	Adult	Probable Female	Vertebral Pathology and Dental Pathology
464	Adult	Probable Female	Vertebral Pathology, Infection and Dental Pathology*
466	Young Adult	Female	Vertebral Pathology, Infection and Dental Pathology*
469	Old Adult	Male	Extraspinal Joint Disease, Vertebral Pathology and Infection*
470	Middle Adult	Male	Extraspinal Joint Disease, Vertebral Pathology, Healed Cribra Orbitalia and Dental Pathology
471	Middle Adult	Probable Female	Extraspinal Joint Disease*
472	Young Child	Subadult	Scurvy**
474	Young Child	Subadult	Scurvy*
476	Young Adult	Female	No visible pathology
477	Old Adult	Probable Male	Trauma and Dental Pathology**
479	Young Child	Subadult	No visible pathology
480	Middle Adult	Unsexed	Vertebral Pathology and Extraspinal Joint Disease*
482	Young Child	Subadult	No visible pathology

Skeleton Number	Age Category	Sex	Pathology
483	Young Child	Subadult	No visible pathology
485	Old Adult	Male	Vertebral Pathology, Extra Spinal Joint Disease and Dental Pathology*
487	Young Child	Subadult	Scurvy**
490	Older Child	Subadult	No visible pathology
491	Adult	Female	Extraspinal Joint Disease*
492	Older Child	Subadult	Infection*
493	Adult	Unsexed	No visible pathology
494	Old Adult	Male	Trauma, Extra Spinal Joint Disease and Infection**
495	Middle Adult	Female	Healed Cribra Orbitalia and Dental Pathology*
496	Infant	Subadult	No visible pathology
497	Young Adult	Male	Vertebral Pathology and Dental Pathology*
498	Adult	Unsexed	Trauma and Infection*
499	Neonate	Subadult	No visible pathology
500	Neonate	Subadult	No visible pathology

References

AlQahtani, S.J., Hector, M.P. and Liversidge, H.M. 2010. Brief communication: The London atlas of human tooth development and eruption. *American Journal of Physical Anthropology* 142, 481–90.

Aufderheide, A.C. and Rodríguez-Martín, C. 1998. *The Cambridge encyclopaedia of human paleopathology.* Cambridge: Cambridge University Press.

Bekvalac, J. 2018. Analysis of the human skeletal remains from St Botolph Billingsgate. In: Schofield, J., Blackmore, L., Pearce, J. and Dyson, T. (eds.) *London's Waterfront 1100-1666: excavations in Thames Street, London, 1974-84,* 386–407. Oxford: Archaeopress.

Brickley, M. 2004. Determination of sex from archaeological skeletal material and assessment of parturition. In: Brickley, M. and McKinley, J.I. (eds.) *Guidelines to the Standards for Recording Human Remains.* IFA Paper No 7, *23*–5. Reading: British Association for Biological Anthropology and Osteoarchaeology (BABAO).

Brickley, M. and Ives, R. 2008. *The Bioarchaeology of Metabolic Bone Disease.* London: Elsevier.

Brook, A.H., Griffin, R.C., Smith, R.N., Townsend, G.C., Kaur, G., Davis, G.R., and Fearne, J. 2009. Tooth size patterns in patients with hypodontia and supernumerary teeth. *Archives of Oral Biology* 54(S1), S63–S70.

Brook, A.H., Jernvall, J., Smith, R.N., Hughes, T.E., and Townsend, G.C. 2014. The dentition: The outcomes of morphogenesis leading to variations of tooth number, size and shape. *Australian Dental Journal* 59(S1), 131–142.

Brooks, S. and Suchey, J.M. 1990. Skeletal age determination based on the os pubis: a comparison of the AcsádieNemeskéri and Suchey-Brooks methods. *Human Evolution* 5, 227–238.

Brothwell, D. 1981. *Digging up Bones.* 3rd ed. New York: Cornell University Press.

Brothwell, D. and Zakrzewski, S.R. 2004. Metric and non-metric studies of archaeological human bone. In: Brickley, M. and McKinley, J.I. (eds.) *Guidelines to the Standards for Recording Human Remains.* IFA Paper No 7, 27–33. Reading: BABAO.

Bytheway, J.A. and Ross, A.H. 2010. A geometric morphometric approach to sex determination of the human adult Os Coxa. *Journal of Forensic Science* 55, 859–64.

Buikstra, J.E. and Ubelaker, D.H. 1994. *Standards for data collection from Human skeletal remains.* Fayetteville: Arkansas Archaeological Survey.

Burke, K.L. 2012. Schmorl's nodes in an American military population: frequency, formation, and etiology. *Journal of Forensic Science* 57, 571–7.

Calcagno, J.M. and Gibson, K.R. 1991. Selective Compromise: Evolutionary Trends. *Advances in Dental Anthropology* Jan 23, 59.

Cheung, E., Mutahar, R., Assefa, F., Ververs, M., Nasiri, S.M., Borrel, A. and Salama, P. 2003. An epidemic of scurvy in Afghanistan: Assessment and response. *Food and Nutrition Bulletin* 24, 247–55.

Clarkson, B.H., Krell, D., Wefel, J.S., Crall, J. and Feagin, F.F. 1987. In vitro caries-like lesion production by Streptococcus mutans and Actinomyces viscosus using sucrose and starch. *Journal of Dental Research* 66(3), 795–8.

Coqueugniot, H., Dutour, O., Arensburg, B., Duday, H., Vandermeersch, B. and Tillier, A. 2014. Earliest Cranio-Encephalic Trauma from the Levantine Middle Palaeolithic: 3D Reappraisal of the Qafzeh 11 Skull, Consequences of Pediatric Brain Damage on Individual Life Condition and Social Care. *PLoS ONE*

9(7), e102822.Cox, M. 2000. Ageing adults from the skeleton. In: Cox, M. and Mays, S. (eds.) *Human Osteology in Archaeology and Forensic Science*, 61–81. London: Greenwich Medical Media.,

Croft, P., Coggon, D., Cruddas, M. and Cooper, C. 1992. Osteoarthritis of the hip: an occupational disease in farmers. *British Medical Journal* 304, 1269–72.

Di Benedetto, A., Gigante, I., Colucci, S. and Grano, M. 2013. Periodontal Disease: Linking the Primary Inflammation to Bone Loss. *Clinical and Developmental Immunology,* 503754. https://doi.org/10.1155/2013/503754.

DeWitte, S.N. 2012. Sex Differences in Periodontal Disease in Catastrophic and Attritional Assemblages from Medieval London. *American Journal of Physical Anthropology* 149, 405–16.

DeWitte, S.N. and Bekvalac, J. 2010. Oral health and frailty in the medieval English cemetery of St Mary Graces. *American Journal of Physical Anthropology* 142(3), 341–54.

Dewitte, S.N., Hughes-Morey, G., Bekvalac, J. and Karsten, J. 2015. Wealth, health and frailty in industrial-era London. *Annals of Human Biology*. 43(3), 241–54.

Duric, M., Rakoceyic, Z., Donic, D., Durić, M., Rakočević, Z. and Donić, D. 2005. The reliability of sex determination if skeletons from forensic context in the Balkans. *Forensic Science International* 147, 159–64.

Fain, O. 2005. Musculoskeletal manifestations of scurvy. *Joint Bone Spine* 72, 124–128.

Fazecas, I.G. and Kósa, F. 1978. *Forensic fetal osteology*. Budapest: Akadémiai Kiadó.

Goodman, A.H. and Armelagos, G.J. 1989. Infant and childhood morbidity and mortality risks in archaeological populations. *World Archaeology* 21, 225–43.

Goodman, A.H., Martinez, C. and Chavez, A. 1991. Nutritional Supplementation and the Development of Linear Enamel Hypoplasias in Children from Tezonteopan, Mexico. *American Journal of Clinical Nutrition* 53, 773–81.

Graunt, J. 1662. *Natural and Political Observations*. London: T. Roycroft.

Guatelli-Steinberg, D. 2015. Dental Stress Indicators from Micro- to Macroscopic. In: Irish, J.D. and Scott, G.R. (eds.) *A Companion to Dental Anthropology, 450-64.* Chichester: John Whiley and Sons.

Harding, V. 2002. *The Dead and the Living in Paris and London, 1500-1670*. Cambridge: Cambridge University Press.

Hayle, R., Carty, N., Henderson, M., Knox, E. and Walker, D. 2017. *The New Churchyard: From Moorfields Marsh to Bethlem Burial Ground, Brokers Row and Liverpool Street*. London: MOLA.

Hillson, S.W. 1997. *Dental Anthropology*. Cambridge: Cambridge University Press.

Hillson, S.W. 2008. Dental Pathology. In: Katzenberg, M.A. and Saunders, S.R. (eds.) *Biological Anthropology of the Human Skeleton* (2nd Ed), 301-*40.* Hoboken: John Wiley and Sons,.

Hillson, S.W. 2014. *Tooth Development in Human Evolution and Bioarchaeology*. Cambridge: Cambridge University Press.

Hoffman, J.M. 1979. Age estimations from diaphyseal lengths: two months to twelve years. *Journal of Forensic Sciences* 24, 461–469.

Hoppa, R.D. 1992. Evaluating human growth: an Anglo-Saxon example. *International Journal of Osteoarchaeology* 2, 275–88.

Hughes, T.E., and Townsend, G.C. 2013. Twin and family studies of human dental crown morphology: genetic, epigenetic and environmental determinants of modern human dentition. In: Scott, G.R. and

Irish, J.D. (eds.) *Anthropological Perspectives on Tooth Morphology: Genetics, Evolution and Variation*, 31-68. Cambridge: Cambridge University Press.

Isaac, C.V., Cornelison, J.B., Castellani, R.J. and de Jong, J.L. 2018. A Unique Type of Birth Trauma Mistaken for Abuse. *Journal of Forensic Science* 63, 602–7.

Iscan, M.Y., Loth, S.R. and Wright, R.K. 1984. Age estimation from the rib by phase analysis: white males. *Journal of Forensic Sciences* 29, 1094–104.

Iscan, M.Y., Loth, S.R. and Wright, R.K. 1985. Age estimation from the rib by phase analysis: white females, *Journal of Forensic Sciences* 30, 853–63.

Jacob, R.A. and Sotoudeh, G. 2002. Vitamin C function and status in chronic disease. *Nutrition in Clinical Care* 5, 66–74.

Janovic, A., Milovanovic, P., Sopta, J., Rakocevic, Z., Filipovic, V., Nenezic, D. and Djuric, M. 2012. Intracranial Arteriovenous Malformations as a Possible Cause of Endocranial Bone Lesions and Associated Neurological Disorder. *International Journal of Osteoarchaeology* 25(1), 88–97.

Kelley, M.A. 1991. Contrasting patterns of dental disease in five early northern Chilean groups. *Advances in Dental Anthropology*, 203–13.

Kozakaitė, J., Piombino-Mascali, D., Miliauskienė, Ž., Girčius, R., Dementavičienė, J. and Jankauskas, R. 2018. A rare case of child abuse from early modern Lithuania. *International Journal of Paleopathology* 22, 189–97.

Kuo, L-C., Polson, A.M. and Kang, T. 2008. Associations between Periodontal Diseases and Systemic Diseases: A Review of the Inter-Relationships and Interactions with Diabetes, Respiratory Diseases, Cardiovascular Diseases and Osteoporosis. *Public Health* 122, 417–33.

Larsen, C.S. 1997. *Bioarchaeology: Interpreting Behaviour from the Human Skeleton.* Cambridge: Cambridge University Press.

Lewis, M. 2002. *Urbanisation and Child Health in Medieval Post-Medieval England.* BAR 339. Archaeopress: Oxford.

Lewis, M. 2004. Endocranial Lesions in Non-adult Skeletons: Understanding their Aetiology. *International Journal of Osteoarchaeology* 14, 82–97.

Lewis, M. 2007. *The Bioarchaeology of Children: Perspectives from Biological and Forensic Anthropology.* Cambridge: Cambridge University Press.

Lewis, M. 2018. *The Palaeopathology of Children.* London: Elsevier.

Lovejoy, C.O., Meindi, R.S., Pryzbeck, T.R. and Mensforth, R.P. 1985. Chronological metamorphosis of the auricular surface of the illium: A new method for the determination of adult skeletal age at death. *American Journal of Physical Anthropology* 68, 15–28.

Maresh, M.M. 1970. Measurements from roentgenograms. In: McCammon, R.W. (ed.) *Human growth and development*, 157–200. Springfield: Charles. C Thomas.

Mays, S. 2008. Metabolic Bone Disease. In: Pinhasi, R. and Mays, S. (eds.) *Advances in Human Palaeopathology*, https://doi.org/10.1002/9780470724187.ch11.

Mays, S., Brickley, M. and Ives, R. 2008. Growth in an English population from the Industrial Revolution. *American Journal of Physical Anthropology* 136(1), 85–92.

McKinley, J. 2004. Compiling a skeletal inventory: disarticulated and co-mingled remains. In: Brickley, M. and McKinley, J.I. (eds.) *Guidelines to the Standards for Recording Human Remains.* IFA Paper No 7, *14*–17. Reading: BABAO,

Meindl R.S. and Lovejoy, C.O. 1985. Ectocranial suture closure: A revised method for the determination of skeletal age at death based on the lateral-anterior sutures. *American Journal of Physical Anthropology* 68, 57–66.

Meindl R.S. and Lovejoy, C.O. 1989. Age Changes in the Pelvis: Implications for Paleodemography. In: Iscan, M.Y. (ed.) *Age Markers in the Human Skeleton.* 3rd ed, 137–68. Illinois: Charles C. Thompson

Meinl, A., Rottensteiner, G.M., Huberm C.D., Tangl, S., Watzak, G. and Watzek, G. 2010. Caries frequency and distribution in an early medieval Avar population from Austria. *Oral Diseases* 16(1), 108–16.

Molleson, T.I., Cruse, K. and Mays, S. 1998. Some sexually dimorphic features of the human juvenile skull and their value in sex determination in immature skeletal remains. *Journal of Archaeological Science* 25, 719–28.

Moore, W.J. and Corbett, M.E. 1971. The distribution of dental caries in ancient British populations 1: Anglo-Saxon period. *Caries Research* 5, 151–68.

Nelson, G.C. 2015. A Host of Other Dental Diseases and Disorders. In: Irish, J.D. and Scott, G.R. (eds.). *A Companion to Dental Anthropology,* 465–84. Chichester: John Whiley and Sons,

Nelson, G.C., Lukacs, J.R. and Yule, P. 1999. Dates, Caries, and Early Tooth Loss during the Iron Age of Oman. *American Journal of Physical Anthropology* 108, 333–43.

Newman, S.L., Gowland, R. and Caffell, A.C. 2019. North and south: A comprehensive analysis of non-adult growth and health in the industrial revolution (AD 18th–19th C), England. *American Journal of Physical Anthropology* 169(1), 104–21.

Novak, M. 2015. Dental health and diet in early medieval Ireland. *Archives of Oral Biology* 60(9), 1299–309.

Novotny, V., Iscan, M. and Loth, S. 1993. Morphologic and osteometric assessment of age, sex, and race from the skull. In: Iscan, M.Y. and Helmer, R.P (eds.) *Forensic Analysis of the Skull,* 71–88. New York: Wiley-Liss.

Obertová, Z. and Thurzo, M. 2008. Relationship between cribra orbitalia and enamel hypoplasia in the early medieval Slavic population at Borovce, Slovakia. *International Journey of Osteoarchaeology* 18(3), 280–92.

O'Connell, L. 2004. Guidance on recording age at death in adults. In: Brickley, M. and McKinley, J.I. (eds.) *Guidelines to the Standards for Recording Human Remains.* IFA Paper No 7, 18–21. Reading: BABAO.

Orme, N. 2001. *Medieval Children.* New Haven: Yale University Press.

Ortner, D.J. 2003. *Identification of Pathological Conditions in Human Skeletal Remains* (2nd edition). New York: Academic Press.

Ortner, D.J. 2008. Differential diagnosis of skeletal lesions in infectious disease. In: Pinhasi, R. and Mays, S. (eds.) *Advances in human palaeopathology,* https://doi.org/10.1002/9780470724187.chp10.

Ortner, D.J. and Eriksen, M.F. 1997. Bone changes in the human skull probably resulting from scurvy in infancy and childhood. *International Journal of Osteoarchaeology* 7, 212–20.

Ortner, D.J., Kimmerle, E.H. and Diez, M. 1999. Probable evidence of scurvy in subadults from archaeological sites in Peru. *American Journal of Physical Anthropology* 108, 321–31.

Ortner, D.J., Butler, W., Cafarella, J. and Milligan, L. 2001. Evidence of probable scurvy in subadults from archaeological sites in North America. *American Journal of Physical Anthropology* 114, 343–351.

Pangan, A.L. and Robinson, D. 2001. Hemarthrosis as initial presentation of scurvy. *Journal of Rheumatology* 28, 1923–5.

Pfirrmann, C and Resnick, D. 2001. Schmorl's nodes of the thoracic and lumbar spine: radiographic-pathologic study of prevalence, characterisation and correlation with degenerative changes in 1,650 spinal levels in 100 cadavers. *Radiology* 219, 368–74.

Phenice, T.W. 1969. A Newly Developed Visual Method of Sexing the Os Pubis. *American Journal of Physical Anthropology* 30, 297–302.

Pimentel, L. 2003. Scurvy: Historical review and current diagnostic approach. *American Journal of Emergency Medicine* 21, 328–32.

Plomp, K., Roberts, C. and Vidarsdottir, U.S. 2015. Does the correlation between schmorl's nodes and vertebral morphology extend to the lumbar spine? *American Journal of Physical Anthropology* 157, 526–534.

Prowse, T.L., Saunders, S.R., Schwarcz, H.P., Garnsey, P., Macchiarelli, R. and Bondioli, L. 2008. Isotopic and dental evidence for infant and young child feeding practices in an imperial Roman skeletal sample. *American Journal of Physical Anthropology* 137(3), 294–308.

Roberts, C. 2007. A bioarchaeological study of maxillary sinusitis. *American Journal of Physical Anthropology* 133(2), 792–807.

Roberts, C and Connel, B. 2004. Guidance on recording palaeopathology. In: Brickley, M. and McKinley, J.I. (eds.) *Guidelines to the Standards for Recording Human Remains.* IFA Paper No 7, 34–9. Reading: BABAO.

Roberts, C.A. and Cox, M. 2003. *Health and disease in Britain. From prehistory to the present day.* Stroud: Sutton Publishing Ltd.

Roberts, C., Lucy, D. and Manchester, K. 1994. Inflammatory lesions of ribs: An analysis of the Terry collection. *American Journal of Physical Anthropology* 95(2), 169–182.

Roberts, C. and Manchester, K. 2010. *The Archaeology of Disease.* 3rd ed. Stroud: The History Press.

Rohnbogner, A. and Lewis, M. 2016. Dental caries as a measure of diet, health, and difference in non-adults from urban and rural Roman Britain. *Dental Anthropology Journal* 29(1), 16–31.

Santos, A.L., and Roberts, C.A. 2006. Anatomy of a serial killer: differential diagnosis of tuberculosis based on rib lesions of adult individuals from the Coimbra identified skeletal collection, Portugal, *American Journal of Physical Anthropology* 130(1), 38–49.

Sarnat, B.G., and Schour, I. 1941. Enamel Hypoplasia (Chronologic Enamel Aplasia) in Relation to Systemic Disease: A Chronological, Morphologic, and Etiologic Classification. *Journal of the American Dental Association* 28, 1989–2000.

Saunders, S.R. 2000. Subadult skeletons and growth related studies. In: Katzenberg, M.A. and Saunders. S.R (eds.) *Biological Anthropology of the Human Skeleton*, 135–62. New York: Wiley..

Schaefer, M., Black, S. and Scheuer, L. 2009. *Juvenile Osteology: A Laboratory and Field Manuel.* London: Elsevier.

Scheuer, J.L., Musgrave, J.H. and Evans, S.P. 1980. The estimation of late fetal and perinatal age from limb bone length by linear and logarithmic regression. *Annals of Human Biology* 7(3), 257–65.

Scheuer, L. 2002. A blind test of mandibular morphology for sexing mandibles in the first few years of life. *American Journal of Physical Anthropology* 119, 189–191.

Schmorl, G. and Junghans, H. 1971. *The Human Spine in Health and Disease*. New York: Grune and Stratton.

Schutkowski, H. 1993. Sex determination of infant and juvenile skeletons I Morphognostic features. *American Journal of Physical Anthropology* 90, 199–205.

Scott, E.C. 1979. Dental wear scoring technique. *American Journal of Physical Anthropology* 51(2); 213–17.

Sima, C., Gastfreund, S., Sun, C. and Glogauer, M. 2014. Rac-null Leukocytes Are Associated with Increased Inflammation-Mediated Alveolar Bone Loss. *American Journal of Pathology* 184, 472–82.

Smisson, R. 2007. *BCP excavation report Trench 5* (Unpublished).

Smith, B.H. 1984. Patterns of Molar Wear in Hunter-Gatherers and Agriculturalists. *American Journal of Physical Anthropology* 63, 39–56.

Sulsky, S.I., Carlton, L., Brochmann, F., Ellegast, R., Glitsch, U., Hartmann, B., Pallapies, D., Seidel, D. and Sun, Y. 2012. Epidemiological Evidence for Work Load as a Risk Factor for Osteoarthritis of the Hip: A Systematic Review. *PLoS ONE 7(2): e31521.*Sun, L., Pechenkina, K., Yanpeng, C., Hai, Z. and Xueyi, Q. 2019. Cases of endocranial lesions on juvenile skeletons from Longshan cultural sites in Henan Province, China. *International Journal of Palaeopathology* 26, 61–74.

Sweeney, E.A., Saffir, A.J. and de Leon, R. 1971. Linear Hypoplasia of Deciduous Incisor Teeth in Malnourished Children. *American Journal of Clinical Nutrition* 24, 29–31.

Temple, D.H. 2015. Caries: The Ancient Scourge. In: Irish, J.D. and Scott, G.R. (eds.) *A Companion to Dental Anthropology, 433*–49. Chichester: John Whiley and Sons.

Thelin, A. and Holmberg, S. 2007. Hip osteoarthritis in a rural male population: A prospective population-based register study. *American Journal of Industrial Medicine* 50(8), 604–7.

Todd, T.W. 1920a. Age changes in the pubic bone: I. The white male pubis. *American Journal of Physical Anthropology* 3, 467–70.

Todd, T.W. 1920b. Age changes in the pubic bone: III. The pubis of the white female. *American Journal of Physical Anthropology* 3, 467–470.

Trotter, M. 1970. Estimation of stature from intact long limb bones. In: Stewart, T.D. (ed.) *Personal identification in Mass Disasters*, 71–83. Washington, D.C.: National Museum of Natural History.

Ubelaker, D.H. and Khosrowshahi, H. 2019. Estimation of age in forensic anthropology: historical perspective and recent methodological advances. *Forensic Sciences Research* 4(1), 1–9.

Ubelaker, D.H. and Volk, C. 2002. A test of Phenice method for the estimation of sex. *Forensic Science International* 47, 19–24.

Vodanović, M., Dumančić, J., Galić, I., Savić Pavičin, I., Petrovečki, M., Cameriere, R. and Brkića, H. 2011. Age estimation in archaeological skeletal remains: evaluation of four non-destructive age calculation methods. *Journal of Forensic Odonto-Stomatology* 29(2), 14–21.

Waldron, T. 2009. *Palaeopathology*. Cambridge: Cambridge University Press.

Waldron, T. and Rogers, J. 1991. Inter-observer variation in coding osteoarthritis in human skeletal remains. *International Journal of Osteoarchaeology* 1(1); 49–56.

Walker, P.L. 1995. Problems of preservation and sexism in sexing: Some lessons from historical collections for palaeodemographers. In: Saunders, S. and Herring, A. (eds.) *Grave Reflections: Portraying the Past Through Cemetery Studies*, 31–48. Toronto: Canadian Scholar's Press.

Walker, P.L. 2005. Greater sciatic notch morphology: sex, age and population differences. *American Journal of Physical Anthropology* 127, 385–91.

Walker, P.L., Bathurst, R.R., Richman, R., Gjerdrum, T. and Andrushko, V.A. 2009. The cause of porotic hyperostosis and cribra orbitalia: A reappraisal of the iron-deficiency-anaemia hypothesis. *American Journal of Physical Anthropology* 139, 109–25.

Walker-Bone, K. and Palmer, K.T. 2002. Musculoskeletal disorder in farmers and farm workers. *Occupational Medicine* 52(8), 441–50.

Walrath, D.E., Turner, P. and Bruzek, J. 2004. Reliability Test of the Visual Assessment of Cranial Traits for Sex Determination. *American Journal of Physical Anthropology* 125, 132–7.

Wapler, U., Crubézy, E. and Schultz, M. 2004. Is cribra orbitalia synonymous with anemia? Analysis and interpretation of cranial pathology in Sudan. *American Journal of Physical Anthropology* 123(4), 333–9.

Weiss, E. and Jurmain, R.D. 2007. Osteoarthritis revisited: a contemporary review of aetiology. *International Journal of Osteoarchaeology* 17(5), 437–50.

Western, G. and Bekvalac, J. 2019. *Manufactured Bodies: The Impact of Industrialisation on London Health.* Oxford: Oxbow Books.

Weston, D.A. 2008. Investigating the specificity of periosteal reactions in pathology museum specimens. *American Journal of Physical Anthropology* 137, 48–59.

Witkin, A., and Prior, S.J. 2014. *Articulated Human Skeletal Remains from Nelme's Paddock, Berkeley, Gloucestershire.* Bristol and Gloucestershire Archaeological Society (Unpublished).

WORD database, Museum of London. Accessed 30/09/20, https://www.museumoflondon.org.uk/collections/other-collection-databases-and-libraries/centre-human-bioarchaeology/osteological-database/medieval-cemeteries/st-benet-sherehog.

Plate 1

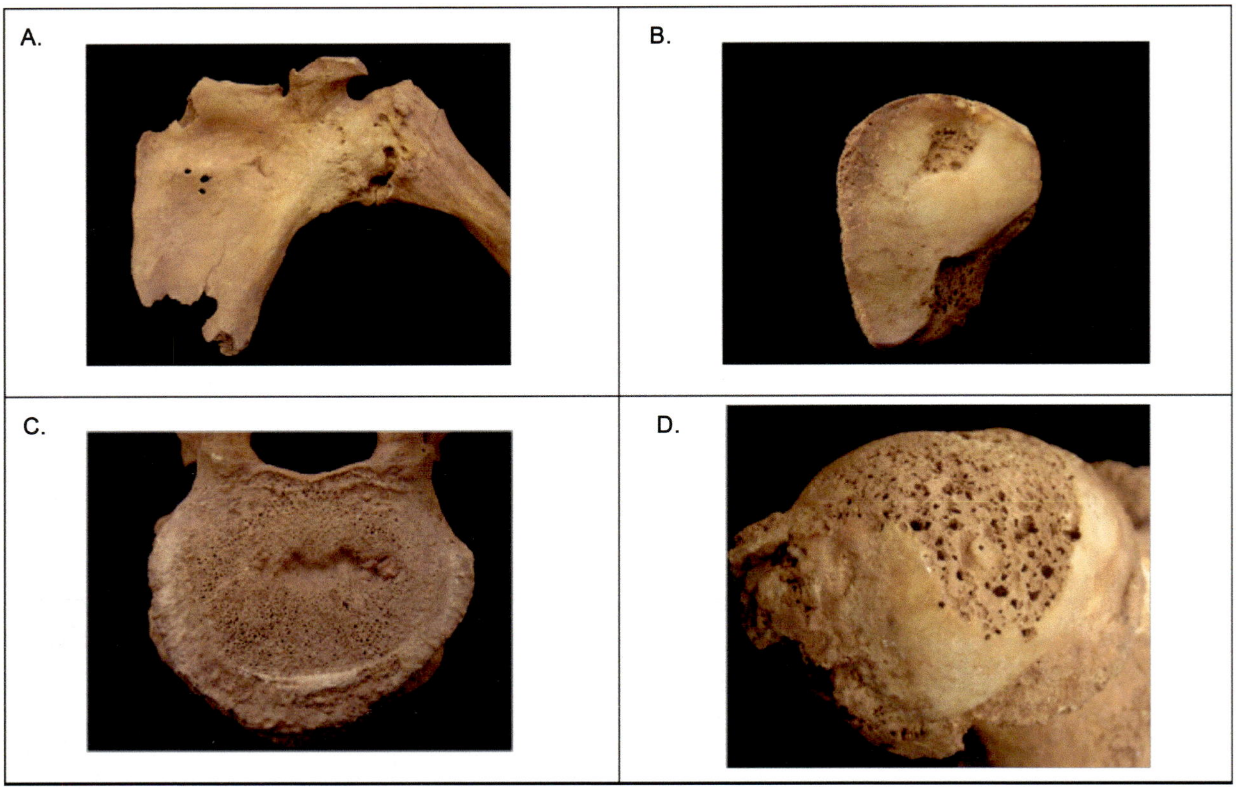

Plate 2

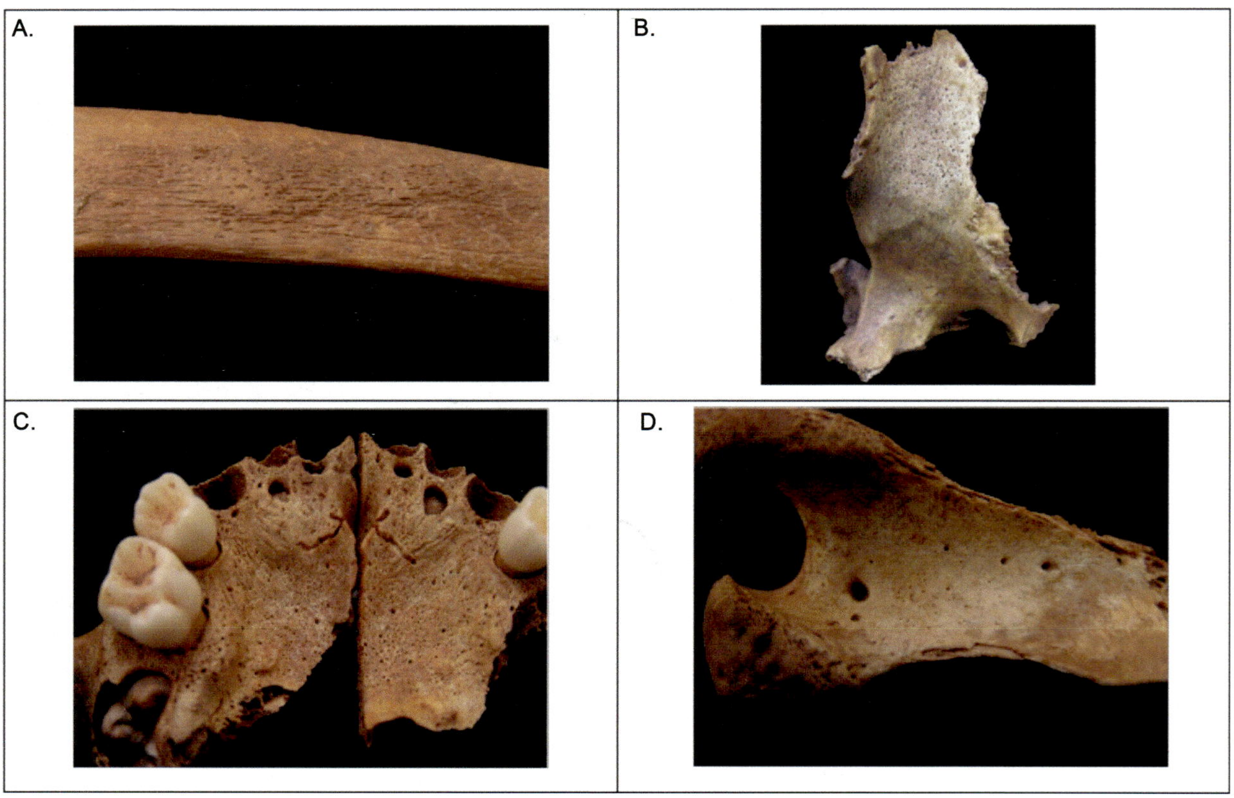

Chapter 9

Berkeley Castle Tales: Narratives from Minster, Manor and Town

Stuart J. Prior and Konstantinos P. Trimmis

Introduction

The Berkeley Castle Project (BCP) set out from the very beginning to rewrite the story around the development of Berkeley town and its homonymous castle using historical and archaeological evidence. Based on the finds presented in the earlier chapters of this volume, we present here the main tales from Berkeley as they have been reconstructed by the excavation. This chapter also brings together conclusions and discussion points that have been addressed in previous publications and reports.

Following the general scope of a 'minster, manor, town' project, the story behind the evolution of Berkeley town is presented first, with the story of the Norman minster in Berkeley as has been recorded by the project. The chapter then explores how Berkeley Castle was established through research on earlier fortifications in the area. Stories from the castle moat unfold afterwards, with a lead to the evidence of an early Tudor pub uncovered in the area of Trench 8. The chapter concludes with archaeological evidence of the Civil War events in Berkeley and an evaluation of the BCP legacy for university teaching-led research projects. Authors and editors of this volume hope that BCP will be a blueprint study for research into the evolution of similar townscapes in Britain and beyond.

The tale of the Berkeley town development

Nucleated settlements such as Berkeley invariably display a high degree of complexity in their overall plan as a result of centuries of expansion, retraction and redevelopment. Evidence for Romano-British occupation at Berkeley and in its hinterland is attested through features and artefacts revealed during BCP excavations (Twinn 2008; Prior 2010–2014), and from excavations to the north-west of Longbridge (Haines 2013, 16–17). Furthermore, a number of Romano-British monuments are known to the east of Berkeley (NMR205255, NMR205272, NMR205273, 1523473, 201622, 205271), although this concentration is almost certainly a result of the higher proportion of excavations in this area associated with the M5 construction, compared to other locales in the parish. A section of Roman road (MN1523473) is particularly interesting as it appears to connect Bitton with Berkeley, indicating a Romano-British settlement at Berkeley. Romano-British pottery scatters are recorded on the banks of the Severn (NMR763738, NMR763743, NMR763778), although due to mechanisms of artefact distribution, these may not indicate occupation in the immediate vicinity.

Cooke (1873, 3) suggests the cross-shaped town plan indicates the presence of a Romano-British fort settlement at Berkeley. While no Roman fort is identical, the typical form is that of a 'squarish playing card with rounded corners' with 'four gateways, one on each side' (Wilson 1980, 14). The crossroads in the centre of Berkeley certainly fit within a typical Romano-British fort layout (Fig. 1). However, if it is assumed that the later Anglo-Saxon town was constructed over some of its footprint, the fort would be extensive, approximately 7 ha, roughly one-third the size of the large legionary fortress of Isca at Caerleon (Boon 1972, 14).

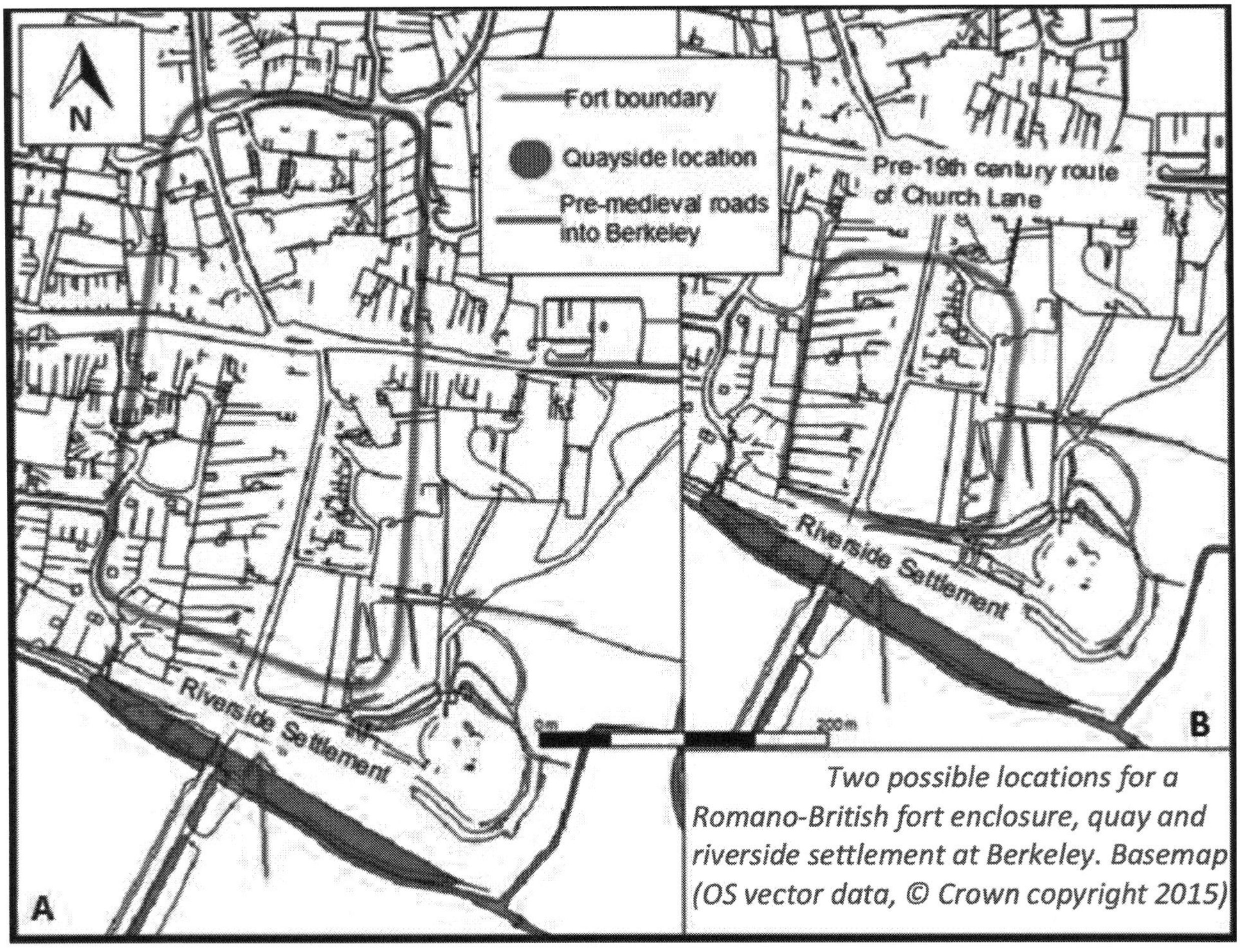

Figure 1. Proposals for possible locations for a Romano-British enclosure at Berkeley.

The layout shown in Figure 1, based on the 1543 route of Church Lane (GRO R41.41GS) and the eastern causeway, would make the fort/settlement more modestly sized at 2.5 ha. The anomalous shape of Church Street, compared to the medieval layout of Berkeley, can therefore be explained as forming the north-east corner of a Romano-British fort, most likely on the line of the Via Sagularis. The possible causeways heading south and east out of town may have Romano-British origins. The quaysides of Roman forts at Gloucester (Heighway and Bryant 1999, 5) and Caerleon (Nash-Williams 1930; Caerleon: General Plan opp. 73) are located outside of the main town enclosure. If a similar plan is assumed for Berkeley then the southern limit of the main enclosure would be sited in the area of Castle Street with a riverside settlement between this boundary and the pill. If the earlier southern course of Berkeley Pill is accurate, then the Romano-British quay at Berkeley would be set in the cut-back face of a meander similar to the Romano-British harbour of Caerleon (Nayling and McGrail 2004, 104).

Archaeological excavations have established the position of Berkeley's Anglo-Saxon minster complex and settlement, which displays a similar plan to that of the Romano-British fort/settlement proposed in Figure 1. Deeds from the last half of the 13th until the early 14th century make reference to the 'old town' (vetus villa), likely centred around the current market square, although a lost deed of late 13th century date makes reference to 'land called the old market-place which lies between Eustace's burgage and the chapel of St Radegund' (Hare 2013, 140). It is possible, therefore, that two marketplaces existed within Berkeley during the Saxon period, a pattern seen in other minster towns such as Bramton in

Oxfordshire and Chesterfield in Derbyshire (ibid, 10). The settlement plan suggests that the Romano-British and Anglo-Saxon settlements and associated quaysides at Berkeley were situated in broadly the same area, similar to the continued usage of Gloucester harbour throughout these periods (Heighway and Bryant 1999, 3). Another feature of Anglo-Saxon Gloucester, potentially pertinent to Berkeley, is the location of St Oswald's Minster on the riverside which, according to Leyland, had a quay associated with it (Smith 1908, 57). The idea of dual quaysides, one for the general population and another for the minster, may reflect the dual marketplace discussed above.

Leech (1981, 4) claims that 'the plan of the town has changed little since medieval times'. As discussed above, 13th–14th century deeds made reference to the 'old town' (vetrus villa) of Berkeley in contrast to the 'new town' (nova villa). The regular burgage plot pattern seen on the west side of the high street, and also revealed to be present on the eastern side from the Nelme's Paddock excavations (Prior 2015, 41–3), strongly suggests a degree of Norman town planning. Several streets are known to have disappeared since the medieval period (Leech 1981, 4), and although some of these have likely changed name and others removed through infill, some may have disappeared through shrinkage of the town. A landscape survey in conjunction with resistivity survey has revealed evidence of a hollow way running through the Park View Playing Fields (see Trimmis *et al.* 2021 in this volume). This street would have formed the western limit of the town, and is comparable to other early medieval planned towns located on a riverside that display similar rectilinear characteristics with a main street and separate curving back lane (Beresford 1967, 438).

The town of Arundel, on the river Arun in Sussex, in addition to displaying a remarkably similar town plan to that of Berkeley, has a comparable development from potential Roman occupation followed by the establishment of a minster and finally planned town built around a castle complex (Hudson 1997, 19). The quays of Arundel, like those of Berkeley, were initially focused around the castle complex, with later expansion associated with plantation development (ibid).

Eighty percent of plantation towns were built in association with castles between 1086 and 1100, while in the period 1101 to 1135 this number fell to slightly more than half (Beresford 1967, 334). It therefore seems more likely that a rectilinear town plan was established in Berkeley during the earlier period. An expansion of Berkeley in a westerly direction along the side of the pill can be seen as a result of a desire to increase the size of available quayside in order to promote maritime commerce in the town. If comparable to towns like Arundel, the original quay at the bottom of High Street would have remained active, although, as discussed below, it may have been a private quay for the castle. New wharfage would have been provided by the expansion of the quayside along Jumpers Lane probably as far as the now defunct road on the western limits of the early medieval town.

The tale of a Norman mynster

'Mynster' was the Old English vernacular word for the latin *monasterium*, a religious community (Blair 1988, 1). These communities were early establishments of the Christian church which evolved during the 200 years following reintroduction of the religion to Britain by the Augustinian mission of AD597. Minsters appear to have been founded as administration centres controlling defined territories (Blair 1996, 8). By the early 8th century a framework of minster parochiae, or parishes, existed over most of England. These foundations were frequently associated with the territorial holdings of royal centres of power (Blair 1985, 116), and were often coterminous with an existing estate unit (Bassett 1992, 19; Croom 1988, 67). It is likely that each minster was served by a group of clergy which ministered to the population of these territorial holdings, though these areas might have varied considerably in size (Gelling 1992, 184).

The simple observation that many known minster churches are located at the centre of a Hundred indicates that these establishments were closely associated with administrative jurisdiction and local control. This has led to the further supposition that the system of Hundreds, recognised in the Domesday Book, can be directly correlated to the parochiae of these early foundations (Turner 2006, 109–11)

However, the idea that minsters were primarily concerned with pastoral care has been questioned and it has been suggested that some might have been closed communities (Cambridge and Rollason 1995; Cubitt 2005). Drawing generalisations about the characteristics of minster sites must be treated with caution. Archaeology of early church sites has not been widespread and there are particularly few well-recorded examples in western England (Heighway 2003, 62). Foot (1992, 213) refutes the idea that there is any such thing as a 'typical Anglo-Saxon monastery' and suggests that each institution adopted its own form and procedures according to the interests of its founders and subsequent inmates, and that no standards were imposed before the widespread monastic reforms of the 10th century. Blair (2005, 5) further proposes that these early churches evolved on a regional basis and were not part of an organisation of uniformly imposed structures. He perceives what he terms as 'ecclesiastical textures' developing across the English regions from the 7th century independently from 'any one channel of religious influence'.

Studies of the early church at Berkeley have been largely concerned with its Domesday Book entry and medieval documentary evidence to support the view of its status as a minster – notably in analyses by Kemp (1968), Moore (1988) and Jones (1992). One of the earliest references to indicate a community at Berkeley dates from the early 9th century and refers to the abbess Ceolburga being appointed as head of the religious establishment (Florence of Worcester 1854, 48; Higgins 2002, 108). The fact that the foundation was presided over by a woman suggests that the Berkeley monasterium was a 'double house' consisting of communities of both monks and nuns. Women played a prominent role in monastic life in the 7th and 8th centuries (Yorke 2003, 1–11; Coulstock 1993, 53) and it was not uncommon for religious communities at this time to be under the charge of an abbess (Thacker 1992, 143).

Domesday is less ambiguous with regard to the size of the estate at Berkeley in the 11th century. Berkeley's entry describes a Hundredal territory of 144½ hides, the largest such landholding in Gloucestershire (Smith 1964, 206). Whether the parochia of the early minster is also described by the Domesday Hundred has also been an area of analysis (Taylor 1895; Kemp 1968). Later documents from the 11th and 12th centuries describe the re-apportioning of the lands associated with Berkeley and its dependent chapels. In many of these the Old English term 'Hernesse' appears as a description of the landholding of the Berkeley estate, including the deed under which the properties were granted to the FitzHarding family (Wells-Furby 2004, 2). The term 'Hernesse' is derived from the Anglo-Saxon word *hyrness* – meaning to 'hear' or 'obey' (Smith 1956, 245) – so in the context of referring to a portion of land it can be seen to identify an area of administration and jurisdiction. This has led to the proposition (Moore 1988, 87) that the continuing use of the term into the 12th century is recognition of a pre-existing unit of Anglo-Saxon territory as a contiguous block of land. The suggestion follows that the hundred outlined by the Domesday Book and the area described by the Berkeley Hernesse are the same unit of territory. If this is the case, the area of land and parochial care associated with the Berkeley community was a district of some substance.

Today, little remains in the landscape to indicate that Berkeley was the base of an important religious community at the administrative core of an Anglo-Saxon estate. One can, however, perceive some landscape features that fit recognised patterns of early minster structures. Minster sites are usually on promontories of land overlooking a floodplain (Blair 1992). In this respect Berkeley occupies a 'typical' minster position which one can observe in other early church sites of the Severn valley such as Deerhurst, Tewkesbury and Bredon.

In her study of minsters in Dorset, Hall (2003, 53) points out that many of these foundations stand in rectilinear enclosures, and it would appear that a physical boundary forms a fundamental element of many minster structures. Although these boundaries rarely survive as earthworks, their outline is often represented in current road systems and pathways (Blair 2005, 196–9). At Berkeley one can detect elements of a possible rectilinear enclosure in the lines of St Mary's Churchyard boundary to the east of the church; the rear of the gardens of the houses which front onto the south side of Canonbury Street to the north; and the rear of the gardens of the houses which front onto the west side of High Street to the west. The southern end of the minster enclosure is almost certainly marked by the south end of the wedge-shaped ridge that the town of Berkeley is situated upon (Fig. 2).

Figure 2. Aerial view of the Castle landscape and the research area of BCP.

Initially, Berkeley Castle Project successfully located the presence of fairly substantial boundary ditches, which appear to have enclosed the minster to the east, north, and northwest, thereby supporting the hypothesis that the minster boundaries follow the above lines (Prior 2005, 2006b; Smisson 2009). Additionally, Tandy (2003, 175–190) suggests that the original road from Ham to Berkeley crossed a field known as Quarf Mead to the south-west of Berkeley: the road was situated about 100 m west of the modern road, running approximately north-south, passing adjacent to the western ends of the gardens which front onto the west side of High Street to meet Maybrook Street in the north. Recent archaeological survey has shown this hypothesis to be correct, and it is highly likely that the old road from Ham to Berkeley marked the minster's western edge.

So what would have been inside this enclosure? Excavations of double minster sites, such as Wimborne (Graham 1985), are testament to the existence of substantial and extensive communities. Alongside the places of worship, buildings to accommodate and support the community would also have existed within the enclosure. Excavations at the minster foundation in Hartlepool (Cramp and Daniels 1987) uncovered a complex of timber buildings. Little remained to inform of the activities associated with these structures, but they appeared to have been part of an organised community.

If Berkeley follows the 'general' pattern of minster communities, then it is probable that more than one church would have existed within its boundary vallum (ditch). Blair (1992, 247–57) describes an accretive process under which successive churches would have been added over time. He perceives that in a few cases, such as Glastonbury and possibly Gloucester, the earliest, and most important, church was dedicated to St Mary. He suggests that these sites are probably very early foundations with possibly pre-English origins. More commonly, a church dedicated to an apostolic saint was founded with a subsequent St Mary church added, usually to the east. These churches were often as close to one another as to be almost touching, as at Canterbury, Wells and Malmesbury. It seems likely that the foundation at Berkeley was arranged similarly, with communal buildings surrounding an alignment of adjacent churches (Blair 2005, 199).

At Berkeley, the surviving church of St Mary the Virgin is in the southern part of the outlined enclosure. The building is unusual for having a separate bell-tower some 20 metres from the main body of the church. The separate bell-tower was rebuilt in 1753 (GSMR entry no. 9344), but an earlier bell-tower that stood roughly on the same spot – the remains of which were identified in recent archaeological excavations (Prior 2009b) – is traditionally believed to have been attached to an additional church (Gethyn-Jones 1992; Leech 1981, 5).

In 1821, Fosbroke wrote that the tower was rebuilt 'on the same spot where the ancient tower stood, to which the ruinous buildings were attached, called the nunnery chapel' (1821, 49). Earlier evidence for a second church comes from Bigland's reference (1791) to Parsons' manuscript, in which it was said that there was 'an ancient church dedicated to our Saviour and his Saints, upon whose wall was written the Apocalypse in Latin. It was joined to the old tower' (microfilm copy of Parsons' manuscript, G.R.O.). A 17th century painting that hangs in Berkeley Castle, by Dutch painter Henry Dankerts, confirms the existence of the earlier church (Fig. 3). The painting shows the eastern side of both the castle and the original tower, and clearly visible on the tower's eastern elevation is a raggle (roof-scar) showing where the main body of the church originally joined the tower. The church would have adjoined the tower's eastern side and would have been parallel to the present church of St Mary's. An early map of Berkeley also appears to support the proposition for a second church. The map, dated 1543, shows the existing church with its adjacent bell-tower and a high cross (now gone) to the west of the church. Two lanes are depicted on this map running from the High Street to the church site – Radegon's Lane and St Michael's Lane. Radegon's Lane approaches the site of the bell-tower from the west. St Radegund was a Frankish queen and abbess of Poitiers who became a popular saint of the early medieval period, often associated with high-status nunneries (McNamara *et al.* 1994, 60–105; Brennan 1985). Reference to Radegund in Berkeley suggests that this may have been the dedication of a nunnery church, and the position of the lane indicates that this church may well have been sited adjacent to where the bell-tower now stands.

The reference to St Michael's Lane on the map is odd in that the surviving Berkeley church is dedicated to St Mary. St Michael's may be a reference to an earlier dedication or possibly a further church on the minster site. Geophysical and earthwork surveys have revealed a 13th century 'designed castle landscape' complete with fishponds and watercourses, the remains of a 12th century hospital, the location and layout of an early Saxon river port (see chapter 2 of this volume), and have successfully defined the boundaries of the minster enclosure (Smisson 2009).

Excavations have recorded two sections of the minster's vallum (boundary ditch) [ST 685 991 & ST 68469 99122], the more substantial of which [ST 685 991] contained numerous sherds of late Saxon pottery,

Figure 3. 17th century painting by Dankerts which confirms the existence of a second church at Berkeley, as a raggle (roof-scar) is clearly visible of the east side of the free-standing bell-tower showing where the main body of the church originally adjoined the tower.

part of a rare Saxon millstone, and two 10th century Saxon coins. The pottery assemblage, which dates from the late 9th to early 11th century, is believed to pre-date the Saxon pottery sequences at both Bristol and Bath, and is the only pottery of its date so far found in southern Gloucestershire (Prior 2005). In 2006, several ditches were discovered near the church tower which were thought to be part of the boundary of the minster. This suggested that Trench 8 and the area containing the High Street houses were all within the Saxon minster, while Berkeley Castle was built by the Normans just on the edge of the minster enclosure. After the consequent excavation seasons, though, it is possible that the two ditches which cut across Trench 8 are valla monasterii: boundary markers for monasteries, which separated the monastery from the outside world and the sacred from the profane (Fig. 4). These valla would instead form the edge of the Saxon minster, meaning that some of the houses along High Street are not part of the Saxon precinct (Fig. 5).

A vallum took the form of long ditches with a bank, stone or clay wall or hedge inside. These have been found through excavation at abbeys in Whitby and Glastonbury; and the D-shaped earthwork valla monasterii of the famous Iona Abbey in Argyll are still extant (Christie and Hodges 2015). Although some valla may have resembled early bank and ditch fortifications, it is likely that they were designed as a symbolic separator of those inside the monastery from the outside world, rather than as actual

Figure 4. Aerial view of trench 8 with the Anglo-Saxon ditches visible.

defensive measures (de Vagvar 1996, 65). Sometimes new valla were not constructed when a monastery was built, and existing boundaries were instead utilised, such as at St Fursey's Monastery at Burgh Castle, which is enclosed by Roman fort walls. Valla monasterii were primarily used in early Anglo-Saxon monasteries but their use continued into the high medieval period.

At Glastonbury, the valla are associated with the earliest layout of the monastery, but were changed several times as the boundaries of the Abbey precinct were moved and expanded. The vallum at Glastonbury was first recorded by C.A. Ralegh Radford, who excavated the site from 1951–1963. The boundary was thought to surround the earliest Saxon church on the site, known as the vetusta ecclesia or Old Church, destroyed in the fire of 1184. The profile of Glastonbury Abbey's vallum bears a striking resemblance to our own, with similar vertical sides and a flat bottom (Rahtz 1993, 93). Other similar valla can be seen at the Saxon Abbey at Whitby. There, the vallum surrounding the 7th century monastery has been found to contain similar material cultural to that found in the Anglo-Saxon layer of Trench 8 surrounding the Berkeley vallum. Upon excavating the ditches now thought of as the valla in 1943, Sir Charles Peers suggested they may have formed part of a roadway, passing between the monastic and the non-monastic buildings on site. This feature has subsequently been reinterpreted as a monastic boundary wall, and the presence of monastic structures outside of the vallum indicates later expansion of the precinct (Daniels 1988, 208).

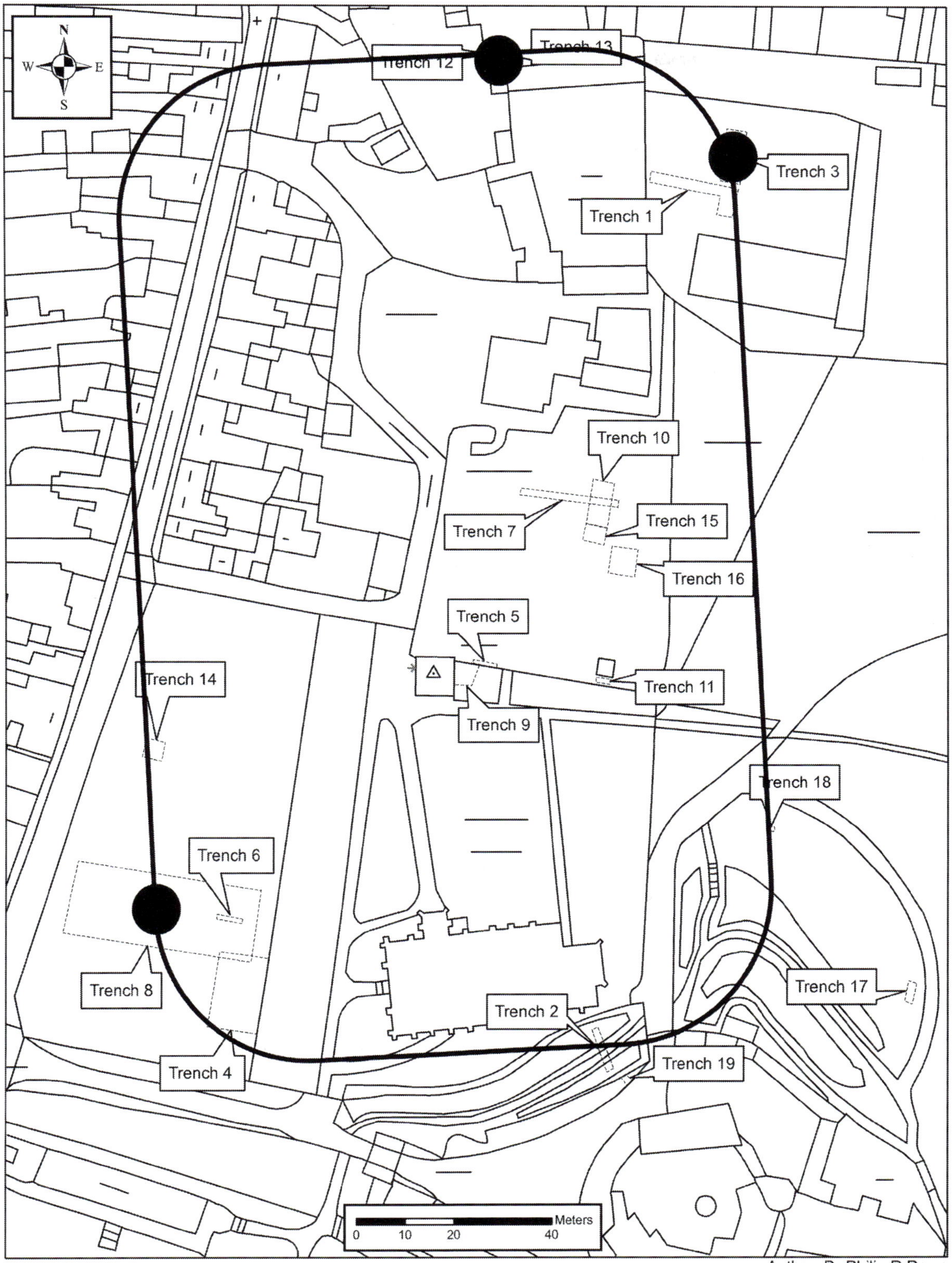

Author: Dr Philip R Rowe

Figure 5. Definitive proposal for the mynster boundaries in Berkeley, after the finding of the two ditches in trench 8.

There are two known Anglo-Saxon monastic structures in the grounds of Berkeley Castle and it is possible that these two monasteries were separated to keep male and female residents separate, with one structure for monks and the other for nuns. The area covering Nelme's Paddock and Trench 8 would have been scattered with cells in which members of the religious order would have lived. Of the valla monasterii at Berkeley, three possible phases of construction can be identified. The first phase is evident at the top of Trench 8, consisting of a shallow, stone-filled ditch which is thought to have fallen out of use by the late 7th or early 8th century. The second phase, a little further down the slope, consists of another, much narrower ditch. The ditches of the first and second phase of construction have an identical terminal, suggesting that despite a 10m expansion of the minster boundary, the entrance into the monastery complex remained the same. The entrance would have been east-facing, and would likely have led between the two Anglo-Saxon minster churches, which would today be between St Mary's Church and the tower. The alignments of these two ditches both mirror the alignment of the church, likely due to it having been built on the foundations of an original Saxon minster building. This alignment follows the natural contour of the small hill Trench 8 is cut into, although the hill contour we see today is slightly different due to topographical changes to this area made in the Civil War. The third phase of boundary construction takes place within the ditch of the second phase; this ditch was backfilled and a fence was constructed within it. The fence was eventually replaced with a stone wall which shows evidence of the reuse of Roman masonry.

Perhaps most important in terms of the minster, however, are two finds of Anglo-Saxon date that were recovered during excavations in Nelme's Paddock in 2008. There are very few finds that can be specifically related to Anglo-Saxon monastic activity – as, for example, anyone could have worn a crucifix – but excavations in Nelme's Paddock in 2008 recovered two artefacts that are unquestionably of monastic origin. The first is an aestel (page-turner) and the second a fine-grained whetstone pendant of the sort recovered in quantity during excavations of the monastic complex at Whitby, North Yorkshire (Fig. 6) (Twinn 2008).

The aestel (Fig. 6a) would have been attached to a thin bone shaft, which would have been used as a pointer to follow text when reading aloud from an illuminated manuscript, such as a bible; the aestel itself was used to turn the page of the manuscript in order to protect the vellum parchment from the grime and acids present on fingers. The whetstone pendant (Fig. 6b) appears to have been utilised to sharpen a small knife used to cut quills for writing and illustration during construction of the manuscripts themselves. These high-status artefacts were found within the precincts of Berkeley minster, and would presumably have been used within a scriptorium.

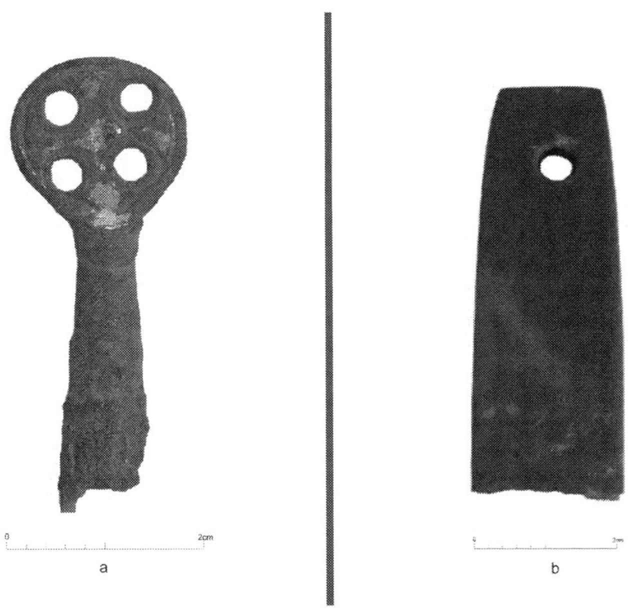

Figure 6. a) The Aestle and b) the whetstone pendant

There is no documentary evidence to clearly identify who founded the minster at Berkeley and when. Carver (2001, 12–14) suggests three varieties of Christian organisations, each of which may have led to the establishment of religious communities: a) royal foundation: communities directly associated with, and geographically close to, the administration centres of royal estates; b) episcopal foundation: territories established by bishops for administrative and revenue purposes; c) monastic foundation: settlements established by an independent community with its own endowment of land. Royal foundation appears to have been common practice and minsters were often wealthy and strongly aristocratic in form (Coulstock 1993, 65). In Dorset, Hall has found that a significant number of minster sites are associated with royal vills (Hall 2000, 40). As yet, no evidence of a royal vill has been found at Berkeley. It is possible that the foundation of the castle in the 11th century has obliterated evidence of an earlier estate centre. Yet royal foundation seems the most likely since the parochial lands that emerge from this establishment is a large territory administering the sort of managed landscape one would associate with a multiple estate.

The tale of a castle

The foundations of one more Anglo-Saxon structure that had been stripped of its masonry have been unearthed in the middle of Trench 8 in Nelme's Paddock. In this structure, which survives only as a right-angle of stone foundations, were the two Anglo-Saxon strap ends and three coins of Coenwulf (796–821), a king of Mercia. The date of these coins coincide with the first record of an abbess of Berkeley, Ceolburh (Ciolburga), the wife of Aethelmund, Ealdorman of Hwicce, who was granted the abbey in 802. As the first waves of Viking raids that devastated Britain's religious communities began to wane in the 9th century, and Scandinavians began to settle here, their new interactions with monasteries were no less lucrative – though rather less bloody. We can see other echoes of these cultural exchanges at Berkeley, with the discovery of a polyhedral-headed pin from Dublin (a Viking-founded town), a small child's bracelet, and honestones made from Scandinavian materials.

At the time Berkeley was a religious site with far-reaching commercial connections – something facilitated by its location on a navigable waterway stemming from the River Severn – and, it appears, inhabitants of some status. One enigmatic object, dubbed the 'Berkeley Gnome', in particular testifies to the wealth of some of the site's early medieval occupants. It is a curious, cone-shaped artefact, with two glass 'eyes' at its base, and the team has interpreted it as an 8th century knife handle terminal.

One impact of the Viking raids along the Severn sees the conversion of the minster into a burh, or fortified settlement, that housed a mint. To date, three coins, now in private collections, have been identified as being struck at Berkeley between 1048 and 1066 – but no trace of the ditched enclosure prescribed for such sites under Anglo-Saxon law has been identified. These defences would also allow the site to continue to flourish into a burh. Berkeley's secular success continued into the later medieval period, traces of which have been located further down Trench 8 towards High Street, where the foundations of late 13th–15th century houses have been uncovered. One of these houses was a substantial, well-built structure in a prime location, fronting directly onto a late medieval/Tudor street that the team still uses to navigate up the length of their trench. Its cobbled surface is shown on Tudor maps, where it is labelled as St Michael's Lane. Remains of a smaller, 12th century building were found at the bottom end of the trench. This was probably one of a number of little burgage plots – small houses with a long strip of land to the rear – that fronted onto both sides of the High Street at this time.

These plots appeared when the town was reorganised by its new Norman lord, at around the same time the castle was being rebuilt in stone. It was originally thought that the first stone castle erected at Berkeley comprised a circular shell keep, but BCP has shed new light on this aspect of the site's past. The architectural evolution of Berkeley Castle was not fully understood before BCP. In a Castle Studies Group Bulletin (CSG Bulletin 18, 2014), Neil Guy suggested that the castle may have had a square or rectangular donjon or keep, which may have been modified as the basis for the Thorpe Tower by Thomas [III] Berkeley (1292–1361). Trench 19 was designed to look for evidence of the north-west corner and west wall of this postulated donjon. The argument here is that Thorpe Tower was not wholly created 'as new' in the 14th century, but was instead a part-relic structure arising from a 1340s re-modelling of the 12th century castle. Namely, two corners and one side of a square donjon which abutted the north side of the 'motte', and for which the shell-keep encasing the motte was an inner (and elevated or upper) bailey.

The archaeological remains observed in Trench 19 appear to demonstrate the presence of a heavily robbed building with structures of two later phases overlying it (Fig. 7). The orientation of the first structural phase (contexts 1912 and 1916) and the robber trench (context 1908) associated with it is in alignment with the south-facing elevation of Thorpe Tower. This orientation suggests that this first phase was associated with, and presumably connected to, Thorpe Tower. It is probable, therefore, that context 1912 represents a heavily robbed wall which is comparable, and most likely contemporary with, wall J3, identified by the 8th Earl, that extended from the northern elevation of Thorpe Tower. As discussed above, it appears that the shell-keep and Thorpe Tower are of a single phase, most likely dating to the mid-12th century. While there is no evidence currently that contexts 1912, 1916 and wall J3 are contemporary with this primary construction phase, it must be noted that the wall (1911) overlaid context 1912 and re-used some of its stone. Further to the evidence from Trench 19, the rear wall of this fortification can still be seen, incorporated into the castle's later form (Fig. 8).

Figure 7. Plan view of trench 19

The tale of a moat

There are several medieval documents that record the cutting of moats around Berkeley Castle, but only two may relate to the cutting of a ditch in the area between the shell-keep and the church. In The Cartulary of St Augustine's Abbey, Bristol, an entry made between 1171 and 1190 records a grant made by Maurice de Berkeley [I] to St Augustine's of a rent of 5s from his mill below the castle, some tithes of pannage, and common pasture for a plough team '*pro emendatione culpe mee de fossato quod feci de cimiterio de Berchel circa castellum meum*' (charter no. 78; Walker, 1998, 46–7), which roughly translated means 'in

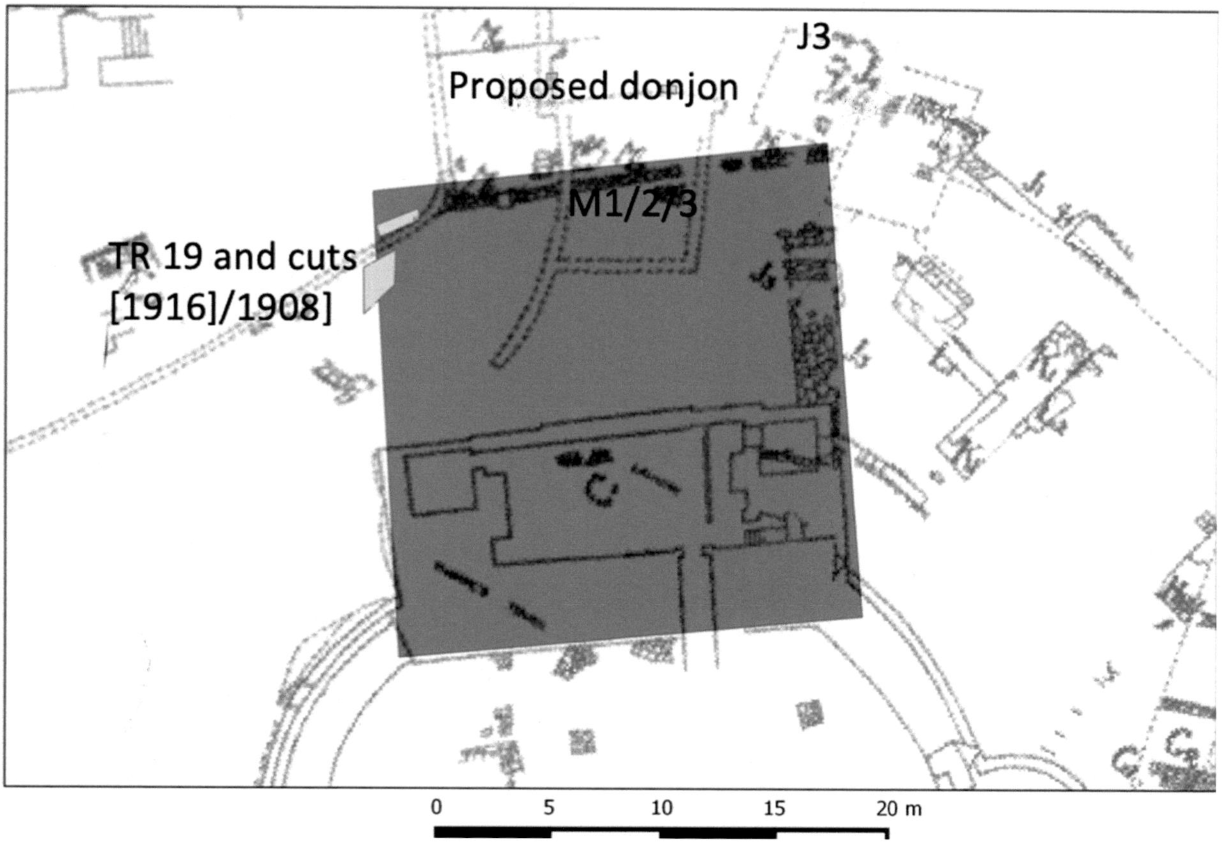

Figure 8. The location of the proposed Donjon

recompense for my offence committed upon the cemetery of Berkeley in cutting a ditch around my castle'. This suggests that Maurice cut a moat around his castle, which encroached upon part of the cemetery, and was subsequently fined for his actions. The grant is again confirmed sometime between 1190 and 1220 by Maurice's son, Robert [II] (charter no. 119; ibid., 69–70). This reference is unlikely to refer to a ditch between the church and the castle, however, as the outer ward was not constructed until 1327–1361; so there was no logical reason to cut a moat in this location between 1171 –1190.

During this period, the castle comprised an ovoid shell-keep with adjacent forebuilding, the curtain wall of the inner ward and the Norman Great Hall, all wrapped around the skeleton of the earlier motte and bailey. Excavations carried out by the 8th Earl between 1917 and 1937 (TBGAS 1938, 321) demonstrated that the shell-keep was already adequately defended by a moat that ran around its base on the south-west, north-west and north-east sides – which may have encircled the earlier motte and bailey – and records show that Maurice [I] dug a deep moat around the south-east side of the castle, presumably to complete the defensive circuit, and diverted the Newport brook and others towards the castle to fill it.

Assuming that Maurice [I] was fined for cutting a moat around the 'north side' of the castle, then there is only one section to which the document can be referring: the north-west terminus of the deep moat that Maurice [I] cut around the south-east side of the castle. The north-west terminus of this moat lies immediately outside the inner court curtain wall and abuts the keep's north-east face, with the moat runing beneath the postern drawbridge 'G'). This suggests that in Maurice's time the cemetery extended to the south-west of the church. This notion is supported by a number of burials found in the area, and a 13th century Latin copy of the original cartulary entry states 'the ditch which I made from the cemetery of Berkeley round my castle' (TBGAS 1938, 330).

Smyth, in his *Lives of the Berkeleys*, writes, under the heading Thomas [IV], year ending 1386, '*He much enlarged the ditch of Berkeley Castle by taking a part of the churchyard which he recompensed with an yearly rent of 6s 8d to the parishioners...whereby the garden that was formerly in that place was destroyed*' (1639, II, 12). As there is insufficient space for a garden between the castle and the church, and as it would be absurd to expect any medieval lord to allow parishioners access to a garden lying directly outside his castle gates, the reference is again unlikely to refer to a ditch in this area. The entry more likely refers to the northernmost section of castle moat, which abuts the current eastern boundary of St Mary's churchyard.

Cooke (1873, 60–1), Tandy (2003, 100) and others, have proposed that, due to its close proximity, the church has always formed a part of the castle's defences, which seems like a plausible suggestion. The moat cut by Thomas [IV] in c.1386, appears to form the eastern side of a new defensive circuit which would have incorporated the church, whilst the moat running under the drawbridge of the outer gatehouse, towards the west end of the church, no doubt comprised the circuit's western section.

Clearly, there is no incontrovertible documentary evidence referring to the cutting of a moat between the shell-keep and the church. Fortunately, the finds recovered from the lower fills of the ditch during excavation suggest a date for its construction, and the profile of the ditch alludes to its function. Finds in the lower contexts of the ditch (221 and 225) indicate that it was cut and in use in the mid to late 17th century, and its size and shape – typical of a mid to late 17th century entrenchment – suggest that it was a Civil War ditch that would have been designed to bolster the castle's defences.

The tale of a pub

In Nelme's Paddock, within the southeastern corner of Trench 8, the team found the remains of a later structure that may have formed a social focus for the Berkeley community: a Tudor tavern. Thanks to the castle's impressive archives, we can identify the building as the Crown Inn – as well as the name of one of its later (perhaps last) owners: by the 1630s, we know that the tavern was being run by a certain John Lemme.

The c.1544 sketch map shows the Crown Tavern positioned between St Michaels Lane and the road to Berkeley Castle. While the pub itself still lies beneath the soil, just outside the extent of the present trench a structure thought to be one of its outbuildings was uncovered by the students. With its eaves drip gulley still clearly visible, the building may have begun life as an animal shelter (possibly the stables) – but later it seems to have been used for metalworking, with burnt patches in its yard yielding quantities of slag. But although the tavern itself remains unexcavated for now, the team has recovered a wealth of finds to shed vivid light on the activities carried out beneath its eaves. The discovery of early tobacco pipes, a large basting dish, pieces of German stoneware, a frying or dripping pan still coated with soot from the fire over which it stood, and so many fragments from a Tudor drinking jug that the team believes it will be almost complete after reconstruction – conjures up a cosy picture of the pub's patrons gathering within its walls to share a drink and a hot meal.

One of the most interesting finds, unearthed in the last excavation season of 2019, was a small die that is very similar to others from the Tudor period. This supports information suggesting that dice games were extremely popular in the Tudor period; Shakespeare regularly referred to dice gambling in his plays. It was a popular activity amongst all classes, with wealthy players using dice manufactured from gold or silver; but most were made from ivory, wood and bone. This popularity meant that cheating was also common in the Tudor period, with weighted dice being found to contain lead to make more likely to land on the higher numbers. Although it does not appear that Berkeley's die was weighted, therefore an honest dice, evidence of this type of cheating has been found previously.

The tale of a battle

At the start of the English Civil War, Berkeley Castle was held for Parliament, but in July 1643 the garrison was withdrawn for the defence of Gloucester. After the Battle of Naseby in the autumn of 1645, the castle was the only fortress of any importance between Bristol and Gloucestershire still in the possession of the Royalists. The castle, at this time, was under the command of Sir Charles Lucas. In September, Sir Thomas Fairfax dispatched Colonel Rainsborough, 'with a considerable party', for the reducing of Berkeley Castle. Fairfax then sent a regiment to join Colonel Morgan and the Gloucestershire forces, and together they were to assist Rainsborough in the taking of the castle.

On the 23rd September, Rainsborough summoned Lucas to surrender, but he refused. The outworks, which included the church, were then stormed. Forty of the defenders were slain and ninety were taken prisoner. The Roundheads allegedly began hauling their ordnance up onto the church roof to enable their cannons to fire down upon the castle. Lucas, realising that further resistance was useless, sounded a parley, and an honourable surrender was arranged. On the 26th September 1645, five hundred horse and foot marched out of the castle: 'the soldiers to march out without arms; the governor, Sir Charles Lucas, with three horses and arms, £50 in money, no more; every field-officer with two horses; foot captains one; lieutenants, ensigns, sword and no horse; the field-officers and captains not to exceed £5. The soldiers not.' (Perfect Diurnal, Sept. 22–29, 1645).

The Church still bears the marks of the Civil War: the west door has loopholes for muskets, which were used by the defenders, and the outside of the church is pockmarked with musket and cannonball scars. The digging of entrenchments around the castle, which almost certainly also included clearing-out and strengthening sections of the medieval moat, probably occurred between July 1643 and September 1645. The work would have been carried out by Royalist forces, under the command of Sir Charles Lucas, who was no doubt expecting the castle to be besieged, and prepared additional layers of defence to counteract the threat. Musket and cannonballs found during BCP further confirm the historic account of the Berkeley siege. As with the finds from the tavern, evidence from the trenches around the castle and St Mary's church bears witness to the community's dramatic end. Berkeley pottery sequence 'stops dead' in the 1640s, ceramics expert Paul Blinkhorn reports – and its outbuilding is sealed by a thick destruction layer dating from the time of the English Civil War. This was a tumultuous period for (Royalist) Berkeley, whose castle was besieged and ultimately captured in 1645.

Evaluating the BCP legacy

The Berkeley Castle Project created a two-fold legacy that future university research-teaching projects can draw upon. The first aspect of the BCP legacy draws upon the hundreds of archaeologists that trained in Berkeley, and the second aspect reflects on the insights that BCP offers to the historical archaeology of the South West of Britain and to methodological advances in field archaeology.

From the very beginning, University of Bristol aimed to have a university excavation project, where, in parallel with other projects, all archaeology students should attend during term time to be trained in all aspects of archaeological work: from geophysics and landscape survey, to excavation, environmental archaeology, archival research, community and public archaeology, post-excavation, reporting and archiving. Only very few programmes can consistently provide this level of fieldwork training and pedagogy to their students. It has been a great pleasure for the project directors and staff throughout the years to see students trained in Berkeley go on to have successful careers in the heritage sector.

Further to the student training, viewing the townscape of Berkeley as part of a fluvial landscape, forming a geographical and political hinterland, has illustrated the integration of maritime and terrestrial settlement patterns, modes of economic exploitation, and changing trends in transport and trade networks of the South West during the Middle Ages. At a local level, the expansion of a post-conquest plantation town along Jumpers Lane, incorporating the hollow way at the west of town, can be viewed in a context of quayside expansion arising from a desire to increase maritime trade. It is likely that the town of Berkeley and village of Newport acted largely as a single entity within the manorial complex, with Berkeley situated for the maritime trade networks of the Severn and Newport established solely to exploit the terrestrial trade along the Bristol-Gloucester road. Goods could easily flow between these two economic centres, and more importantly could be controlled by the manor. The fact that institutional regulation stretched beyond trade to control the landscape indicates not only the wealth which could be made from such control but also the collective imperative of maintaining the fluvial landscape.

On a more regional scale, the changes in goods imported into Berkeley demonstrate changing economic and political influences along the Severn. Certain materials from the artefactual assemblage of Romano-British and Anglo-Saxon periods from Berkeley, such as the Severn Valley Wares and the sandstone millstone fragment, appear to show a preference for regional goods imported along the Severn. Throughout the medieval period luxury goods imported from Bristol are more frequently represented through historical accounts. Apart from the growing importance of Bristol during this period, the holdings of the Berkeley estate in the city no doubt contributed to the increase in trade from this port.

Imports from the Forest of Dean can also be seen from at least during the Anglo-Saxon period until the 20th century. Having a ready supply of raw materials, particularly building materials, undoubtedly aided the expansion of Berkeley. That said, we must be careful to observe, particularly when analysing the archaeological material, an evidential bias. A depositional preference of artefacts comprising the local archaeological record must either have been produced locally or imported. While, as Schofield & Vince (2003, 174) have suggested, analysis of non-local products, particularly ceramics, may prove to be the most 'reliable indicators of trade'. In a local study such as this it is important not to neglect the exports of any locality, the products of which, by their nature, are absent from the local archaeological record.

Conclusion and notes to the future

There is more to be uncovered in Berkeley and it is the hope of the authors that similar local studies in the future will allow more general themes to emerge regarding not only the exploitation and modifications of fluvial landscapes but how these landscapes interact with those inland. Research in the BCP still aims to analyse the skeletal assemblages and the bioarchaeological remains, and to correlate these with similar evidence from the medieval South West. As more archaeological evidence becomes available, it will be possible to refine the BCP early outcomes presented in this volume and to understand more about the early ecclesiastical landscape of Berkeley and its surroundings. As has been noted though, the one thing that is no-longer in doubt is that underlying the present settlement of Berkeley are the remains of a high-status Anglo-Saxon minster.

Bibliography

Bassett, S. 1992. Church and Diocese in the West Midlands: The Transition from British to Anglo-Saxon Control. In: Blair, J. and Sharpe, R. (eds). *Pastoral Care before the Parish*, 13–40. Leicester: Leicester University Press.

Beresford, M. 1967. *New Towns of the Middle Ages*. London: Lutterworth Press.

Blair, J. 1985. Secular Minster Churches in Domesday Book. In: Sawyer, P. (ed). *Domesday Book: A Reassessment*, 104–42. London: Edward Arnold.

Blair, J. 1988. Introduction: From Minster to Parish Church. In: Blair, J. (ed). *Minsters and Parish Churches: The Local Church in Transition*, 1–19. Oxford: Oxford University Committee for Archaeology.

Blair, J. 1992. Anglo-Saxon Minsters: A Topographical Review. In: Blair and Sharpe, R. (eds). *Pastoral Care before the Parish*, 226–266. Leicester: Leicester University Press.

Blair, J. 1996. Churches in the Early English Landscape: Social and Cultural Contexts. In: Blair, J. and Pyrah, C. (eds). *Church Archaeology Research Directions for the Future.* CBA Research Report 104, 6–18. York: Council for British Archaeology.

Blair, J. 2005. *The Church in Anglo-Saxon Society*. Oxford: Oxford University Press.

Boon, G.C. 1972. *Isca: The Roman Legionary Fortess at Caerleon, Mon.* Pontypool: Hughes & Son Ltd.

Brennan, B. 1985. St Radegund and the Early Development of Her Cult at Poitiers, *Journal of Religious History* 13 (4), 340–54.

Cambridge, E. & Rollason, D. 1995. Debate: The Pastoral Organisation of the Anglo-Saxon Church – A Review of the 'Minster Hypothesis', *Early Medieval Europe* 4, 87–104.

Carver, M. 2001. Why that? Why there? Why then? The Politics of Early Medieval Monumentality. In: Hamerow, H. and MacGregor, A. (eds). *Image and Power in the Archaeology of Early Medieval Britain - Essays in Honour of Rosemary Cramp*, 1–22. Oxford: Oxbow Books.

Christie, N. and Hodges, R. 2015. Anxious Abbots? Questions of monastic security and insecurity in early medieval Europe. In: Christie, N. and Herold, H. (eds). *Fortified Settlements in Early Medieval Europe: Defended Communities of the 8th–10th centuries*. Oxford: Oxbow Books.

Cooke, J.H. 1873. *A Sketch of the History of Berkeley, Its Castle, Church, and the Berkeley Family.* Gloucester: G. Sinderly.

Coulstock, P.H. 1993. *The Collegiate Church of Wimborne Minster*. Woodbridge: Boydell Press.

Cramp, R.J. & Daniels, R. 1987. New Finds from the Anglo-Saxon Monastery at Hartlepool, Cleveland, *Antiquity* 61, 424–32.

Croom, J. 1988. The Fragmentation of the Minster Parochiae in South-East Shropshire. In: Blair, J. (ed.) *Minsters and Parish Churches: The Local Church in Transition*, 67–81. Oxford: Oxford University Committee for Archaeology.

Cubitt, C. 2005. The Clergy in Early Anglo-Saxon England, *Historical Research* 78(201), 273–87.

Daniels, R. 1988. The Anglo-Saxon Monastery at Church Close, Hartlepool, Cleveland. *Archaeological Journal* 145(1), 158–210.

Earl of Berkeley, 1927. Berkeley Castle. *Transactions of the Bristol and Gloucestershire Archaeological Society* 49, 183-193.

Earl of Berkeley, 1938. Excavations At Berkeley Castle. *Transactions of the Bristol and Gloucestershire Archaeological Society 60*, 308-339.

Florence of Worcester, 1854. *The Chronicle of Florence of Worcester*, translated by T. Forester. London: H.G. Bohn.

Foot, S. 1992. Anglo-Saxon Minsters: A Review of the Terminology. In: Blair, J. and Sharpe, R. (eds). *Pastoral Care before the Parish*, 212–25. Leicester: Leicester University Press.

Fosbroke, T.D. 1821. *Berkeley manuscripts. Abstracts and extracts of Smyth's lives of the Berkeleys, illustrative of ancient manners and the constitution; including all the pedigrees in that ancient manuscript. To which are annexed a copious history of the castle and parish of Berkeley, consisting of matter never before published; and biographical anecdotes of Dr. Jenner ....* London: J. Nichols and Son.

Gelling, M. 1992. *The West Midlands in the Early Middle Ages.* Leicester: Leicester University Press.

Gethyn-Jones, J.E. 1992. The Church in Berkeley, *Transactions of the Bristol and Gloucestershire Archaeological Society* 110, 59–60.

Graham, A.H. 1985. Wimborne Minster, Dorset: Excavations in the Town Centre, 1983, *Dorset Natural History 7 Archaeological Society Proceedings* 106, 77–86.

Haines, C. (2013). Land at Berkeley Gloucestershire: Archaeological Evaluation. CA Project 4627/CA Report 13676. Unpublished archaeological evaluation report.

Hall, T.A. 2000. *Minster Churches in the Dorset Landscape.* BAR British Series 304. Oxford: Archaeopress.

Hall, T.A. 2003. The Reformation of the British Church in the West Country in the 7th Century. In: Ecclestone, M., Gardner, K., Holbrook, N. and Smith, A. (eds). *The Land of the Dobunni: Sons of Woden - Soldiers of Christ? Papers submitted to the Symposia organised by the Bristol & Gloucestershire Archaeological Society's Committee for Archaeology in Gloucestershire and The Council for British Archaeology South-West 2001-2002*, 49–55. Oxford: Parchment (Oxford) Ltd.

Hare, M. 2013. *Anglo-Saxon Berkeley: history and topography.* Anglo-Saxon Studies in Archaeology and History 18, 119–156.

Heighway, C. & Bryant, R. 1999. *The Golden Minster: The Anglo-Saxon Minster and Later Medieval Priory of St Oswald at Gloucester.* CBA Research Report 117. York: Council for British Archaeology.

Heighway, C. 2003. Not Angels but Anglicans – The Origins of the Christian Church in Gloucestershire. In: Ecclestone, M., Gardner, K., Holbrook, N. and Smith, A. (eds). *The Land of the Dobunni: Sons of Woden - Soldiers of Christ? Papers submitted to the Symposia organised by the Bristol & Gloucestershire Archaeological Society's Committee for Archaeology in Gloucestershire and The Council for British Archaeology South-West 2001-2002*, 56–64. Oxford: Parchment (Oxford) Ltd.

Higgins, D.H. 2002. The Anglo-Saxon Charters of Stoke Bishop: A Study of the Boundaries of Bisceopes Stoc. *Transactions of the Bristol and Gloucestershire Archaeological Society* 120, 107–31.

Hudson, T.P. & University of London. Institute of Historical Research (1997) Arundel in Hudson, T.P. (ed.) A History of the County of Sussex. Vol 5.Pt. 1: The Victoria history of the counties of England. Oxford: Oxford University Press.

Kemp, B.R. 1968. The Churches of Berkeley Hernesse. *Transactions of the Bristol and Gloucestershire Archaeological Society* 87, 96–110.

Leech, R. 1981. *Historic Towns in Gloucestershire.* Gloucestershire: Committee for Rescue Archaeology.

McNamara, J.A. Halborg, J.E. and Whatley, E.G. 1994. *Sainted Women of the Dark Ages.* Durham/London: Duke University Press.

Moore, J.S. 1988. The Gloucestershire Section of Domesday Book, Geographical Problems of the Text, Part 2. *Transactions of the Bristol and Gloucestershire Archaeological Society* 106, 87–106.

Nash-Williams, V.E. 1930. *The Roman Legionary Fortress at Caerleon in Monmouthshire: Report on the Excavations Carried Out in Jenkins Field in 1926.* Cardiff: National Museum of Wales.

Nayling, N. & McGrail, S. 2004. *The Barland's Farm Romano-Celtic Boat.* CBA Research Report 138. York: Bowes Morrell House.

Neuman de Vagvar, C. 1996. Saints and companions to saints: Anglo-Saxon royal women monastics in context. In: Szarmarch, P. (ed). *Holy Men and Holy Women: Old English Prose Saints' Lives and Their Contexts.* New York: New York Press.

Prior, S. 2005. *Archaeological Excavation & Earthwork Survey in The Butterfly Garden & Water Meadow at Berkeley Castle, Berkeley, Gloucestershire.* BCP Report No 05/01 (Unpublished excavation report).

Prior, S. 2007. *Archaeological Excavations in the Edward Jenner Museum Garden. BCP Report No 7. 2007: Archaeological Excavation Report for the Edward Jenner Museum, Gloucestershire, 2007* (Unpublished archaeological report).

Prior, S. 2010. *Project Specification for a Programme of Archaeological Work at Berkeley Castle and the Edward Jenner Museum. Berkeley, Gloucestershire, 2010* (Unpublished archaeological report).

Prior, S. 2011. *Project Specification for a Programme of Archaeological Work at Berkeley Castle and the Edward Jenner Museum. Berkeley, Gloucestershire, 2011 and Interim reports for Trench 8, Nelme's Paddock, 2008–10; Trench 9, St Mary's Churchyard, 2009; Trench 10, Jenner Museum Garden, 2008–10* (Unpublished archaeological report).

Prior, S. 2012. *Project Specification for a Programme of Archaeological Works (BC12) at Berkeley Castle and the Edward Jenner Museum. Berkeley, Glous. 2012 and Interim reports for Trench 8, Nelme's Paddock, 2011; Trench 15, Jenner Museum Garden, 2011* (Unpublished archaeological report).

Prior, S. 2013. *Project Specification for a Programme of Archaeological Works (BC12) at Berkeley Castle and the Edward Jenner Museum. Berkeley, Glous, 2013 and Interim reports for Trench 8, Nelme's Paddock, 2012; Trench 16, Jenner Museum Garden, 2012* (Unpublished archaeological report).

Prior, S. 2014. *Project Specification for a Programme of Archaeological Works (BC12) at Berkeley Castle and the Edward Jenner Museum. Berkeley, Glous, 2014 and Interim reports for Trench 8, Nelme's Paddock, 2013; Trench 16, Jenner Museum Garden, 2013; Trenches 17 & 18, Berkeley Castle Grounds, 2013; St Mary's Churchyard Project, 2013; Geophysical Survey Project, 2013, Social Media Project, 2013* (Unpublished archaeological report).

Prior, S. 2015. *Project Specification for a Programme of Archaeological works (BC15) at Berkeley Castle, Berkeley, Gloucs. 2015 and Interim reports for Trench 8, Nelme's Paddock, 2014; Social Media Evaluation Report, 2014; Geophysical Survey Report Watermeadow, 2014* (Unpublished archaeological report).

Rahtz, P. 1993. *Glastonbury.* London: English Heritage.

Schofield, J. & Vince, A. 2003. *The Archaeology of Medieval Europe 1100–1600: Medieval Towns.* London: Continuum.

Smisson, B. 2009. *Geophysical Survey Investigations to locate the Boundary of Berkeley's Monastic Enclosure, Berkeley, Gloucestershire, 2009.* Bristol University: unpublished report (BC09): BCP Report 11.

Smith, L.T. 1908. The Itinerary of John Leyland in or about the years 1535-1543. Parts IV & V. London: George Bell and Sons.

Smith, A.H. (1964) The Place-Names of Gloucestershire, Part II: The North and West Cotswolds.Cambridge: Cambridge University Press.

Smith, A.H. 1956. *English Place-Name Elements, Part 1.* Cambridge: English Place-Name Society.

Smyth, J. (of Nibley) (1567-1641). The Berkeley Manuscripts: Lives of the Berkeleys. 3 Vols. Maclean, J. (ed.), Bristol and Gloucestershire Archaeological Society (1883-1885). Gloucester: John Bellow.

Tandy, D. 2003. *Berkeley, A Town in the Marshes.* Chippenham: Anthony Rowe Ltd.

Taylor, C.S. 1895. Berkeley Minster. *Transactions of the Bristol and Gloucestershire Archaeological Society* 19, 70–84.

Thacker, A. 1992. Monks, Preaching and Pastoral Care in Early Anglo-Saxon England. In: Blair, J. and Sharpe, R. (eds). *Pastoral Care before the Parish*, 137–70. Leicester: Leicester University Press.

Turner, S. 2006. *Making a Christian Landscape*. Exeter: Exeter University Press.

Twinn, P. 2008. *Research Excavation on the Berkeley Estate and at the Edward Jenner Museum Garden* (Unpublished finds report).

Walker, D. 1998. The Cartulary of St Augustine Abbey, Bristol. Gloucester: Bristol and Gloucestershire Archaeological Society.

Wells-Furby, B. 2004. A Catalogue of the Medieval Muniments at Berkeley Castle I. *Bristol and Gloucestershire Archaeological Society*17.

Wilson, R. 1980. *Roman Forts: An Illustrated Introduction to the Garrison Posts of Roman Britain*. London: Bergstrom & Boyle Books Ltd.

Yorke, B. 2003. *Nunneries and the Anglo-Saxon Royal Houses*. London/New York: Continuum.

The Photographic Tales from Berkeley

During the 14 years of the Berkeley castle project, hundreds of Bristol students trained on the Berkeley grounds and numerous staff members and volunteers were involved in the project activities. Over the next few pages, snapshots of the Bristol journey at Berkeley are presented: From views of the trenches to aerial images of the Berkeley grounds, then to the community driven Town Museum project, the development and different stages of works are showcased. The story is completed with a presentation of some of the most interesting finds from the Berkeley excavations. Mostly photographed by Pete Twinn, the finds demonstrate the rich material culture from the different periods of occupation and activity around the castle and the town.

Plate 1. Berkeley castle front approach by Leonard Knyff, c.1676 (Berkeley Castle Archives)

Plate 2. Berkeley castle south front by Leonard Knyff, c.1676 (Berkeley Castle Archives)

Plate 3. View from Nelme's Paddock towards St Mary's during the 2007 excavation season (photo BCP- Department of Anthropology and Archaeology).

Plate 4. Aerial view of St Mary' and the graveyard (photo by Aerial Cam 2008)

Plate 5. Aerial view of Jenner Museum and gardens with the University of Bristol at the back excavating trench 10 (photo by Aerial Cam 2008).

Plate 6. The inner gatehouse of Berkeley Castle (photo by Aerial Cam 2008).

Plate 7. Professor Mark Horton is launching the deturfing of Trench 1 on 2005, first season of the Berkeley Castle Project (photo BCP - Department of Anthropology and Archaeology).

Plate 8. General shot of works at trench 3 (photo BCP - Department of Anthropology and Archaeology).

Plate 9. Dr Stuart Prior while he is photographing one of the skeletons found in trench 4 (later to be incorporated into trench 8) (photo BCP - Department of Anthropology and Archaeology).

Plate 10. General shot of works during the earthwork Survey at Quarf Mead (photo BCP - Department of Anthropology and Archaeology).

Plate 11. A window display during the Berkeley town museum project (photo BCP - Department of Anthropology and Archaeology).

Plate 12. A display in a local shop, during the Berkeley town museum project (photo BCP - Department of Anthropology and Archaeology).

Plate 13. General shot of works at trench 3 during the summer season of 2013 (photo BCP - Department of Anthropology and Archaeology).

Plate 14. A panoramic view of St Mary's church the graveyard and the tower (photo by Aerial Cam 2008).

Plate 15. A rare Anglo-Saxon gold ring that was first recorded in the castle's collections in 1860. However, in recent years it has only been shown in public once at an exhibition at the Victoria and Albert Museum in 1972. The ring is an exceptional example of goldwork, with intricate filigree work, and four beasts' heads with inlaid blue and yellow glass eyes. The quality of the craftsmanship places it as one of the finest pieces from the Anglo-Saxon period. Dr Leslie Webster dated it to the early part of the ninth century. This was the period of great artistic achievement in the English Midlands initiated by Mercian king Offa (757-796) which continued until the Viking raids of the mid ninth century. (photo BCP - Department of Anthropology and Archaeology).

Plate 16. A selection of Saxon coinage found in Berkeley (photo BCP- Department of Anthropology and Archaeology).

Plate 17. SF 122b an Alexander II Halfpenny (photo P. Twinn - Department of Anthropology and Archaeology).

Plate 18. SF 125a a Constantine I Urbs Roma (photo P. Twinn - Department of Anthropology and Archaeology).

Plate 19. SF 123a Anglo Saxon Page Turner (photo P. Twinn - Department of Anthropology and Archaeology).

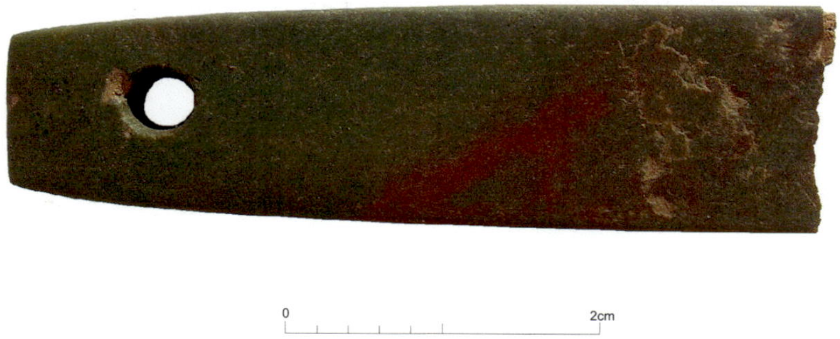

Plate 20. SF 157a Whetstone Pendant (photo P. Twinn - Department of Anthropology and Archaeology).

Plate 21. SF 151b an Edward II Penny (photo P. Twinn - Department of Anthropology and Archaeology).

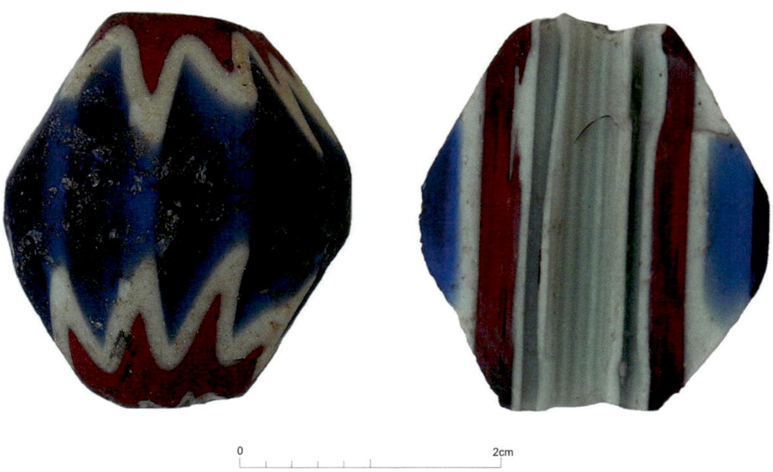

Plate 22. Venetian Trade Bead 15th-16thC (photo P. Twinn - Department of Anthropology and Archaeology).

Plate 23. SF4 Tudor Hawking Bell 15thC (photo P. Twinn - Department of Anthropology and Archaeology).

Plate 24. 7th-18th century musket balls (photo P. Twinn - Department of Anthropology and Archaeology).

Plate 25. SF 121a Mount or Washer. 13th-17thC. (photo P. Twinn - Department of Anthropology and Archaeology).

Plate 26. SF 143b Button 18th-20thC. (photo P. Twinn - Department of Anthropology and Archaeology).

Plate 27. The porpoise tale bones discovered during the last season of 2019 (photo BCP- Department of Anthropology and Archaeology).

Plate 28. The Tudor bone dice found in the last season of 2019 (photo BCP- Department of Anthropology and Archaeology).